D1544061

ENGLISH COURT CULTURE IN THE LATER MIDDLE AGES

Frontispiece. Herman Scheerre. Unidentified owner kneeling before the Virgin and Child. Berkeley Castle, Nevill Hours, folio 7.

English Court Culture
in the
Later Middle Ages

edited by

V. J. Scattergood

J. W. Sherborne

St. Martin's Press   New York

All rights reserved. For information, write:
St. Martin's Press, Inc., 175 Fifth Avenue, New York, NY 10010
Printed in Great Britain
First published in the United States of America in 1983

ISBN 0–312–25412–1

Library of Congress Cataloging in Publication Data
Main entry under title:

English court culture in the later Middle Ages.

Includes indexes.
Contents: Introduction/J.A. Burrow – Aspects of English court culture in the later fourteenth century/J.W. Sherborne — Literary culture at the court of Richard II/V.J. Scattergood — [etc.]
1. Great Britain—Court and courtiers—Addresses, essays, lectures. 2. England—Civilization—Medieval period, 1066–1485—Addresses, essays, lectures.
I. Scattergood, V. J. II. Sherborne, J. W.
DA185.E63 1983   942   82–25023
ISBN 0–312–25412–1

Contents

Contents

Plates

Frontispiece. Herman Scheerre. Unidentified owner kneeling before the Virgin and Child. Berkeley Castle, Nevill Hours, folio 7.

(between pp. 148 and 149)

Plate 1. Pseudo-Aristotle, *Secreta Secretorum.* BL MS Additional 47680, folio 17.

Plate 2. Initial 'A' with Edward III (?) kneeling before the Virgin and Child. Oxford, Bodleian Library, MS Douce 131, folio 110.

Plate 3. East end of St. Stephen's Chapel, Westminster. Magus with a bird-topped staff (after Smith).

Plate 4. East end of St. Stephen's Chapel, Westminster. Adoration of the Magi with Edward III and his children kneeling below (after Smith).

Plate 5. The Black Prince kneeling before the Trinity. University of London Library MS 1, folio 3v–4.

Plate 6. Scenes from the life of Christ. John Rylands University Library, Manchester, MS Latin 22, folio 9.

Plate 7. Hoccleve presenting the book to Henry, Prince of Wales. BL MS Arundel 38, folio 37.

Plate 8. Annunciation with arms of Queen Catherine. Private Collection, Lancs.

Plate 9. A king, Henry V (?), praying at Mass. Trinity College, Cambridge, MS B 117, folio 31v.

Plate 10. Henry VI adoring Christ as Man of Sorrows. BL MS Cotton Domitian A XVII, folio 98.

Plates 15 and 17 are reproduced with the kind permission of the Huntington Library.

Introduction

'I am in time, and I speak of time,' said Augustine, and straightway added, 'I know not what time is'. With like wonderment can I say that I am in the court, and speak of the court, and know not – God alone knoweth – what the court is.
(Walter Map, *De Nugis Curialium*, trans. Tupper and Ogle)

Modern students of the middle ages, historians and others, often speak of the court; and 'courtly' is a key term in many studies of medieval art, literature and music. These terms, however, are often applied at once too precisely and too loosely – too precisely, because it is assumed that the court was a fixed and clearly distinct body of people, like an order of chivalry, and too loosely, because little attention is paid to the actual evidence for what particular men and women associated with the king in fact thought, read, listened to, and looked at. This book, containing the text of ten papers delivered at the Colston Research Society Symposium held in Bristol in the spring of 1981, presents some of this evidence – evidence for 'court culture' – so far as concerns England in the fourteenth and fifteenth centuries. One of the essays considers Scotland. Education, patronage, crusades, architecture, painting, manuscripts, literature and music are the main topics discussed.

The rich and authoritative body of material presented in this book prompts two main general reflections. The first is that we, like Walter Map, must give up hope of defining the 'court' with any precision. The difficulty arises not from lack of evidence (Map did not lack that) but from the nature of the circle which surrounded the king and his immediate family. Close to the centre of this circle, clearly, was the king's chamber or *camera regis*, to which only chosen intimates were regularly admitted. The circumference of the circle, on the other hand, was indistinct and varied continuously with times, seasons, and places. Therefore it is not surprising that, where artefacts are concerned, the best modern scholars are often least dogmatic in assigning a given work to court patronage (see, for instance, the essays of Dr Doyle and Dr Colvin here).

Something, however, *can* be discovered about the 'court culture' of late medieval England from the evidence to be found in the following pages. The most striking discovery, in which a number of our contributors agree, is that the English kings and their associates were not, in

this period, notably energetic patrons of the arts – not by comparison
with their French contemporaries, or indeed with some of their English predecessors and successors. Even Richard II, often represented
as a man of high and strenuous culture, is treated here as a doubtful
case (in the essays of Mr Sherborne and Professor Scattergood). Like
his grandfather Edward III and his Lancastrian and Yorkist successors, Richard certainly possessed books, read poems, and listened to
songs; but none of these kings, it would seem, commissioned such
works on quite the lavish scale one might expect of royalty; nor can
they readily be shown to have encouraged, by the active exercise of
taste, any distinctive English 'court style' in manuscripts, or buildings,
or music, or poetry. The following remarks are representative of the
reservations expressed by several contributors to this volume: 'If one
does not look too closely, it is easy to see Richard II as presiding at
the centre of a literary court culture based on the English language'
(Scattergood); 'It is hard to fashion a portrait of Richard as a significant cultural force, let alone a cultural leader' (Sherborne); 'there is
[in the poetry of Dunbar and Douglas] no special court style' (Fox);
'the concept of a "court style" [in architecture] remains ill-defined and
requires careful handling if it is not to degenerate into a mere cliché
devoid of any real historical validity' (Colvin); 'No English king, not
even Henry VI, seems to have had the interest in books and learning
of Charles V [of France]' (Alexander); 'The tendency of this cursory
treatment of selected examples has been to doubt a uniquely distinguishable influence of the royal court on the character of book-production in English' (Doyle). Dr Wilkins strikes a more positive note,
showing how large a part music and song played in the daily life of
noble households; but even here we can hardly credit the *English*
court with a 'uniquely distinguishable influence', since courtly song
was, as Wilkins amply demonstrates, largely French in influence, and
often in language too.

Perhaps Professor Scattergood is wrong to imply that one can in
fact never 'look *too* closely' in a matter such as this; but even if the
overall effect of these essays is a little too sceptical, they cannot fail
to be salutary. As a term in the critical description of books and
buildings, poems and paintings, 'courtly' neither can nor should be
used all the time in full awareness of its historical bearings. The term
has, however, sometimes seemed in danger of losing these bearings
altogether; and the effort to recover them leads to results which are,
even in this case, by no means only negative. Insofar as the evidence
casts doubt on the cultural supremacy of the metropolitan court, it
testifies to the creativity and civility of other groups and other centres
in the kingdom. 'Courtliness' was not, in England, the preserve of an
exclusive group at Westminster.

Bristol   J. A. Burrow

Contributors

J. J. G. Alexander is Reader in the History of Art in the University of Manchester.

J. A. Burrow is Wintersboke Professor of English in the University of Bristol.

H. M. Colvin is a Fellow of St John's College, Oxford.

A. I. Doyle is Keeper of Rare Books in the University of Durham.

Denton Fox is Professor of English in Victoria College, University of Toronto.

Richard Firth Green is Professor of English in Bishop's University, Quebec.

M. H. Keen is a Fellow of Balliol College, Oxford.

Nicolas Orme is Reader in History in the University of Exeter.

V. J. Scattergood is Professor of Medieval and Renaissance English in Trinity College Dublin.

J. W. Sherborne is Senior Lecturer in History in the University of Bristol.

Nigel Wilkins is a Fellow of Corpus Christi College, Cambridge.

1

Aspects of English Court Culture in the Later Fourteenth Century

J. W. Sherborne

I begin my essay with some definition of its title. Part of what I have to say about the later fourteenth century will be born out of time, because it is unhelpful to write of Edward III during the last thirty years of his reign without setting the scene, and for this reason some references to the 1330s are desirable. Secondly all who are familiar with the extensive literature on royal courts and, more particularly, on the 'cultures' of these courts will acknowledge that scholars are by no means at one in their conception and interpretation of their themes. Culture is a difficult word, for it carries different meanings. What, therefore, do I mean by culture? I shall be concerned with enlightenment and excellence of taste in the arts and in the humanities among those who through interest, experience, observation and commitment had learned to value and promote beauty and distinction. But the word culture may also be used in the broader sense of a society's pattern of behaviour in thought, speech and actions. Today we hear much of the 'cultural gap' between generations or of differences between social classes and geographical areas. So it has always been; what is true of the 1980s was inevitably also so in the Middle Ages. I intend to write of culture in both these senses, for only by reference to the broad framework can the distinguished and distinctive creativity of a generation be put in perspective.

It is scarcely suprising that historians have written of the royal courts of medieval England with contrasting thoughts in mind, for with the long passage of time the king's household changed and developed and in the process new forms and fresh characteristics evolved. Despite innate traits of conservatism, a flexible approach to the court is, therefore, necessary.

The courts of Edward III and Richard II were naturally synonymous with the presence of the king, but day by day and month by month the company the king kept varied greatly in size, purpose and dignity. In its most extended form parliament was a meeting of the king's court and by the year 1399 parliament had become highly formal. Yet one hundred years earlier parliaments had only started to develop from those embryonic gatherings of Henry III's reign when the officers of state, the bureaucrats and the familiars who were in more or less constant attendance upon the king within his household were afforced by men who met the king only occasionally, but without whose temporary presence it had become impossible or impolitic to conduct the *magna negotia regis et regni*. Using the word courtier in its widest sense, all those who came to parliaments whether by individual summons or as a result of communal elections were courtiers.

In the parliaments of the fourteenth century, among the company of several hundred men who sat or stood in the king's presence on the opening day, there were many who were not courtiers in the normally accepted usage of the word. This was true of the majority of elected members. In the November parliament of 1351, on the other hand, when the archbishops of Canterbury and York were present, together with eighteen bishops, eleven earls, fifty lay lords, twenty-four abbots and the priors of Lewes and of the Hospital of St John of Jerusalem, there were many whom it is correct to describe as courtiers. Among this number, however, there were some who scarcely cast a political or social shadow. Their familiarity with the king was minimal; such men we might describe as institutional courtiers who were present because their father and grandfathers had been summoned in earlier years. Lords of the blood royal and those bound to the crown by marriage were very different, as were others who spent much time in the king's company, sharing the burdens and the recreations of the king's changing round. Had there been a court circular in the middle ages, we should be able greatly to amplify knowledge which can now only be impressionistic. Other essays in this collection will reiterate how patchy is the survival of evidence crucial to important themes.

Like parliament the king's council had grown out of the king's household, and here is another much older facet of the king's household. Sadly, detailed knowledge of its composition before the 1390s has not advanced much since the works of N. H. Nicolas and J. G. Baldwin.[1] Only in the last decade of the fourteenth century does a *dramatis personae* of those who were present sometimes emerge, and thus we gain insight into the workings of the royal executive which had previously been largely a matter for conjecture. Yet the composition of the Great Council which met at Eltham in the king's presence

1. J. F. Baldwin, *The King's Council in England during the Middle Ages* (Oxford, 1913), 115–46, 489–505, N. H. Nicolas, *Proceedings and Ordinances of the Privy Council*, 7 vols (London, 1834–7), i. 6–9, 11–12b, 14c–14d, 17–18a, 64–5.

on 22 July 1395 was much as we would have expected it to be and, stressing the ancestral tradition of English government at its highest level, a comparison with witness lists of Anglo-Saxon royal charters is not anachronistic. Often the council debated and made important decisions without the king's presence, but Richard II's absences were not a reflection of indifference or indolence. Richard II was not a king to entrust significant issues to others without his consultation, and by decree certain categories of business were reserved for royal participation. By any definition the king's councillors were courtiers and were in varying degree *persona grata* with the king. The chancellor and the treasurer were almost always present and there was an evident rapport between Richard and the small number of knights of the chamber (like Sir Richard Stury or Sir Edward Dalingrigg) who were regular attendants, as was from time to time the Steward of the Household. Those earls, barons or bishops who figure intermittently were men trusted by the king and would not have been present without his blessing: they may well have attended by royal command. Mutual respect and personal friendship intertwine in the private and the public profiles of kingship.

The courts of parliament and of council, however, made relatively small demands upon the time of Edward III and Richard II. In the years 1390–8, for example, the seven parliaments only occupied 173 days. During the period covered by John Prophet's Journal, Richard only attended the council for five days.[2] Yet between 1330 and *c.* 1372 Edward III never lacked application in meeting demands made upon him as king, nor can Richard II be faulted in this respect between *c.* 1381 and 1386 or after May 1389. In his case an accusation of pursuing his own opinionated initiative too much would be more appropriate. Yet in both reigns there were long periods when government was safely entrusted to the chancellor and the treasurer, who acted in consultation with civil servants of long experience, men who had moved up the rungs of the offices of state assimilating experience and proving through their reliability and intelligence that they could be relied upon to serve the king well. The onus upon these men was the exercise of constant discretion in deciding whether action or decision were proper without reference to the king. The endless sequence of entries upon the Issue Rolls of wages paid to messengers carrying letters (often described as 'urgent') to the king proves that the king, wherever he might be and whatever he might be doing, was always present in the minds of those who bore his trust. With chancellors of the calibre of William Edington (1356–63) and William of Wykeham (1367–71), Edward III was handsomely served in this respect. And

---

2. Baldwin, op. cit., 489–504. Between 20 January 1392 and 21 February 1393 meetings of the council on only forty-two days are recorded.

Wykeham, as we shall see, was a courtier who made an outstanding contribution to the culture of his generation.

Yet though Edward III or Richard II might be separated from the executive, their courts were always with them. The composition of the court might vary in number from several hundred to perhaps fifty or less. Information for Edward III is drawn from the fortunate survival of the books of the keepers of the wardrobe for the years 1353–4, 1366–7, 1369, 1371–3 and 1376–7. Four books survive of Richard II's wardrobe accounts covering parts of the years 1383–84, 1389–90, 1393–4 and 1395–96. The keepers of the wardrobe were the financial controllers of the king's household. The staff of the household was very large and, as Dr Given-Wilson has recently shown, between 1360 and 1377 the number employed varied between 350 and 450.[3] It has always been of the nature of kingship to be lavishly served. Edward III and Richard II employed clerks, squires, valets, yeomen, palfreymen, sumptermen, messengers and carters by the score. Within the household there were eleven different offices, each serving different needs of the king and queen, their family and their familiars. At the core of the household was the king's chamber and it is here for the first time that we draw near to court intimacy and the privacy of the king. Access to the chamber was restricted. It was there that he usually took his meals, there he slept, there he kept his most cherished possessions and there he relaxed. We shall have more to say of the chamber in due course.

The reigns of Edward III and of Richard II both began with minorities: Edward III was crowned at the age of fourteen and Richard when he was ten. Each shared an inheritance which in different ways was politically contaminated. The contrast in character between the two kings could scarcely have been greater: in somewhat similar fashion both were quite unlike their fathers. The sharp dissimilarity between Edward III and his father Edward II was as stark as that between Richard II and Edward, Prince of Wales, the Black Prince. From the day in 1330 of his emancipation from the corrupt ambience of his mother, Queen Isabella, and her lover, Roger Mortimer, first earl of March, Edward III began the redemption of a country which had been politically and militarily scarred for a generation. In a famous proclamation of 20 October 1330 Edward declared that 'we wish all men to know that in future we will govern our people according to right and reason, and as is fitting our royal dignity'. (Interestingly Richard II might have argued, whatever his critics might be saying, that such words expressed his own political intent.) 'And that the matters which touch us,' Edward continued, 'and the estate of our realm are to be

3. C. J. Given-Wilson, 'Court and household of Edward III, 1360–1377' (unpub. Ph.D. of the University of St Andrews, 1976), 172–5.

disposed of by the common counsel of the magnates of our realm, and not in any other manner.'[4] These words were to prove most relevant in the character of Edward III's court and to the culture which is our concern. For the greater part of the forty-seven years which followed, Edward fulfilled his undertaking and as a result commanded the respect and admiration of his subjects in a manner unparallelled since the Norman Conquest.

It is doubtful, on the other hand, whether Richard II ever commanded the respect of more than a minority of his subjects, even in the relatively quiet years from 1389–97. As early as November 1381, when Richard II was only fourteen, there were ominous signs of disquiet about the king and his household expressed by the actions of the Lords and the words of the Commons in the parliament of that month. The composition and the cost of the king's court had already become a political issue. We may well conjecture how the opinionated Richard voiced his unrecorded displeasure. Almost certainly the seeds of his stark and frightening response to Haxey's petition in February 1397 were firmly planted earlier in the reign. Nor do I think that the allegedly heady experience of Richard II's coronation had contributed to an excessive preoccupation with his royal dignity, any more than too much exhortation about becoming a great king as his grandfather had been, or as his father might have been, had anything to do with his conscientious misunderstanding of the rights and duties of kingship. The conventionalism of Edward III came naturally to him; he wore his crown lightly. Richard's crown, on the other hand, much as he loved to wear it and to be seen wearing it, pressed heavily upon him and in the end he lost it.

Inevitably politics and court composition were as warp and woof in the reigns of Edward III and Richard II. Commonly it was the custom of contemporaries to refer to individuals as courtiers only if they were disliked, distrusted or controversial. Edward III's courtiers were virtually taken for granted – were they not a credit to the royal prudence? – for most of his long reign. It was only towards the end that a small, untypical clique of courtiers emerged in an entirely unprededented way and lightning struck in the Good Parliament of 1376. Nothing like this had happened before and, granted the dotage of the king, it is uncertain whether the rot which had set in would have assumed the character it did, had not the problem of financing the *damnosa hereditas* of fighting France and Castile virtually exhausted the resources of the government and lightened the purses of increasingly reluctant tax-payers. There was irony in the manner in which warfare, once the crowning glory for Edward III, led to suspicion and distrust which carried over into the 1380s and sharpened the angularities of

4. T. Rymer, *Foedera*, ii, 799.

Richard II, distorting understanding of his by no means entirely perverse attempts to establish himself. Richard unquestionably created difficulties of his own making, but he was also a victim of the past.

Great claims have been made for the personal culture of Richard II and also that of his court. One historian has written that 'the work done for Richard II was instinct with a vividness and unity of aim which stamp the masterpieces of the end of the fourteenth century as the high-watermark of English achievement'.[5] I find it hard to accept hyperbole of this kind. Nor can I echo the words of Joan Evans who wrote 'historians of art cannot but regard Richard's death with a certain regret. Under his leadership all the arts of England enter upon a phase of fruition'.[6] One of the purposes of the colloquium from which the papers in this book derive was to re-assess judgments of this kind in the light of more recent scholarship. As will appear, Richard II's court as a 'notable centre of the arts, the most notable perhaps since the court of Eleanor of Aquitaine' expresses a view which no longer commands respect.[7]

Underlying these generalisations are to be found some of those imprecisions of thought and definition of which I wrote earlier. Also – and this is a point of major substance – these judgments lack perspective. Let us now return to Edward III – to the culture of the king himself and that of his courtiers, and in doing so we must be alert for evidence of continuity in the 'court cultures' of the two reigns.

Yet before I proceed, one further quest for a definition is essential. *Court culture* – what does the concept mean? Let me return to the alternative definitions of culture with which I began. Using the word in a broader sociological sense, we may expect to find many patterns of behaviour which were common to the king and those who were close to him. If, however, the activities considered originated with the king himself and were deliberately adopted or pursued by others possibly in a quest for royal favour, patronage or enhanced status, by men who might not have acted as they did had they not been courtiers of the king, then we may use the phrase court culture meaningfully. We must also allow scope for a royal enthusiasm which, while it was not creatively original, had a dynamic which served to heighten or intensify what was already intrinsic in accepted practice. Is it mistaken to emphasise Edward III's conventionality, in his passion for tournaments and for fighting, in his love of pageantry and ceremonial, in his delight in personal display, expressed in expensive dress and jewellery, or his zest for hawking and hunting? I shall return to these matters

5. J. Harvey, *The Plantagenets* (London, 1948), 152.

6. J. Evans, *English Art 1307–1461* (Oxford, 1949), 399.

7. J. Taylor, 'Richard II's views on kingship', *Proceedings of the Leeds Phil. and Lit. Soc.*, xiv (1971), 202.

in more detail shortly, but it is impossible to see anything new here. In may ways Edward III and his friends had much in common with William I or Henry II and their familiars. If we feel obliged to establish distinctiveness, we might perhaps say that Edward III was unusually extravagant. But this is scarcely a contribution to the history of culture. Some of the king's exchanges with his bankers and with the Commons in parliament were embarrassing and sometimes irresponsible to the point of financial dishonesty. And if the king's crowns and jewellery sometimes served as pawns to money-lenders, can we be confident in assuming that all his financial difficulties arose from the heavy costs of warfare?

When I turn to my second definition of culture – enlightenment and excellence of taste in the arts and in the humanities – I find myself in immediate difficulties. Were I convinced that either Edward III or Richard II originated cultural patterns which might not otherwise have occurred and that they communicated their taste and discrimination to friends who adopted their leadership, anxious to emulate or even outshine their monarch, I would write of court culture with greater confidence. In fact I cannot find signs of original artistic taste consciously fostered and promoted either by Edward III or by Richard II, nor evidence of a royal leadership which created an intellectual or artistic climate which laid the foundations for the emergence of a coherent growth of courtly taste.

Edward III was a companionable man. Despite an irascible temper, unreliability in money matters and a tendency to go back on solemn promises made (often, it is clear, with evident reluctance) in parliaments, he made friendships of a kind which commonly lasted a lifetime. He was regularly handsome in the gifts and patronage which he bestowed upon those who commanded his liking and respect. He was not afraid of his magnates and regarded their participation with himself in the joint enterprise of the government of the realm as axiomatic. It was natural that his subjects, whether of great or lesser degree, should revere one who epitomised the chivalric values and practices which were highly esteemed during the fourteenth century. Edward III loved warfare and his campaign against Scotland in the first year of his reign was the first of numerous expeditions over the northern border of England or across the Channel against France which were to follow until his final landing on French soil in 1359. In the victories at Halidon Hill in 1333 and at Crécy in 1346, Edward showed courage and resource as a tactician. At Sluys in 1340 and on other occasions, his personal bravery was much admired, and as a general his fine leadership was clear. However, whether Edward III was a truly great soldier is another matter. It is difficult to give Edward the benefit of the doubts which are prompted by the apparent lack of systematic strategic thinking behind many, if not most, of his campaigns. The king's contemporaries, if we may judge by their enthusiasm to fight under his command, thought better of Edward than some scholars have been disposed to do. What is not in doubt is that until the treaty of 1360 Edward III's court was dominated by his companions in war.

It is arguable that Edward III's military prestige reached its apogee in August 1347, when Calais surrendered; almost exactly a year had passed since the decimation of the French army at Crécy had won for the soldiery of England a European esteem which was unprecendented, and which, despite an uncomfortable number of setbacks later in the fourteenth century, was last until 1421. Whatever the year of the foundation of the Order of the Garter may have been – let us assume it was 1348 – the creation of this 'Society, Fellowship and College' of twenty-six knights (Edward III himself and twenty-five others chosen by the king) was an event of cultural import. It was also deeply meaningful in the history of Edward III's court and its membership. When the king returned from Calais in 1347 he was generally lionised, an experience which Edward heartily enjoyed and thought entirely proper. If contemporaries drew upon the unforgettable twelfth-century fantasies of Geoffrey of Monmouth and compared their king with that greatest of all British soldiers, King Arthur, they were speaking Edward III's own language, for he, like his grandfather Edward I, thought in the tradition of the Nine Worthies and saw himself as another Arthur. In 1344 he had made his first move towards the creation of a Round Table for his own companions in war. By 1348 the formulation of his plan had changed in detail, but the essence of the idea remained the same. In 1348 Edward was celebrating and honouring the blessing which God had bestowed upon him and his realm through the great victories at Crécy and Calais. These had demonstrated that the Almighty endorsed the justice of Edward's claim to the throne of France. Through the Order of the Garter, which has survived unbroken in continuity until the present day, Edward III projected himself and his courtier captains as chivalric heroes, who had won divine benediction for their bravery and their perseverance.

Among the original knights of the Garter were Edward, Prince of Wales, only recently blooded in combat, and four earls – Henry of Derby, Thomas Beauchamp of Warwick, William Bohun of Northampton and Robert Ufford of Suffolk – who were already war veterans. Northampton and Suffolk, for example, had campaigned with Edward in 1339, 1340, 1342–3 and 1346–7; Derby had shared their experience, except that in 1345–7 he was busily engaged in restoring English fortunes in Gascony, which until 1345 had been almost entirely neglected. Each of these earls had been raised to highest status on that remarkable day, 16 March 1337, when Edward had made six new creations. In honouring William Bohun and Robert Ufford, Edward was in part expressing his gratitude for the support these men had given him when Isabella and Mortimer had been ousted in 1330. Henry of Grosmont, earl of Derby, later (1351) first duke of Lancaster was, as we shall see, a man of many parts and he, like Northampton and Suffolk, fought with Edward III in France to the end, leading a retinue in the sadly disappointing campaign of 1359–60. Other courtiers made Garter knights in 1348 were peers of the realm, like the lords Lisle, Mohun and Grey of Rotherfield. Several were of families of the Norman Conquest, while others, if not distinguished across so many generations, were of blood as blue as the colour of the robes and of the garters provided for them by the Great Wardrobe on 23 April 1348, the feast of St George. Neither the feast nor its date were new, but St George, once the patron saint of all warriors, now became the patron saint of English soldiery and of England itself. Other creations of 1348 came of more modest station, but their names read like a roll call of honour, echoing across the fields of France, where they had fought with their king, perhaps exchanging urgent words of comfort and exhortation during the night before Crécy was fought; they included Jean de Grailly, Miles Stapleton, James Audley and John Chandos. They may not have been men of parliament or council, but their campaign medals gave them an entrée to the king's chamber.

Let me pick out one Garter earl, Henry of Grosmont, for more particular attention.[8] He was the epitome of the aristocratic courtier of Edward III's reign. The nephew of Thomas of Lancaster and, in due course, father-in-law of John of Gaunt, who married Henry's daughter Blanche in 1359, Henry was a remarkable and fascinating man. Certainly there is no other English courtier of the fourteenth century of his stature and significance. Henry, duke of Lancaster, was unique. Some of his peers shared wealth, loyalty, piety and belligerence with him; all were literate and are likely to have owned books. How greatly these books mattered and the extent to which they were read or possibly read aloud for entertainment and instruction during leisure hours are questions which usually cannot be answered. Later I shall mention several of Richard II's courtiers who were authors, but Henry of Lancaster stands alone as an author among the courtiers of Edward III. His *Livre des Seyntz Medicines* has much to say about courtly life. What is interesting is that the duke apologises for his indifferent command of the French language, claiming that he was self-taught, and late in life at that. If this was not a stylistic conceit, the remark is significant, for it is at variance with our understanding of the educational practices of the day.

Lancaster was a rich man; Professor Fowler has suggested a gross income from his estates in England and Wales of over £8,380, and we

8. K. Fowler, *The King's Lieutenant, Henry of Grosmont* (London, 1974), 189–96, 214–18, 225–6, J. Barnie, *War in Medieval Society* (London, 1974), 60–5.

can be sure that this territorial income was, over the years, supplemented by profits of war. A contemporary estimated that his Savoy palace, which was built between 1349 and 1357, cost £35,000. Building was one of the duke's enthusiasms and we may assume that, interested in nothing less than the best, he was willing and able to afford what he set his heart on. He felt most at home at Leicester, where his castle, with its great chamber, apartments for his family and guests and its dancing chamber, was civilised and comfortable; in common with much other new buildings at this time, Leicester castle was more of a private residence than a fortified position. Henry was a generous benefactor of the church. He died, as he wished, in Newarke College, Leicester, which he had financed and endowed.

These remarks about Henry prompt two considerations about Edward III and the culture of his courtiers. If in this context we exclude dress as an art form, Edward III's sole claim to outstanding patronage was the amount of money he spent upon building. In what sense should we represent Henry of Grosmont's architecture as a manifestion of an Edwardian court culture? The answer must be that this was only the case in a very general fashion. Granted that duke Henry was a courtier, he did not build as he did because he was a courtier. He did so rather because his homes were symbolic of his lineage, his personal status and of his wealth. He was a great man and he liked to be seen by the world as such. But ostentation was of less importance to him than the pleasure of comfortable living and an anticipation that, when he returned from pilgrimage or his repeated forays in France, he might enjoy eating, sleeping and sharing the company of his family and friends in style. There were other courtiers who thought as he did and built for much the same reasons.

But what of the literary culture of Edward III and his courtiers? As Professor Scattergood shows, we know that Edward III possessed books and evidence might be cited of the king spending money upon them. Edward III's mother, Queen Philippa, also possessed books, and they are of much the same kind as those of her son – the literature of *chansons de gestes*, of romance and of chivalry. Here we have what may be described as the dominant literary currency, not only of Edward III's reign, but also of that of Richard II. But here we must be on our guard. All courtiers in all generations have much common cultural ground, but we may recall Chaucer's remark about 'diversité in Englissh and in writyng of oure tonge' and John Burrow's thought that Chaucer and Langland who were 'probably very near neighbours in the London of the 1370s and 1380s show no clear sign of having read each other's work'.[9] Granted the popularity of Arthurian literature in fourteenth-century England, we are confronted by the problems posed

9. *English Verse 1300–1500*, ed. J. A. Burrow (London, 1977), xxi.

by *Sir Gawain and the Green Knight*, which has with reason been judged the finest piece of writing on an Arthurian subject of the century. But we do not know who was the author of this magisterial work, written in the dialect of the north-west Midlands. Did the author enjoy the patronage of some aristocratic household of those parts, or may the audience for which *Gawain* and other contemporary alliterative verse was written have been primarily one of educated gentry?[10] I will not venture into controversial literary ground. Yet royal courtiers only spent part of their time in the king's company, and in their homes, far removed from Westminster, Windsor, Sheen, Eltham or Langley, they may have experienced and taken pleasure in poetry which was quite alien from anything which might appropriately be called court culture.

Let us now direct our attention to royal culture, and in particular to Edward III's patronage of architecture. Here he made a distinctive contribution which followed in the tradition of his forebears, Edward I, Henry III and other great builders before them. Edward III was consciously proud of the dignity and the tradition of the crown he had inherited. Also his pre-occupation with his duty to pursue his inherited royal rights in France and Scotland provided him with what he regarded as rightful targets against which to direct his innate belligerence. Richard II also, as we shall see, was much concerned with the historic rights of the English crown; but the inspiration which fired his concern was of a different and, in the event, more dangerous kind.

Since the reign of Edward I a rebuilding of St Stephen's Chapel at Westminster had made intermittent progress. This chapel provides our first instance of Edward III's architectural designs. Westminster was important to Edward III, as it had been to earlier kings, as a symbolic and physical attribute of the English monarchy. And so it was that in 1331 as an act of piety the young king set men to task to resume work which had been interrupted in the late days of his father.

One contemporary wrote of Edward that he was 'assiduous and eager in the construction of buildings: in many parts of his kingdom he completed buildings most excellent in craftsmanship, most elegant in design, most beautiful in location and in cost of great value'. I emphasise design and craftsmanship. These were the accomplishments of an unbroken succession of craftsmen – of masons, carpenters, painters and glaziers – upon whose talents the crown and the royal administration drew (often by impressment) to give substance to the wishes of Edward III and Richard II. There is much that might be said of William of Ramsay, John Sponle, William of Wynford, Henry Yevele, Hugh and William Herland, and their like. In the case of each man, his skill and aptitude were promoted by the challenge of royal com-

10. Ibid, 46.

missions which helped him on the way to his greatest achievements, but none of these men was a royal discovery, picked out by a perceptive royal official in the course of a talent-spotting itinerary. Nor, once Henry Yevele, for example, had been confirmed in full-time appointment by the crown with a daily payment for life, as well perhaps as an annuity, did he confine his services to the king. Significant though the royal works at Windsor and Westminster were, the record of English architectural achievement in the fourteenth century would still have been remarkable without them.

After the completion of the fabric of St Stephen's Chapel in 1348, the carpenters, the painters and the glaziers moved in. Glazing began in July 1349 with the glass being brought not only from London, as we might expect, but also from Shropshire. During the exchequer year 1351–2 twenty to thirty glaziers were working at St Stephen's under the direction of five or six masters. The coloured glass which they used may well have been imported. In March 1350 Master Hugh of St Albans appears in charge of the painters assigned to decorate the walls. It would be pleasant to know whether he discussed with the king the themes which Edward thought appropriate to the chapel. We cannot be certain. Yet in the absence of evidence showing direct royal supervision, the king must at least have let it be known that he would settle for nothing less than best. Let Hugh the painter have the materials he needs, and do not quibble about the cost of gold leaf. If he wants extra men, save him time and trouble by seeking out those whom he names.

And so we may presume it was when William of Hurley was given charge of making the stalls with the help of William Herland in 1351. Some years later, in 1355, the services of a quality carpenter from Newstead in Notts, Master Edmund of St Andrews, who 'had no equal in carver's work in England', were requisitioned. Master Edmund seems to have brought several assistants with him and for six or seven years he is described in exchequer accounts as 'master of the stalls in the king's chapel'. Time, patience, enquiry and money were essential to enterprises of this kind. The completion of St Stephen's Chapel, however, was not an expensive enterprise, costing somewhere between £2,700 and £3,700.[11]

We may now move from Westminster to Windsor, which was the home of the Order of the Garter, and consider the Chapel of St George which with a warden or dean, twelve canons and thirteen vicars served as the collegiate church of the Order of the Garter. New buildings for the college were necessary: a vestry, chapter-house, treasury, warden's lodge and accommodation for the clergy. The chapel also needed at-

11. *History of the King's Works*, ed. R. Allen Brown, H. M. Colvin and A. J. Taylor (London, 1963), i, 510–22.

tention. Work began in 1350 and was completed in 1357 at a cost of over £6,000. The chief carpenter in the chapel was William Hurley, whom I have already mentioned, with William Herland as his assistant. The glaziers were Master John Lincoln and Master John Athelard. They had their workshops in London and had already made glass for St Stephen's Chapel. The commission for the reredos was given to Master Peter of Nottingham; here we have an excellent example of the use of a provincial craftsman. His work was eventually transported to Windsor in 1367 in ten carts, each drawn by eight horses.

The chapel and the college of St George at Windsor mattered greatly to Edward III because they were integral to the Order of the Garter, but architecturally the great works in the upper bailey at Windsor were of more importance. A major reconstruction of the royal lodgings was essential to meet the needs of Edward and Philippa of Hainault, his queen. Most of the work was done between 1357 and 1365, and very impressive it was too. The continuator of the *Polychronicon* wrote that about 1359 Edward 'at the instance of William Wikham, clerk, caused many excellent buildings in the castle of Windsor to be thrown down, and others more beautiful and sumptuous to be set up'. In time Wykeham proved to be a patron of architecture of importance comparable to Edward III and Richard II. 'The said William,' the continuator wrote, 'was of very low birth . . . yet he was very shrewd, and a man of great energy. Considering how he could please the king and secure his goodwill, he counselled him to build the said castle of Windsor in the form in which it appears today to the beholder.' Wykeham made himself indispensable to the king – Froissart wrote of him, using the same phrase which he used of Robert de Vere, 'by Wykeham everything was done, and without him they did nothing'. There is what Sir William Hayter called a 'not well authenticated legend' that Wykeham inscribed somewhere on the castle walls the words *hoc fecit Wykeham*.[12] When later accused of arrogance, William explained that the words meant 'this (castle) made Wykeham', not 'Wykeham made this castle'. Very large sums were spent on the secular work at Windsor, and 'the whole range of buildings was most sumptuously re-fitted and refurbished throughout'. The principal works were the rebuilding in stone of the half-timbered buildings of the west block originally built by Henry III, the conversion of the existing hall into a great chamber for the king, and a great new hall.

William of Wykeham was clerk of the works at Windsor during the crucial period October 1356 to November 1361. Planning, organisation and co-ordination were his responsibilities. In 1360, for example, the sheriffs of thirteen counties were ordered to send a total of 568 masons to Windsor; and in the next year seventeen sheriffs were ordered to

---

12. Ibid, ii. 876–82, W. Hayter, *William of Wykeham* (London, 1970), 15.

dispatch 1360 masons to Windsor. It is hardly surprising that there were complaints that the king's works were depriving other builders of skilled labour. This reminds us that Edward III was by no means the only important builder at this time. It is interesting too to learn that others were ready to pay more than the statutory labour rates per day, and as a result the king was angered to learn that, whatever the statute said, the laws of demand and supply were costing him the services of skilled men who were drawn away by better offers. It was difficult to devise an effective remedy. It would have been unhelpful to imprison good carpenters or glaziers.

But to return to Wykeham's office. A great variety of stone was used at Windsor. It was brought from Oxfordshire, Yorkshire, Surrey, Lincolnshire and nearby Bisham in Berkshire. Ambitious architecture on the grand scale involves sustained attention to detail, and it was vital that key craftsman like Master John Sponle, master mason throughout the Windsor works and the great William of Wynford, Sponle's colleague, who first appears in royal employment in 1361, or the chief carpenter William Hurley who was assisted by his warden William Herland, should not be delayed in their work.

Thus Edward III and Queen Philippa came to possess accommodation of unprecedented grandeur and scale. Within the upper bailey the king had a number of chambers, as well as a chapel and a hall. The queen had a first chamber, a second chamber with a small chapel, a chamber with mirrors, and a dancing chamber. The cost was heavy; it was in excess of £51,000 between April 1350 and June 1377. But let us keep our perspective. We are talking of a sum which was less than the yield of one and one-half lay subsidies granted by parliament. In relation to expenditure on armies and fleets, £51,000 was a relatively small sum. The money spent on the upper bailey was less than three times the annual cost of the garrison at Calais. When war with France was renewed in 1369, all the structural work at Windsor was finished. Here there was a new monument built not to the greater glory of God or the saints in heaven, but, in an entirely proper way, as a memorial to the English regality and to Edward III himself.

If time allowed I would have liked to say something about Edward's concern for his country houses, recalling that the king was very much a 'saddle king', never staying for very long at one place. At Langley Edward spent £3000, at Hadleigh £2450, £2000 at Sheen, £966 at Moor End (acquired particularly for the hunting), £650 at Havering, £1500 at Leeds and £500 on hunting lodges in the New Forest.[13] One work which demands a little comment was Queenborough castle on the Isle of Sheppey. Queenborough is of particular interest to the

13. *King's Works,* ii. 975–6 (Langley), 662–6 (Hadleigh), 995–8 (Sheen), 742–5 (Moor End), 958–9 (Havering), 699–702 (Leeds) and 984–5 (New Forest lodges).

historian of military architecture. There was no precedent for its concentric design when work began in 1366, with an eye to the defence of the Thames estuary. If the king was not present on the day the first sod was cut, he certainly often visited Queenborough in later years, enjoying the site, it would seem. It was the only new castle built by the king, and as the cost approached £26,000 it consumed a significant proportion of Edward III's building expenditure.[14]

The most prominent of Edward III's courtiers was Edward, Prince of Wales, the Black Prince. The prince was cast in the same mould as his father, and the excellent rapport which prevailed between them, as well as within the family as a whole, contributed to an atmosphere of goodwill and mutual support at court. Both Edwards loved jousting and were as cynosures for their skill. Tournaments were part of the court way of life, colourful and expensive, exciting and sometimes dangerous. Men and women (always keen attendants) dressed for them as they would today for Ascot or for royal garden parties. Commoners flocked to watch their betters in these enjoyable, but hugely competitive, pastimes. Edward III always ordered new clothes for a tournament. He might appear as a 'simple knight' as he did in the company of the earls of Derby, Warwick, Northampton, Pembroke, Oxford and Suffolk at Dunstable on 11 February 1342. On other occasions the king's garb and that of magnate courtiers sharing his enthusiasm, was more fanciful, whimsical or satirical. Both Edward and his son spent lavishly on clothes and jewellery, traits which they shared with Richard II, who was criticised for his extravagance in a way neither his father or grandfather experienced. Edward III did not, it seems, blink at spending £500 on a dress for Queen Philippa to be worn on St George's Day, and commissioning embroidered vests costing £100, £200, or even more, lost him no sleep. He often gave rich clothes as presents, like the gowns of sanguine-coloured cloth in grain presented to the queen, Lancaster, Warwick and the earl of Duff in 1361.[15] On one occasion the Black Prince paid £715 to an embroiderer for work for himself, for his wife Joan and for her daughter; his fascination for jewels was shared by many of more modest means. In 1362, for example, he paid £200 for jewelled buttons for his wife.[16] They must have been splendid buttons, for they would have paid the daily wages of an esquire or master craftsmen for more than ten years. The sharp attacks directed against Richard II and his friends for their sartorial excesses were anticipated in the 1360s by John of Reading, who attributed the return of the Black Death to the fact that the rich, as

14. Ibid, ii. 574–7.
15. S. M. Newton, *Fashion in the Age of the Black Prince, a study of the years 1340–1365* (Woodbridge, 1980), 27.
16. R. Barber, *Edward, Prince of Wales and Aquitaine* (London, 1978), 174.

well as the not so rich, wore their hose so tight and so revealingly that they could not kneel in prayer; and there were those dreadful shoes (we hear of these again in Richard II's reign) with long beaks at their toes. Who was to blame for this shameful display? The French blamed the Italians and the English blamed the Flemings. In the late 1340s courtier dress became richer and more elaborate with increased use of imported silks and furs. An inventory of the Great Wardrobe shows stocks of linen of Rheims (4s an ell), Paris (15d an ell), Hainault and Flanders (12d an ell) and of Westphalia (10d an ell).[17] Queen Philippa had lavish tastes in clothes, owing money in 1360 to tailors, furriers, embroiderers, jewellers and goldsmiths.[18] The acquisitiveness of the king's mistress, Alice Perrers, for jewels and rich clothing is well-known. Thus the two chief women in Edward III's life had expensive tastes; both involved Edward III in financial embarrassment as a consequence. I cannot tell you whether Richard II spent more on personal adornment than his grandfather had done, but much of the evidence cited in this context by Gervase Mathew had ample precedent. If there were times when Richard owed money for his tailory, there might be reward in patience, for when the king spent, he might really lash out. Unfortunately detailed accounts are rare, but in the years 1392–4 the Great Wardrobe spent over £13,000 on mercery (£6,204), furs (£2,219) and drapery (£4,431). The merchant who supplied much of the mercery was the famous Richard Whittington; velvets, damasks, cloths of gold, taffetas and gold embroidered velvets were bought from him. Some years earlier, Whittington had done good business, to the tune of £1,900, with Robert de Vere, earl of Oxford. Another customer, someone as yet respectable politically, unlike de Vere, was Henry of Derby who also maintained a fashionable wardrobe.[19]

Edward III was aged fifty-four when he returned from his last venture in France, and the treaty of 1360 was sealed. It is impossible to chronicle with precision the changes in the habits of the king who had for so long been colourfully flamboyant and socially extrovert; but after 1360 the great days of tournaments and pageants ebbed away; there was less dressing up, fewer parties and less dancing. The king,

17. Newton, op.cit., 31–8, 44, 53–4.
18. Given-Wilson, op. cit., 106–7.
19. *The Reign of Richard II, Essays in honour of M. McKisack*, ed. F. R. H. Du Boulay and C. M. Barron: C. M. Barron, 'The quarrel of Richard II with London 1392–7', 197 n.98; *Studies in London History presented to P. E. Jones*, ed. A. E. Hollaender and W. Kellaway (London, 1971), C. M. Barron, 'Richard Whittington: the man behind the myth', 200.

however, continued to listen to music and song. Time had started to take its toll upon one who had lived life to the full, almost around the clock. His continuing zest for hunting and hawking, however, shows that he was by no means the invalid that he became in the 1370s; but he was drawing in his horns.

The Wardrobe books which survive for the 1360s and 1370s show that Edward spent increasing amounts of time away from his household, which was likely to remain at Windsor. The king rarely went to Westminster, except when a parliament or a meeting of the great council required his presence. He never failed, however, to be present at Windsor on 23 April, the day of the Garter Feast. More and more he can be observed with his *privata* or *secreta familia* at one of his country houses which he had begun to build or to restore in the late 1350s at Eltham or Sheen, Langley, Havering or Moor End.[20]

It is appropriate to amplify what has already been said about the king's chamber, for although it was part of the household, it might physically separate itself from it. The *camera regis* was indissolubly linked with the royal presence and the *secreta familia* of Edward III were members of the *camera*. The king's steward and his chamberlain usually accompanied him, as did chaplains, a physician and the king's confessor. John Woodrow, a Dominican, held this office from 1360 to 1377. The knights of the chamber were amongst Edward III's closest friends. They are an interesting group, and upon another occasion it might be illuminating to make a detailed comparison between the chamber knights of Edward III and Richard II. It would prove helpful to compare the generous patronage which Richard bestowed on the men upon whom he so closely relied in the period 1382 or 1383 to 1386 with the munificence enjoyed earlier by Edward III's chamber knights. Were Richard II's alleged excesses as great as his critics declared? Certainly Edward III had rewarded his chamber knights well with annuities (which were customary), castellanships and offices which were often sinecures. This group requires a systematic analysis throughout Edward III's reign, but Dr Given-Wilson has gathered material for the years after 1360, as Dr Tuck has done for the disturbed years before 1386.[21] As he grew older, Edward III allowed the number of his chamber knights to run down. He did so, perhaps, as a consequence of the peaceful years between 1360 and 1369, which were accompanied by his growing withdrawal from public life. Knights and

20. T. F. Tout, *Chapters in the Administrative History of Mediaeval England* 6 vols (Manchester, 1920–33) iv, 175–85, Given-Wilson, op.cit., 111f.

21. Ibid, 127–44. J. A. Tuck has examined Richard II's patronage of his chamber knights in his unpub. Univ. of Cambridge Ph.D. (1966), 'The Baronial Opposition to Richard II, 1377–89'. Both authors stress the close friendships which existed between Edward III and Richard II and their chamber knights; these men were not second-class courtiers.

esquires of the household, on the other hand, were prominent in the company Edward prepared to escort him to France in 1369. In the event Queen Philippa's death prevented him from campaigning; the household soldiers accompanied John of Gaunt, who acted as leader in his father's stead.

We know less about the presence of aristocratic courtiers in the king's company after 1360 than we would like; but an analysis of the witness lists of royal charters is helpful, if not as informative as might be wished. Several of his old companions in war witness from time to time, but age took its toll with the deaths of Warwick and of Suffolk in 1369, Oxford in 1371, Stafford in 1372, Hereford in 1373 and last, but by no means least, the rich and mighty Richard FitzAlan, earl of Arundel in 1376. In the 1370s John of Gaunt (duke of Lancaster since 1362), and his brother Edmund, earl of Cambridge, habitually attended the king when they were in England. Thomas of Woodstock, Edward's youngest son, first witnessed in 1375 at the age of nineteen and was regularly at court until 1377. In contrast the Black Prince scarcely appeared, but by this time he bore the stamp of death. Thus by his last years Edward had lost most of the courtiers whose support and friendship had once meant so much to him. The sinister Richard Lyons, who with others *privez le roi* faced the wrath of the Commons in 1376, was a very different kind of courtier. His accusers in the Good Parliament asserted that he had been prominent *a la maison et al Conseil du Roi*.[22]

The Black Prince died at Kennington on 8 June 1376 at the age of forty-six, and thus Richard, his second son (born at Bordeaux on 6 January 1367), became heir to the throne. At the time of his birth, his succession would scarcely have been predicted. For Thomas Walsingham, 16 July 1377, the day of Richard's coronation, was one 'of joy and gladness ... the long-awaited day of the renewal of peace and of the laws of the land, long exiled by the weakness of an aged king and the greed of courtiers and servants'.[23] As a background to Walsingham's rhetoric, however, the political and military scene in July 1377 did not inspire 'joy and gladness', for the war with France and Castile had just been renewed, and a dilatory English council had made wholly inadequate preparations for the defence of the realm. The south coast of England accordingly suffered heavy landings, and it was not surprising that in the parliament of October 1377 the Speaker, Sir Peter de la Mare, referred sadly to the loss of England's past greatness, and asked whether the spirit of chivalry, which had once made English soldiers daunting and of wide repute, was now dead.[24]

22. Given-Wilson, op.cit., 179f.
23. T. Walsingham, *Chronicon Angliae*, ed. E. M. Thompson (*RS*, London, 1874), 155.
24. *Rotuli Parliamentorum*, iii, 5.

The future was to prove that chivalry, as it had been understood under Edward III, was almost a thing of the past. Thomas of Woodstock's military campaign against France in 1380–81 ended disastrously, his naval expedition of November 1377–January 1378 was unhappy in its timing, and the great expense lavished on Lancaster's naval expedition of 1378 proved a disappointing investment. With the exception of the naval campaign led by the earl of Arundel in 1387, the English government found neither profit nor comfort in the war, until at last, much to Richard II's satisfaction, and as a result of the reluctant conclusion of his belligerent opponents of 1387–8 (Gloucester, Arundel, Warwick, Derby and Nottingham) that there could be no advantage in more fighting, a truce was made in 1389. Well before that date there were grounds for questioning Richard II's commitment to the French war, as well as reason to doubt whether he possessed any aptitude for war. His venture against Scotland in 1385 collapsed after verbal fighting between the king and John of Gaunt, which was all too characteristic of Richard's relations with several of his greater subjects at this time.

It is an historian's cliché to emphasise the problems inherent in the minorities of medieval kings. Edward III, it is true, passed into political manhood with success and had few problems with his magnates, nor were the criticisms directed by the Commons in parliament often aimed at him personally. Richard II's minority, on the other hand, began with anxiety and fear that through abuse or manipulation disaster might strike. Within four years anxiety had advanced to overt criticism. The royal household, for example, spent too much money on hospitality. Parliament would never have presumed to criticise Edward III in this way, nor to have demanded that the king's confessor should absent himself from court except at the main Christian festivals of the year. Thomas Rushook, the clerk in question (later bishop of Llandaff in 1383 and of Chichester in 1385), was not perhaps much exercised with concern for Richard II's immortal soul. Nor, it seems, can Sir Simon Burley and Sir Aubrey de Vere have been helping the young king to learn political discretion. Court and country were drifting apart, and for this reason Richard, earl of Arundel, and Michael de la Pole were appointed by the Lords 'to attend the king in his household and to govern his person'. The household, furthermore, and its officials, it was thought, required investigation: the Lords and Commons believed that they had smelled smoke. In July 1382, Richard, lord Scrope, an outraged chancellor, vacated office because he found himself unable to reconcile his sense of duty with the orders sent to him by the king. In 1384 the king's court and his council were exposed to a barrage of criticism, to which Richard II reacted pugnaciously. If the earl of Arundel thought the realm was ill-governed, he could go to the devil. In October 1386 the king was threatened with deposition by his uncle, Thomas of Gloucester, and by Thomas Arundel, bishop of Ely, two men who in happier circumstances might have been expected to have been active courtiers. Parliament lasted until 28 November 1386 and, as it ran its course, Richard seethed with anger. Impotently, he observed his faithful chancellor, de la Pole, impeached and sentenced for offences which, to the king, seemed either imaginary or non-existent. At a later date, during the Merciless Parliament (3 February to 4 June 1388), the king listened helplessly as the duke of Gloucester and the earls of Arundel, Warwick, Derby (the king's cousin and the son of John of Gaunt) and Nottingham charged de la Pole and Robert de Vere with putting kingship in bondage and causing Richard to hate the loyal lords of the realm. In addition, they had impoverished the king and by the levy of unnecessary taxation had bankrupted the realm. To Richard this was arrant falsity. This talk of his 'bondage' was propagandist nonsense, as were the charges against four of his chamber knights, Sir Simon Burley, Sir John Beauchamp of Holt, Sir James Berners and Sir John Salisbury. Far from placing him in servitude, they had been his friends and they had executed his will. If Burley had 'dwelled about the person of the king and had been with him since his youth', Richard had delighted in his presence, and in saying that Burley had 'procured' the advancement of Robert de Vere and had caused the king 'to have many aliens, Bohemians and others in his Household', the Commons were insulting the king. The actions attacked and the patronage dispersed had been determined by Richard himself.

The period October 1386 to June 1388 was the fulcrum in the political history of the reign. Richard II suffered experiences which he never forgot, and the fate of many of the members of his chamber – unhelpfully labelled Richard II's 'first court party' by some historians – was a savage affront to the king's understanding of his office. Earlier in 1387 he had withdrawn from Westminster when his household was exposed to an examination by a commission appointed in parliament. In December 1387, there was a brief phase of civil war, and in the following month household servants were dismissed by the score. Four courtiers whom the king had until then implicitly trusted were charged with treason (and later executed after parliamentary judgment); others were banished from the king's presence. The court which Richard had created and which had helped to create him had been decimated.

With this argumentative political background in mind, we may now examine the validity of the concept of a Ricardian court culture. Once again it is essential to remind ourselves that this phrase can only be used to advantage if we can recognise a coherence of literary and artistic interests shared by the king and his companions. Notwithstanding the confident judgments of those scholars whose opinions have already been quoted, it is hard to fashion a portrait of Richard as a significant cultural force, let alone a cultural leader. As we have seen he shared with his father and grandfather a love of richly ostentatious dress and jewellery.[25] He was also devoted to hunting and hawking, which occupied much of his time. On the other hand, he lacked their belligerence, and while he was ready to watch a tournament from time to time, or to promote one for diplomatic reasons, Richard never jousted himself and tournaments played a smaller part in court entertainment than they had done earlier. We do not know whether the Black Prince had devoted as much thought to Richard's education as Edward III seems to have done for his sons, or Gaunt for his heir. His facility in reading French pleased the self-important Froissart in 1395 but was entirely predictable; it would have been remarkable had it been otherwise. We must accept on trust his report that Richard was delighted with a collection of poems about love stories. Richard must also have been accustomed to reading English. Had this not been so, John Gower, flattered and anxious to please when receiving an invitation from the king to write him 'something new', would have played safe and written in French. It would not appear that the contents of the *Confessio Amantis* reflect more than Gower's expectation of what was likely to be acceptable to Richard; and his later re-dedication of his work, which, judging by the relatively large numbers of early copies surviving, had something of a vogue, does not suggest an attempt by Gower to fashion a work for a man whose literary interests were known to be unusual. Richard's spontaneous request to Gower indicates some liking for literature, but to see it as an act of patronage, in more than a loose sense, would be unsound. There is no evidence that Gower was ever beholden to the king for anything and, when Richard's behaviour displeased him, Gower was uninhibited in writing what he thought. We are uncertain whether the author of the *libellus* on geomantics, written in March 1391, chose a theme which he understood to be of particular interest to the king, or if the same author was responsible for all the contents of MS Bodley 581.[26] There is nothing strikingly unusual or original in its diverse contents. The *De Quadripartita Regis Specie Libellum*, it is true, was expressly intended to help the king in exercising his office, but most of it derives from the pseudo-Aristotelian tract *Secreta Secretorum*, which was widely read at the time. It is in fact impossible to write with conviction about the king's literary preferences, but we do know that upon occasion he recognised the pragmatic value of written words which might be used to justify or buttress his ideas

25. G. Mathew, *The Court of Richard II* (London, 1968), 26–9, 38–9.
26. *Four English Political Tracts of the Later Middle Ages*, ed. Jean-Philippe Genet, Camden Society, 4th series, xviii (1977), 22–39.

about kingship. How much thought Richard had given before 1386 to the misfortunes of his great-grandfather, Edward II, we cannot tell; but in 1387 he was advancing a case for Edward's canonisation, and in 1395 a record of miracles attributed to Edward was sent to Rome.[27] Legal and political precedent mattered greatly to Richard II, and we can assume he had learned advisers who helped him articulate historical arguments against the humiliations inflicted upon him by the parliament of October-November 1386. This is evident from the skilfully devised questions to the judges of August 1387, which not surprisingly frightened the advocates of the reform programme of the previous year. In this context the compilation of statutes contained in St John's College, Cambridge, MS A.7 has not received the attention it merits. The statutes chosen in the manuscript have yet to be analysed in detail, but the illumination on f.113, portraying an enthroned king (Richard II himself) receiving a book from a kneeling clerk, suggests a presentation copy of a work which the king had commissioned. The inclusion of the *Articuli super Cartas* of 1301 and of the Ordinances of 1311 together with the *statutum come Hugh le Despenser* proves that Richard II had been thinking hard about earlier episodes of crown-magnate hostilities.[28] The dating of the last entry (1 December 1388) places the text close to the king's experiences during the Merciless Parliament and strongly suggests that Richard remained consistent in the reasoning behind his hostility to his opponents in that year. It is virtually certain, however he behaved between May 1389 and July 1397, that he remained convinced of the rightness of his cause. As we know, this inflexibility of thought, combined with his obsessional vindictiveness, ultimately led to his deposition. If Richard II was sure that history was on his side, Roger Dymock was equally confident of the king's orthodoxy, when, some time after January 1395, he presented his carefully argued case (written in Latin and drawing upon a host of learned authorities) against the Lollard *Conclusions* (probably presented in their original English) advocating the reform of the church, to the king. We cannot be sure that Dymock anticipated that Richard had either the capacity or the application wholly to assimilate his arguments, but clearly he did not underestimate the king's intelligence. As regent master of the Dominicans in England, Dymock was well-informed about his religious habits. Richard respected Dominicans and particularly liked sermons preached by members of that order.[29]

27. E. Perroy, *L'Angleterre et le Grand Schisme d'Occident* (Paris, 1933), 301, 330, 341–2.

28. *Descriptive Catalogue of the manuscripts in the library of St John's College Cambridge* (Cambridge, 1913), ed. M. R. James, 111–13.

29. *Rogeri Dymmok liber contra XII errores et hereses Lollardorum* (London, 1922) ed. H. S. Cronin.

Richard II was a devout king, and this was something he shared with his much-loved queen, Anne of Bohemia. Her father, Charles IV (1346-1378), had been a cultured king, presiding over a court wholly dissimilar from those of Edward III or Richard II. He was a patron of artists, and his court offices were held by eminent scholars whom he had gathered together through generous patronage. In 1348 he had established the Caroline University at Prague and in his youth he had known the University of Paris. Anne's intelligence is obvious, for she acquired some mastery of English and a later defence of the translation of the bible into the vernacular alleges that in his funeral oration in 1394, Thomas Arundel, then archbishop of York, praised Anne 'for, notwithstanding that she was an alien born, she had in English all the four gospels' together with vernacular glosses upon them. There are, as Dr Hudson has warned us, problems in this reference and it should be treated with caution.[30] There may, however, have been some residual element of truth in this posthumous and almost certainly embellished story. If Anne with her impeccable orthodoxy was not attracted by writing in English which helped her better to understand the New Testament, there were knights of the king's chamber who undoubtedly were.

At this point we may refer briefly to the fact that among the king's chamber and household knights there were several men who interest the literary historian. This is the concern of Professor Scattergood, but in our search for court culture the literacy of Richard's chamber knights deserves emphasis and the fact that two of them were poets calls for mention. Sir John Clanvowe wrote in English, whereas the lost verses of Sir John Montague (Steward of the king's Household from October 1381 to January 1387, and later earl of Salisbury) were in French, and judging by the testimony of Christine de Pisan, they were of some quality. Sir Richard Stury, Sir Philip de la Vache and Sir Lewis Clifford were book-owners (though this is not in itself surprising) and several were on more than nodding terms with Chaucer. It is uncertain, however, how much this grouping of men owed to the king himself, for most of them had previously been servants or associates of the Black Prince or of Princess Joan. The point I would stress here is that we are concerned with royal familiars who had cultural interests. These interests were shared, but they were not of a kind or coherence which would justify any suggestion that proximity to the king or interaction within his court noticably promoted them or gave them a common stamp of a particular kind.

It is interesting to compare the scale and the character of royal building under Richard II with that of Edward III. Only one work of major importance was undertaken during his reign and this was the

---

30. *English Wycliffite Writings*, ed. A. Hudson, (Cambridge, 1978), 166–8.

reparacio of the great hall at Westminster. In 1394, when John Godmaston was put in charge of the project, the mighty hall which had
been built three hundred years earlier by Rufus showed signs of age.
It is also possible that it was judged old-fashioned and inconvenient
for the state occasions for which it was used. The strengthening of the
east wall with a flying buttress in 1387 and the use of the word 'repair'
in Godmaston's letter patent prompts the thought that physical de-
terioration had set in. In the event, as we know, the hall was transformed. The masonry was entrusted to Henry Yevele and the
carpentry to Hugh Herland, and with such talents employed it is not
surprising that instead of a patching-up operation a magnificent reconstruction took place. By 1401 Westminster Hall had become one of
the great glories of contemporary secular architecture in Western
Europe. The glorious hammer-beam roof commands admiration for its
beauty and for its technical expertise.[31]

It is at this point important to conjecture the character and extent
of the king's involvement with this work. Some have written as if the
new hall should be seen as a proof of the artistic vision of the king
himself. Scholars may wish to differ here, for the evidence discourages
confident judgment. We may assume that when a building of such
importance was an issue the problem was discussed with the king in
some detail. What was his will? He probably asked for advice, and this
required recourse to experts. Yevele and Herland must have enquired
how much money the king was prepared to spend, for they could not
make more than general suggestions unless they were given some
indication of what the king wanted.

There is no evidence to suggest that either Edward III or Richard
II identified themselves with the royal architectural achievements of
their reigns with the dedicated concern which had characterised Henry
III's supervision of the rebuilding of the abbey at Westminster. Tout's
comment that 'after 1397 Richard hardly ventured to show his face at
Westminster unless strongly protected, although Westminster Hall
was being rebuilt' is interesting in this context, and it is notable that
between 1 October 1395 and 30 September 1397 Richard II only visited
Westminster to honour the anniversary of the death of Queen Anne
on 7 June.[32] It may be prudent to play down Richard II's personal
contribution to Westminster Hall. On the other hand the repeated
occurence of the symbol of the white hart in the carving and masonry
of the hall deserves mention. The king was doubtless gratified by what
he saw of the new work. His taste for the splendid was gratified, and
in the work of Yevele and Herland he saw the dignity of Westminster
enhanced. Whatever instructions he may have given about the hall,

31. *King's Works*, i, 527–33.
32. Tout, loc.cit., 218–22.

we may be sure that he expressed a concern that the job should be a credit to himself. He liked things done in style, even if he may have possessed no outstanding insights. It is ironical that Richard II's historical reputation as a patron of architecture, based as it is almost wholly upon the survival of Westminster Hall, should rank higher than that of his grandfather whose expenditure on the royal palace at Windsor, which has not survived, was vastly greater than the suggested sum of perhaps £8,000 – £9,000 spent on Westminster Hall. There can be no suggestion that the work done for Edward III – who, spent more than double this sum on Queenborough Castle alone – was lacking in quality.

Gervase Mathew, drawing upon the material cited in the *History of the King's Works*, has described Richard's commissions for his country palaces.[33] When allowance has been made for some decline in the relevant evidence, two points are clear. Richard II spent much less than his grandfather had done, for the younger king was able to enjoy the fruits of Edward III's enthusiasms. One of the attractions of Langley, Eltham or Sheen was that Edward III had made them such hospitable residences. Secondly, when we read of Richard II's new bath-house at Eltham, we may recall that a bath-house had been built by Edward III at Langley at some cost in 1368–69; it had ten windows. Despite Richard II's invention of the handerchief, I doubt whether one king was more fastidious about personal cleanliness than the other. Both kings spent money on dancing chambers, and for all that contemporaries wrote, I doubt whether Richard II and his courtiers were more prone to pass their leisure hours in thoughtless hedonism at vast expense than Edward III and his friends had been. Proof of more sophistication in Richard II's court and of a greater prominence of ladies than had prevailed under Edward III is not readily apparent. Dance and song, conjurers and acrobats, masques and charades were to be found in the courts of both men. The line of continuity seems to have been strong, and in our quest for royal patronage Queen Philippa's hospitality to Froissart probably owed as much to his talent for writing pleasing verse and lyrics as to their common background in Hainault. My impression is that until at least 1360 the court of Edward III was probably more fun than that of his grandson.

Space forbids extended examinations of Richard II's pursuit of architecture and of its embellishments. Westminster Abbey, for example, was patronised by the king, which was scarcely surprising;[34] the amenities of the collegiate church of St Stephen's, Westminster were

33. Mathew, op.cit., 22–37.
34. R. B. Rackham, 'The nave of Westminster Abbey', *Proc.Brit.Acad.* iv (1909–1910). 40, 91; Richard II gave less than £300 to the rebuilding of Westminster nave, whereas he contracted to spend £250 on Queen Anne's tomb and £400 for effigies of Anne and himself: *Reign of Richard II*: J. H. Harvey, 'Richard II and York', 209 and n.5.

improved (work left incomplete by Edward III); there is interesting evidence of rich decorative work executed at the Tower of London in the 1390s; and during 1394–6 more than £1,100 was spent on a new residence in Windsor Park. York (a grant of 100 marks) and Canterbury (£160 in unpaid taxation pardoned) received tiny contributions towards the costs of their great rebuilding schemes. It is hard to argue that here was a great artistic patron.[35]

In conclusion I wish to say a little more about some English architecture of the late fourteenth century in order to present Richard II in perspective. Elsewhere in this book Dr Colvin explores the concept of a 'court style' of architecture in England in the later middle ages. My concern is to return to the theme of architecture as an aspect of court culture in the years 1350–1400. I would like to keep the rebuilding of Westminster Hall and Richard's modest royal patronage of building within a proper context. In doing so I must allow myself some latitude in using the term 'courtier'. Some of the men I mention were true *familiares* of the king, while others enjoyed proximity to the king only intermittently and, when they did so, it was more a matter of royal prudence than pleasure. Thomas Beauchamp, earl of Warwick (1339–1401), for example, was rarely much more than a nominal courtier of Richard II; but continuing the tradition of his father, one of Edward III's warrior friends, he built extensively at Warwick, adding to the proud family castle and rebuilding the parish church of St Mary. Not far away, and at much the same time, John of Gaunt was lavishing money on gracious accommodation at Kenilworth Castle. It will be interesting to learn more in due course about the scale of Gaunt's spending on architecture. At Warwick and Kenilworth there was evident concern for domestic space and comfort. This was a major concern too for John Holand, duke of Exeter (the king's half-brother) when Dartington was built with its magnificent hall, graced by another striking hammer-beam roof. Away in the north, lord Scrope of Bolton built a fine new castle on the Yorkshire moors. Much of it still stands, and from its battlements the historian of today may peer northwards across a largely unchanged landscape, trying in his mind's eye to catch sight of the Scots riding south, as had been their custom six hundred years earlier. Scrope was a generous patron of Durham Cathedral, providing a magnificent reredos. To the east Henry Percy, earl of Northumberland, who had striven for political moderation and reconciliation in late 1387, but who, twelve years later, had become (for reasons by no means clear) the implacable opponent of Richard II, was

35. *King's Works*, ii, 123, 469.

financing work at Warkworth which is regarded as some of the finest accomplished by any medieval English architect. The size of the castle provided ample accommodation for the earl, his family and his retainers. Warkworth was comfortable and plenty of light shone through a great central lantern and ingeniously placed interior windows. All of this work might loosely be described as Ricardian architecture, but I would rule out the suggestion that it was court architecture as inappropriate. As a final thought, may I close with a few words about William of Wykeham, bishop of Winchester? He had, as we have seen, made himself indispensable to Edward III, and he continued at least in an official capacity – councillor or minister of state – to be a courtier of Richard II. The architectural patronage of this remarkable man was only a part of his cultural legacy, but the buildings which he financed and inspired at Winchester – the college and a continuation of the rebuilding of the cathedral nave – and at Oxford, through the foundation of New College, represent some of the finest architectural work of his generation. But I would be reluctant to describe them as part of the court culture of our period.

2

Literary Culture at the Court of Richard II

V. J. Scattergood

Anyone who seriously attempts to come to terms with questions about the development of English literature needs to face problems which are properly the province of the historian, particularly the social historian. In order to do his work the literary scholar with any commitment to historicism needs to be able to speak with some certainty about the level of culture at any particular time, especially about the level of literary culture. He will wish to know about the extent of literacy, about the general and particular availability of books, about the cost of books; he will wish to know about the characteristic reading habits of the public and about ownership and use of books. Crucially, he will wish to know which books were important in the establishment of taste, and he will want to know also about the impact of new literature – particularly if that literature turns out to be important.

For recent times these questions are relatively easy to answer; at least, the evidence is available (usually in an official form). But as one goes back further in time it becomes more and more difficult to generalise about the state of literary culture and about the impact of individual writers and books on that culture. The evidence not only does not exist in any completeness, but it often does not exist at all; and when it does exist the scholar who seeks to generalise from it often has the uneasy feeling that his material consists largely of, perhaps unrepresentative, chance survivals. Of course, something can be established even about the conditions of literary culture in medieval England. Some measure of the popularity of a medieval book can be approximately deduced from the number of manuscript copies in which it survives, and the number of references to it. The ownership of books can be established in general terms by determining whether the surviving manuscript copies were *de luxe* products for an aristocratic market, or whether they were relatively plain, cheaper copies; exceptionally, precise ownership, can be established by an inscription claiming ownership, or by means of a coat of arms. There are a few official documents – wills and inventories being the most useful – which list books amongst other things. But the evidence is scanty and hard to apply. What there is, however, literary scholars sometimes ignore, and this leads to faulty generalisations about the state of literary culture and the impact of certain authors, even when the literary culture is that of a court as well documented as Richard II's.

If one does not look too closely, it is easy to see Richard II as presiding at the centre of a literary court culture based on the English language and having as its most famous representatives John Gower and Geoffrey Chaucer.[1] There is evidence which can be read to support this view. In the Prologue to the first recension of *Confessio Amantis* Gower refers to his poem as 'A bok for King Richardes sake' and to himself as 'liege man' to the king with all his 'hertes obeissance' in everything that he 'may doon or can' (24–8); and he goes on to describe the way in which the king invited him on to his barge on the Thames and encouraged him to write his poem.[2] What is more, the frontispiece to the Corpus Christi College, Cambridge, MS 61 copy of Chaucer's *Troilus and Criseyde* appears to show the poet reading his poem to a court audience: those about the poet, in a variety of postures signifying everything from rapt attention to utter boredom, are dressed in an elaborate and highly fashionable way; and some scholars have even gone so far as to identify individual figures with actual people – the man dressed in gold in the lower left centre of the picture, for example, is usually said to be Richard II.[3] Once the assumption is made that the picture records an actual occasion, or that it is the accurate embodiment of a tradition which represents Chaucer as delivering his poems in this way, it is not difficult to find, in the rest of his work, evidence that might be interpreted to mean that he was the poet of the court. Some poems certainly have clear connections with the royal family or the higher aristocracy: it is plain from lines 1314–20 of *The Book of the Duchess* that, whatever else it is, that poem is a sort of consolatory elegy on the death of Blanche of Lancaster, wife of John of Gaunt; and it is plain that the witty *Complaint to his Purse* is a request to Henry IV for money.[4] Moreover, it is an easy step from assuming that Chaucer wrote for royal or aristocratic audiences to the

1. For example, Gervase Mathew, *The Court of Richard II* (London 1968), 62–82.

2. All references are to *The English Works of John Gower*, ed. G. C. Macaulay, *EETS* ES 81, 82 (1900, 1901).

3. See, for example, Aage Brusendorff, *The Chaucer Tradition* (Copenhagen, 1925), 19–25; Margaret Galway, 'The *Troilus* frontispiece', *MLR* xliv (1949), 161–77; George Williams, 'The *Troilus and Criseyde* frontispiece again', *MLR*, lvii (1962), 173–78.

4. All references are to *The Complete Works of Geoffrey Chaucer*, ed. F. N. Robinson (2nd edition, London, 1957).

notion that the marks of favour he received – annuities, gifts, relatively important administrative positions – were to some extent rewards for his literary efforts.

It is an attractive argument, but not one which can be sustained. Gower was in no sense dependent on Richard II's patronage: he was relatively well-off, owning land in East Anglia and Kent; he made provision in his will for a chantry in Southwark Cathedral and made bequests to churches and hospitals in London; he provided generously for his wife. He could, and evidently did, write to please himself, for when he revised *Confessio Amantis* in 1393 he suppressed the references to the king, so it is unlikely that he was totally committed to Richard II or reliant on him. In fact, approving references to Henry Bolingbroke, present in the poem from the first, begin to increase in the later versions – probably not because he owed anything to Bolingbroke (though he did accept a 'collar' in 1393) but because he admired him, and perhaps because he felt his name lent weight to the poem.[5] In 1374 Chaucer received an annual pension of £10 from John of Gaunt, but there is nothing to connect that with the writing of *The Book of the Duchess*; indeed, Chaucer's wife appears to have been more honoured by Gaunt than Chaucer was.[6] None of the surviving manuscripts of the *Confessio Amantis* has a standard presentation picture – the poet kneeling before his patron presenting his book – nor do any of Chaucer's.

What the *Troilus* frontispiece is, however, is not easy to determine. Of the two scenes depicted, the upper one shows two decoratively attired companies meeting outside an ornate castle – it seems to be based on 'procession' pictures.[7] The lower picture, though, appears to be based on fairly standard 'preaching' or 'teaching' pictures.[8] The 'poet' (if that is what he is) stands in what looks like a pulpit; he has no book from which to read; and he gestures admonishingly at his audience with his right hand – a typical 'preaching' or 'teaching' posture. The manuscript evidently dates from after Chaucer's death, and it may well be that the scene depicted has no historical authenticity at all – though the appearance of the poet is similar to other portraits of Chaucer. It may be that the compiler of the manuscript needed a frontispiece and that a refashioned 'procession' picture was

5. For an account of the successive dedications of *Confessio Amantis* see Macaulay, op. cit., i, xxi–xxviii; and for a view in the context of other double dedications K. J. Holzknecht, *Literary Patronage in the Middle Ages* (Philadelphia, 1923), 147–9.

6. *Chaucer Life-Records*, ed. M. M. Crow and C. C. Olson (Oxford, 1966), 271–4; and for Philippa Chaucer see 67–93.

7. *Troilus and Criseyde, A Facsimile of Corpus Christi College Cambridge MS 61* with introductions by M. B. Parkes and Elizabeth Salter (Cambridge, 1978), 15–23.

8. Derek Pearsall, 'The *Troilus* frontispiece and Chaucer's audience', *Yearbook of English Studies*, vii (1977), 68–74.

what his artist chose to illustrate one of the central incidents in the poem[9] – Criseyde's parting from Troilus and meeting with Diomede (v.57–91) – and that a refashioned 'preaching' picture was the closest approximation the artist could find to communicate the myth of oral delivery, the sense of a listening group that Chaucer cultivates in the poem itself with his references to 'al this compaignye' of lovers 'in this place' (i.450, ii.30). It may well be therefore that Chaucer's relation to the court was very different from the one implied in this picture. The prominence he attained as an administrator and civil servant – controller of customs for the port of London, clerk of the king's works and so on – was probably the result of his ability and efficiency in these areas; and the gifts and marks of favour he received are not out of line with those received by people (who were not poets) in similar positions. No reward that Chaucer received can be directly connected with his activity as a poet; he did not owe his career to his literary ability.[10] It looks rather as if the positions he attained – which were comparatively well-paid and relatively unarduous – gave him the leisure to write.

That Gower and Chaucer were not poets patronised by the aristocracy ought, in many ways, to create no surprise. One cannot be sure, of course, what sort of literature the king and the aristocracy listened to, but it is fairly clear from the books they owned that their tastes were settled on a literature very different from that which Chaucer and Gower produced.

One needs to begin with Richard II's books, about which there is a certain amount of information (though it is not easy to interpret). According to a Memoranda Roll list compiled in 1384–5[11] he owned 'vne Romance de Roy Arthure', the chanson de geste *Aimeri de Narbonne*, another on *Garin le Loherenc*, the *Queste del Saint Graal*, the Vulgate *Mort Artu*, a version of the Alexander romance *Fuerre de Gadres*, a *Generides* in French, and *Enseignements Robert de Ho* ('vn Romance de Trebor'). A few other items cannot be identified: 'vn Romance de Darry et ffloridas' which may be a version of *Fuerre de Gadres*, 'vn liure des laies mon' Lowys Counte de Cleremond', and 'vn Romance q'comence "Seignours voillez oier vn bon chauncon. . ." '. On the dorse of the same document are listed a two-volume Bible, a *Roman de la*

9. See Elizabeth Salter and Derek Pearsall, 'Pictorial illustration of late medieval poetic texts: the role of the frontispiece or prefatory picture', *Medieval Iconography and Narrative: A Symposium* (Odense University Press, 1980), 100–23.

10. A point well made by F. R. H. du Boulay, 'The historical Chaucer' in *Writers and their Background: Geoffrey Chaucer*, ed. D. S. Brewer (London, 1974), 33–57.

11. This list has frequently been studied: see Edith Rickert, 'Richard II's Books', *The Library*, 4th series, xiii, (1933), 144–7; and R. S. Loomis, 'The library of Richard II', *Studies in Language, Literature and Culture of the Middle Ages and Later*, ed. E. Bagby Atwood and A. A. Hill (Austin, Texas, 1969), 173–8. (For some of the indentifications I follow Loomis).

Rose, and what is probably Chrétien's *Conte del Graal* ('vn Romance de Perciuall et Gawyn'). There is no doubt that Richard II owned these books, but what they can reveal about his literary tastes is limited. Recent evidence has been brought forward to show that he purchased none himself: all fourteen were inherited from his grandfather Edward III, and by 1384–5 'it seems more than likely that the books and other valuables on the Memoranda Roll had been sold or pawned to raise cash for chamber expenses'.[12]

Aside from this list a certain amount of other information about books owned by Richard II has survived.[13] At some time between 1394 (the death of Queen Anne) and 1396 (the marriage of Richard II to Princess Isabella) he acquired the exquisite two-volume *Breviaire de Belleville* which had miniatures by Jean Pucelle. On Richard II's death it passed to Henry IV, who sent it back to France to Jean, Duc de Berry. It survives as Bibliothèque Nationale MSS Latin 10483–4. In 1395, according to his own account, the Hainault chronicler and poet Jean Froissart presented a book of poems to Richard II:

> . . .Then the King asked me what it (the book) dealt with. I said to him, 'Of love'. He was pleased with this reply and looked into the book in various places and read, for he spoke and read French very well, and then he gave it to one of his knights who was called Sir Richard Credon to take to his [i.e. the King's] private chamber, and he welcomed me even more pleasantly and entertained me marvellously well.[14]

A little later Richard II received a copy (now BL MS Royal 20 B VI, complete with presentation picture) of Philippe de Mézières's *Epistre d'un Viele Solitaire des Celestins de Paris*, a propagandist work urging the princes of Christendom (especially Charles VI and Richard II) to forget their differences and combine in a crusade against the infidel. There is no evidence that Richard II asked for any of the last three books. In fact, the only book he probably commissioned is the *Libellus Geomancie* (now extant in MS Bodley 581 and BL MS Royal 12 C V) a collection of pseudo-science and advice (see Appendix A). He also owned the *Forme of Cury*, a collection of recipes written for him by his master cook, two books of statutes (now St John's College, Cambridge, MS A 7 and BL MS Cotton Nero D VI) and Dymmok's *Liber contra Duodecim Errores* (now Trinity Hall, Cambridge, MS 17) a polemical attack on Lollard heresies presented to him in 1396.

12. Edith Rickert, *loc. cit.*, pointed out that several of Richard II's books belonged to Queen Isabella, and R. S. Loomis, op. cit., suggested inheritance from Edward III. For the idea that the books on this list were being sold or pawned in 1384–5, see R. F. Green, 'King Richard II's books revisited', *The Library*, xxxi (1976), 235–9.

13. For good brief accounts of some of these books see R. S. Loomis *loc. cit.* 175–7 and Gervase Mathew op. cit., 40–42.

14. *Chroniques*, ed. Kervyn de Lettenhove, 25 vols. (Brussels, 1870–7), xv, 164 (my translation).

Richard II seems to have been anything but an assiduous book collector, and one cannot, with any confidence, make generalisations about the nature of literary culture at his court simply on the basis of the books he at some stage owned. Yet the main features of the books which come into his possession – that they tended to be in French primarily, though a considerable number were in Latin, and that for entertainment reading the staple was romance – are also found in other aristocratic collections.

A list of books appears among the possessions of Thomas Woodstock, duke of Gloucester (the king's uncle) who died, probably murdered, in 1397.[15] It is both larger (it contains more than 80 items) and more varied than the king's. A good many of the books were theological or philosophical: a two-volume Bible, a versified Bible, the 'histories of the Popes', a book on the evangelists, a book on the Apocalypse, St Augustine, St Bernard's meditations, Gregory's *Cura Pastoralis*, a collection of decretals (perhaps Gratian's), a Boethius, a *Barlaam and Ioasaph*, various prayers, a life of St Thomas of Canterbury, and so on. He had some law books: a Latin book on civil law and the statutes of England and France. Several were historical: Livy's Roman histories, Nicholas Trivet's *Chronicles*, and various other books on English history including MS Bodley 316 (a *Polychronicon* and several other works by Higden and Walsingham). Some books were of a more or less practical nature: Giles of Rome's *De Regimine Principum*, Vegetius on the art of war, Bartholemew's *De Proprietatibus Rerum*, two books on physic, one on geography. His leisure reading, apart from the almost obligatory *Roman de la Rose* (which he acquired from the executors of Sir Richard Stury), seems to have consisted primarily of romances: one on Hector of Troy, two on Merlin, a French Lancelot, two books in French on the Trojan war, 'la gest de Fouk Filtz Waryn', an Alexander, a book on Arthur, and one on Godefray of Bouillon. Less predictably, he had a book on the art of poetry, two versions of *Les Voeux du Paon*, and a French Mandeville's *Travels*. He also had a large book of 'tretes amoireux & moralitez & de caroll' in French, which may have been a book of lyrics or shorter poems. It is not always possible to decide in what language each particular book was written, but it looks likely that forty-eight were certainly in French, twenty-five in Latin, and only three in English. The English books, though, are interesting: two are on the 'evangelists' and one of these is described as 'new' ('novel') as if such books were unusual; the third is 'un bible en Engleys' which

15. Viscount Dillon and W. H. St John Hope, 'Inventory of the goods and chattels belonging to Thomas, duke of Gloucester', *Archaeological Review*, liv (1897), 275–308. See also the useful account of Anthony Goodman, *The Loyal Conspiracy: the Lords Appelant under Richard II* (London, 1971), 74–86.

was almost certainly Wycliffite. This is now BL MSS Egerton 617 and 618. He also had thirty-nine service books in his chapel.

This is by far the largest collection of which evidence remains from the reign of Richard II. But the contents of smaller aristocratic collections give evidence of much the same taste – a taste shared by noble ladies too. On 28 January 1391 Margaret Courtenay, Countess of Devon bequeathed two primers, a book on medicine, a book of vices and virtues and three romances: on Tristram, Merlin and 'Arthur de Britaigne'.[16] On 6 December 1392 Isabel, Duchess of York left two Bibles, two primers, a book of vices and virtues to Sir Lewis Clifford, and two books called 'marchart' and 'Launcelot' to her son Edward.[17] A rather larger collection, but one which has similarities to the two previous ones, was bequeathed by Eleanor Bohun, duchess of Gloucester on 9 August 1399.[18] She had a two-volume Bible in French, a book of decretals also in French, Comestor's *Biblia Scholastica*, the *Vitae Patrum* by Jerome and John Cassian, Gregory's *Cura Pastoralis*, four psalters – two of which were glossed, one was 'richly illuminated', and the other included the 'primer and other devotions' (perhaps National Library of Scotland MS 18.6.5). She also had a *Legenda Aurea* in French and a book of vices and virtues. Her collection was predominantly religious in character, therefore, but she had three secular books: a chronicle of France in French, a version of Egidus's *De Regimine Principum*, and a single verse romance – the 'Histoire de Chivaler a Cigne'. Though a few of these books may have been in Latin, the majority were in French; none of them was in English.

Among non-aristocratic courtiers there are indications also of the same set of literary preferences, though the evidence is not very plentiful. The best of this evidence concerns Sir Simon Burley who, though not an aristocrat, came to prominence in Richard II's court perhaps because the Black Prince, Richard's father, had made him Richard's tutor. At his execution in 1388 Burley possessed 22 books.[19] Several were on religious subjects – a Bible, two books on the commandments, and a book of saints' lives. But he also had a book of philosophy (unspecified), a French Gile's *De Regimine Principum*, the prophecies of Merlin, and the *Sompniale Danielis* in French (which he had lent to John Acton 'clerk'), and what appears to have been a multi-lingual dictionary. Eight of his books were French romances, including one

16. *Testamenta Vetusta*, ed. N. H. Nicolas, 2 vols (London, 1826), i, 127–8; K. B. McFarlane, *The Nobility of Later Medieval England* (Oxford, 1973), 236.
17. McFarlane op. cit., 236–7.
18. *Testamenta Vetusta* i, 146–9; McFarlane, op.cit., 236. There is some useful material also in E. G. Millar and M. R. James, *The Bohun Manuscripts* (Roxburghe Club, 1936).
19. V. J. Scattergood, 'Two medieval book lists', *The Library*, xxiii (1968), 236–9; Maude Clarke, *Fourteenth Century Studies* (Oxford, 1937), 120–1.

on Arthur, another on Bevis, and another on Maugis d'Aigremont. Only one of his books was in English – 'I liure de englys del forster & del sengler' – probably a book on hunting. One could do with knowing more about other knights who were not aristocrats, but the information is very scanty. In 1389 Sir William Trussell bequeathed 'all his books of romances', but unfortunately did not specify what they were.[20] Sir Richard Stury owned a copy of *Le Roman de la Rose* (now BL MS Royal 19 B XIII). Sir Lewis Clifford, as well as receiving the book of vices and virtues from Isabel, duchess of York, also bequeathed to Sir Philip de la Vache 'my mass-book and my porhoos' and 'my book of tribulation to my daughter his wife'.[21]

Of course, wills and forfeitures simply record the ownership of books; it does not follow necessarily that the recorded owners sought to possess the books in question. They may have been heirlooms, and, in fact, the care with which some testators bequeath books makes one suppose that they were valued objects (they often had highly ornamental covers and fastenings) irrespective of literary merit. It does not follow necessarily either that the owners of these books actually read them, or that they did not read (or listen to) anything else. Nevertheless, this evidence does show what books were around, and the consistency of the evidence suggests that these documents do not represent something casual but a distinctive aristocratic and knightly taste in literature.

If this is indeed the case, it seems clear that Gower and Chaucer were hardly essential reading among the aristocracy or among certain members of the knightly class who are known to have owned books. In fact, the available lists of books suggest that the culture of the court was still overwhelmingly Latin and French, and French of a somewhat old-fashioned sort too: most of the French books are romances evidently of some antiquity; apart from *Le Roman de la Rose*, the newer sort of love poetry as written by Machaut and Deschamps is not represented and the only book of Froissart's is the one presented to Richard II. There are no Italian books. And of all the books so far mentioned as appearing in lists, only four were certainly in English. English evidently had far to go before it acquired any sort of prestige – despite, for example, legislation in 1362 which made it (theoretically, if not actually) the language of pleading in the law-courts.[22] In the Prologue to *Confessio Amantis* Gower makes the point that 'fewe men endite/In oure Englissh' (22–3), and it may well be that to choose to

---

20. Lambeth Library, Reg. Sudbury f. 104v (quoted by McFarlane op. cit., 236).

21. *Testamenta Vetusta* i, 164–5.

22. For the ineffectuality of the 1362 legislation in the higher courts of law see G. E. Woodbine, 'The language of English law', *Speculum*, xviii (1943), 395–436.

write in English, as Gower did in this instance and as Chaucer did habitually, was felt to be somewhat anomalous and *avant garde*.

It is not impossible that some members of the aristocracy and knights who frequented the court read the sort of literature produced by Gower and Chaucer. Gower dedicated the *Cinkante Balades* and *Traitie pour Essampler les Amantz Marietz* to Henry IV 'por desporter vo noble court roial' (though it is possible the poems may have been composed earlier), and it may be that Richard II read the *Confessio Amantis* since he evidently took such as interest in its inception. He may also have read Chaucer's *Lack of Steadfastness*, a ballade which is usually assumed to have been addressed to him:

> O prince, desire to be honourable,
> Cherish thy folk and hate extorcioun. . . (22–3)

– this is said in a note to BL MS Harley 7333 to be King Richard 'thanne being in his Castell of Windesore', and though the manuscript dates from much later than Chaucer's lifetime it is difficult to know who the 'prince' could be if not Richard II.

It may be also that Chaucer found some of his early readers among courtly ladies – perhaps including the queen. At the end of *Troilus and Criseyde* Chaucer addresses himself directly to 'every lady bright of hewe' and 'every gentil woman' in his audience, and asks them to forgive him for writing about Criseyde's unfaithfulness; he offers instead, if they would prefer it, to write about 'Penelopees trouthe and good Alceste' (v.1772–8) – the faithful wife of Ulysses and the wife of Admetus who was willing to die herself and go to Hell in order to prolong her husband's life. It is difficult to assess Chaucer's tone in this passage, which may not be entirely serious. But whatever the level of the joke it appears to be continued in the *F Prologue* to *The Legend of Good Women* where Alceste appears to Chaucer and instructs him to write 'Of wommen trewe in lovyng al hire lyve' so that he may make some recompense for the slurs on the constancy of woman implicit in his translation of *Le Roman de la Rose* and in his characterisation of Criseyde (435–41). The poet makes various arguments in mitigation of what he has done, but is dismissed with the following lines:

> Goo now thy wey, this penaunce is but lyte.
> And when this book ys maad, yive at the quene.
> Oh my byhalf, at Eltham or at Shene. (495–7)

Eltham and Sheen were royal palaces near to London, and 'the quene' must be Anne of Bohemia. There is no evidence that the book was ever so presented, however, and in the later *G Prologue* mention of 'the quene' and the two royal residences is omitted.

It is difficult to know what importance to attach to these references, and similar uncertainty surrounds the final stanza of *Lenvoy de Chaucer a Scogan*:

> Scogan, that knelest at the stremes hed
> Of grace, of alle honour and worthynesse,
> In th'ende of which strem I am dul as ded
> Forgete in solytarie wildernesse –
> Yet, Scogan, thenke on Tullius kyndenesse;
> Mynne thy frend, there it may fructyfye. . . (42–8)

If the reference in line 47 is to Cicero's *De Amicitia* it looks as though Chaucer is asking his friend for a favour, though exactly what sort of favour is no longer clear. In the manuscripts of this poem 'the stremes hed' is glossed as 'Windsor' (a royal palace on the Thames) and 'th'ende of which strem' as 'Greenwich' (lower down the Thames, where Chaucer lived), and on the basis of this it has been argued that Chaucer is here asking Scogan to put in a good word for him at court. It is not by any means certain, however, that the word 'strem' is meant to be taken literally – the passage would make good sense if it were metaphorical[23] – and the identification with precise places through the manuscript glosses is a product of the fifteenth century. As evidence that Chaucer wished to be a 'court poet' this ballade is extremely uncertain. What is not in doubt, however, is the easy familiarity which evidently existed between Chaucer and Scogan (himself a poet and tutor to the sons of Henry IV), for the ballade talks in gently mocking terms about how both he and Chaucer are too old for love affairs, and Chaucer is feeling too old even for writing poetry. Whoever else read Chaucer's poems, Henry Scogan certainly appears to have,[24] and probably other people like Henry Scogan too.

The poetry of Gower and Chaucer, therefore, appears to have been written, on occasions, with an aristocratic courtly audience in mind; but its more significant readers appear to have been career diplomats, civil servants, officials and administrators who were attached to the court and the government.[25] Gower and Chaucer, who both belonged to this world and who knew each other, evidently read each other's poetry (see *Confessio Amantis* viii.2941; *Troilus and Criseyde*

23. See J. A. Burrow, ed. *English Verse 1300–1500* (London, 1977), 196; J. M. Manly argues that in 1393 Chaucer may have been living in North Petherton (*Some New Light on Chaucer* (New York, 1926), 40ff.).

24. Henry Scogan's *Moral Balade* (see *Chaucerian and Other Pieces*, ed. W. W. Skeat (Oxford, 1897), 237–44) is a meditation, for the sons of Henry IV, on Chaucer's ballade *Gentilesse*, which he quotes. For Scogan see G. L. Kittredge, 'Henry Scogan', *Harvard Studies and Notes*, i (1892), 109–17.

25. This is the conclusion reached by other means, by both Pearsall *loc. cit.* 73–4 and by Paul Strohm, 'Chaucer's audience', *Literature and History*, v (1977), 26–41.

v.1856).[26] Another Londoner, Thomas Usk, under-sheriff for Middlesex until he was beheaded in 1388, praises Chaucer as a love poet in his *Testament of Love* iii.iv and had evidently read *Troilus and Criseyde* (which he mentions) and *Boece* (from which he takes ideas and phrases).[27] Sir John Clanvowe, soldier, diplomat, and chamber-knight quotes from *The Knight's Tale* 1875–6 and uses ideas from elsewhere in Chaucer in *The Boke of Cupide* (if Clanvowe is indeed the author, as I think).[28] Ralph Strode, who is addressed specifically with Gower at the end of *Troilus and Criseyde* v.1858, was another Londoner, in fact Chaucer's neighbour in Aldgate: he was a lawyer, common sergeant and pleader of the city, and had evidently had an earlier career as a philosopher at Oxford (hence Chaucer's epithet 'philosophical').[29] Thomas Hoccleve, a rather improvident clerk at the London office of the Privy Seal and a prolific poet, was one of the copyists of Trinity College, Cambridge, MS R III 2 (581), a collection of Gower's work including *Confessio Amantis*;[30] he also admired Chaucer's work, he tells us, and claims to have known him personally.[31] It may well be that Chaucer's work was known in France to the poet Eustache Deschamps: in a ballade dating from perhaps 1386 Deschamps pays handsome tribute to Chaucer and commends to him a copy of his own poems, which he says he is sending by Sir Lewis Clifford, one of Richard II's chamber knights and a friend of Chaucer's. Deschamps evidently knew something of Chaucer's work and it would not be too surprising if Clifford took some of Chaucer's poems to France for Deschamps.[32] Most of these men were writers or intellectuals themselves, and so one may suppose that Chaucer felt a special rapport with them. But two of his poems, beside the ballade to Scogan, are directed to people with whom – if the tone of the poems is any indication – he felt particularly at ease. One ballade, to Sir Peter Bukton, who, among other things, managed Henry Bolingbroke's estates dur-

26. When Chaucer went to Italy in 1378 he appointed John Gower and Richard Forester his general attorneys (*Chaucer Life-Records*, op. cit., 54).

27. For *The Testament of Love* see *Chaucerian and Other Pieces*, op. cit., 1–145, and for details about Usk's life see Skeat's introduction.

28. See *The Works of Sir John Clanvowe* ed. V. J. Scattergood (Cambridge, 1975); and K. B. McFarlane, *Lancastrian Kings and Lollard Knights* (Oxford, 1972), especially 177–206.

29. For Chaucer's relations to Strode see *Chaucer Life-Records* 281–4.

30. See A. I. Doyle and M. B. Parkes, 'The production of copies of the *Canterbury Tales* and *Confessio Amantis* in the early fifteenth century', in *Medieval Scribes, Manuscripts and Libraries: Essays Presented to N. R. Ker*, ed. M. B. Parkes and A. G. Watson (Cambridge, 1978), 182–5.

31. *Regement of Princes* ed. F. J. Furnivall, *EETS* ES 72 (1897), 2077–107, 4978–98. But for a sceptical view of this evidence see Jerome Mitchell, *Thomas Hoccleve* (Urbana Ill., 1968), 110–23.

32. For Clifford see G. L. Kittredge, 'Chaucer and some of his friends', *Modern Philology*, i (1903), 1–18.

ing his exile, contains ironic warnings about the perils of marriage and an injunction to read the Wife of Bath (*Lenvoy de Chaucer a Bukton* 29–32). The second, to Sir Philip de la Vache, commiserates with him for (probably) losing some of his positions during the period in which the Lords Appelant ran the country (*Truth* 22–8). If one has to reconstruct the original audience for the poetry of Gower and Chaucer it probably consisted of men like these. It was essentially a London audience, but there is no evidence that the merchant class were part of it (see Appendix B).

From all this it might appear that there was some division in the literary culture of the court of Richard II: from the evidence of books owned by the aristocracy it appears they preferred literature in Latin and French on a variety of serious subjects, but that for entertainment they relied almost exclusively on romances; the career diplomats, civil servants, officials and administrators, on the other hand, appear to have been open to the new, serious-minded poetry dealing with philosophy and love, often written in the vernacular. This may have been the case. Sir John Clanvowe, in 1391, attacks the values of the court and the literature which sustains these values in the following memorable passage:

> . . .þe world holt hem worsshipful þat been greet werreyours and fiȝteres and þat distroyen and wynnen manye loondis, and waasten and ȝeuen muche good to hem þat haan ynouȝ, and þat dispenden outrageously in mete, in drynke, in clooþing, in buyldyng, and in lyuyng in eese, slouþe, and manye ooþere synnes. And also þe world worsshipeþ hem muchel þat woln bee venged proudly and dispitously of euery wrong þat is seid or doon of hem. And of swyche folke men maken bookes and soonges and reeden and syngen of hem for to hoolde þe mynde of here deedes þe lengere heere vpon eerth, ffor þat is a þing þat worldely men desiren greetly þat here naame myghte laste loonge after hem heere vpon eerth. But what so euere þe world deemeþ of swiche forseide folke leerne we wel þat God is souuerayn treuþe and a trewe iuge þat deemeth hem riȝt shameful. . . (*The Two Ways*, 485–501)

The 'bookes' he is attacking may be romances which, above all other genres, celebrate the sort of quasi-heroic values he deplores, or he may be thinking of contemporary examples of celebratory history such as the Chandos Herald's *Life of the Black Prince*, written in French for an English audience perhaps in 1385 or earlier.[33] Clanvowe, of course, had Lollard sympathies by 1391, and the religious convictions he held no doubt in part account for the position he takes up here. He may,

---

33. *Life of the Black Prince by the Herald of Sir John Chandos*, ed. M. K. Pope and E. C. Lodge (Oxford, 1910), 1v. The date is based on line 1816 which says that since the conquest of Castile by Henry of Trastamare 'ne passa mye des ans vint'. But more recent scholars have suspected that there may have been an earlier version of the poem.

therefore, be somewhat unusual, though it is fair to say that a number of courtiers were Lollards or accused of Lollardy.

Though there may have been some split in the literary culture, however, it cannot have been absolute. Certain tastes appear to have been common to both groups, and so too were certain books: Sir Richard Stury's copy of *Le Roman de la Rose* passed, after his death, to Thomas Woodstock, duke of Gloucester;[34] and Isabel, duchess of York bequeathed her book of vices and virtues to Sir Lewis Clifford. And by the first and second decades of the fifteenth century the works of Gower and Chaucer were being acquired and known by members of the aristocracy: between 1405 and 1413 MS Christ Church, Oxford, 148, a version of the first recension of *Confessio Amantis*, was completed, perhaps commissioned, for one of the sons of Henry IV, perhaps Thomas, duke of Clarence;[35] and between 1406 and 1415 in the Preface to his translation of Gaston Febus's *Livre de la Chasse*, Edward Langley, second duke of York, referring to the permanence of writing, says 'for as Chaucer saith in his prologue of The 25 Good Women : By writing have men mind of things passed, for writing is the key to all good remembrance.'[36] Though certain broad groupings and literary preferences at the court of Richard II may hold good, the situation is not a simple one. There does, however, appear to have been a good deal of literature of one sort or another, religious and secular, old and new, in Latin and in the vernaculars, circulating in and around the court of Richard II. Though there is little evidence of widespread patronage, the circumstances for the production and dissemination of literature were obviously not unfavourable.

APPENDIX A

It is worth considering briefly just what MS Bodley 581 consists of, since it was evidently made for Richard II: fol.1r mentions 'dominus Ricardus, dei gracia, rex Anglie et Francie'; on fol.9r he is mentioned again and the item occupying fols.87v–89v is entitled *Rosarium Regis Ricardi*. The manuscript is extensively illuminated and a portrait of the king appears in an initial on fol.9r, so perhaps it was a presentation copy. On the same folio appears the date of March 1391.

MS Bodley 581 is made up of three main groups of items, all in Latin. It opens with two brief treatises based loosely on the *Secreta Secretorum*: on fols.1r–3r appears the *De Quadripartita Regis Specie Libellum*, a political tract on the nature of kingship, followed on

---

34. On Royal MS 19 B XIII fol.2r appears the statement: 'ceste liure est a Thomas, fiz au Roy, duc de Gloucestre, achates des executours monsire Richard Stury'.
35. See A. I. Doyle and M. B. Parkes, op. cit., 208.
36. *The Master of Game*, ed. W. A. and F. Baillie-Grohmann (London, 1904), 2–3.

fols.3r–5v by the *Phisionomia Aristotelis*. Then comes the *Sompniale Danielis* on fols. 7r–8v preceded by an introduction on fols.6r–7r. The main item in the manuscript is the *Liber Judiciorum*, a geomantic tract which occupies fols.9v–74v, and this is followed by two items of the same sort related to it – *Flores Questionum et Iudiciorum Veritatis Artis Geomancie* (fols.75r–87r) and the *Rosarium* already mentioned. On fol.89v appears a *Tabula Regni Planetarum Singulis Horis Diei et Noctis*. BL Royal MS 12 C V is obviously related to MS Bodley 581 but it contains only the geomantic items. On fol.3v appears the ascription 'Liver regis Ricardi secundi quem fecit fieri motu proprio anno regni sui Anglie et Francie quarto decimo' (i.e. 1390–1); but there is no portrait.

In the prefatory material to *De Quadripartita Regis Specie* the author describes himself as 'minimus regis massarum erulus Hibernie' which Jean-Philippe Genet renders 'the most humble servant of the Treasurers in Ireland'.[37] He goes on to suggest that this same man could 'have been responsible for the entire volume, and he would have been the compiler of the geomantic items.'[38] His preferred candidate for authorship is John Thorpe, Treasurer of Ireland in 1393–4 – though the evidence for any definite ascription is meagre. If the volume were put together by a single compiler, however, it would help to explain its nature: the first item is obviously a piece of advice to a prince, and a very popular piece at that; and a knowledge of physiognomy and divination was sometimes held to be important for rulers.[39] It would seem that the book was put together to counsel and help Richard II as a ruler. (It is worth recalling also that Sir Simon Burley, Richard II's tutor, possessed a book called 'songes de Danyell' which must have been a French version of the *Sompniale Danielis*.)

APPENDIX B

Though literacy of a practical sort was becoming an increasingly desirable thing among late fourteenth-century merchants, there is no evidence to show that merchants were particularly assiduous as collectors of books, or that their tastes favoured the new vernacular literature. William Walworth, a fishmonger knighted in 1381 for killing Wat Tyler, was perhaps the biggest collector: he bequeathed nine religious books to various churches and a library of law books worth

37. *Four English Political Tracts of the Later Middle Ages*, ed. Jean-Philippe Genet, Camden Society, fourth series, xviii (1977), 24. On the Bodley and Royal MSS, see also below, pp. 145–6.

38. Ibid., 27.

39. See, for example, Lydgate and Burgh's *Secrees of Old Philisoffres*, ed. R. Steele, *EETS* ES 66 (1894), 1184–218, 2465–723.

£100 to his brother.[40] The vintner Richard Lyons, killed by the rebels in 1381 had a 'regestre', a 'livre appelle manual oue diuerse trehotez', a 'livre appelle Breton escript en frauncais' (possibly a copy of Bracton's law book), and a saints' legends.[41] According to the wills proved and enrolled in the Court of Husting (London) for the reign of Richard II, a number of merchants left a few books, usually religious and usually either to churches or chantries or to men in religious life. John de Cantebrigge left 'a Legend of the Saints called the Golden Legend' to his chaplain in 1377.[42] Walter de Berneye, a mercer, in 1379 left a *Summa de Abstinencia* and a saints' legend to Friar Thomas de Elsyng; and to William de Norton, a draper, he left a portiforium and 'all his books on canon and civil law'.[43] In the same year, Beatrix Barton, a vintner's widow, left a portiforium.[44] In 1381 Margery Broun left an 'ancient missal' and 'a book of the service of St Anne'.[45] In 1385 Richard Glemesford left a missal and money to buy a 'Legend' for the parish church of St Stephen Colman Street.[46] In 1389 Thomas Carleton, a broiderer, left a Bible and a saints' legend.[47] In 1394 William Kyng, a draper, left a French Bible and a book called *Liber Regalis*.[48] In 1395 Gilbert Prynce, a painter, left a missal;[49] and in 1396 Henry Herbury left a missal and a portiforium.[50] Two grocers who became bankrupt in the 1390s had between them four 'libros de romance', two 'libros de Englysshe', a calendar and a primer – but these items were from among what they intended to sell, not from among their personal possessions.[51]

40. Sylvia Thrupp, *The Merchant Class of Medieval London* (Chicago, 1948), 161.

41. A. R. Myers, 'The wealth of Richard Lyons' in *Essays in Medieval History, presented to Bertie Wilkinson*, ed. T. A. Sandquist and M. R. Powicke (1969), 327.

42. *Calendar of Wills Proved and Enrolled in the Court of Husting, London*, ed. R. R. Sharpe, 2 vols (London, 1890), ii, 198.

43. Ibid., ii, 205–6.

44. Ibid., ii, 210.

45. Ibid., ii, 220–1.

46. Ibid., ii, 249.

47. Ibid., ii, 273.

48. Ibid., ii, 312–13.

49. Ibid., ii, 320.

50. Ibid., ii, 322.

51. Sylvia Thrupp, op. cit., 162.

3

Chaucer's Knight, the English Aristocracy and the Crusade

Maurice Keen

The question that I hope to look at in this chapter is one that was suggested to me a long time ago when I happened to be reading the description of the Knight in Chaucer's prologue to his *Canterbury Tales*. The lines in question are very familiar ones:

> A knyght ther was, and that a worthy man,
> That fro the tyme that he first bigan
> To riden out, he loved chivalrie,
> Trouthe and honour, fredom and curteisie.
> Ful worthy was he in his lordes werre,
> And therto hadde he riden, no man ferre,
> As wel in cristendom as in hethenesse,
> And evere honoured for his worthynesse.
> At Alisaundre he was whan it was wonne.
> Ful ofte tyme he hadde the bord bigonne
> Aboven alle nacions in Pruce;
> In Lettow hadde he reysed and in Ruce,
> No Cristen man so ofte of his degree.
> In Gernade at the seege eek hadde he be
> Of Algezir, and riden in Belmarye.
> At Lyeys was he and at Satalye,
> Whan they were wonne; and in the Grete See
> At many a noble armee hadde he be.[1]

This litany of battles and voyages done in the cause of Christendom is clearly important in defining what sort of a figure the Knight is. They appear to present him to us as a model of chivalry, and to identify him with a particular chivalrous concern, the crusade against the heathen, and in that sense they are striking lines. There is another respect too in which the picture that they draw of the Knight is rather

---

1. *Canterbury Tales*, General Prologue, 43–60, ed. Robinson.

striking. Those who have written footnotes to the *Prologue* have been
able, it is true, to find an English knight who played some part in
each of the campaigns and engagements that Chaucer's Knight had
a hand in. They have never, though, found a knight who had a hand,
as he is supposed to have had, in all of them; and besides, the commitment to the crusade with which his experience identifies him is
out of line with what is usually considered to be the tone of English
knightly attitudes in the second half of the fourteenth century. If it
had been the great battles of the Hundred Years War with France in
which the knight had won the sovereign prize for prowess – Sluys,
Crécy, Poitiers, Nájera – then there would be no cause for surprise.
In that war Chaucer had himself made his apprenticeship in arms,
along with hosts of his contemporaries, a good many of whom made
themselves rich and famous through service in it. But his contemporary generation of knights and esquires is not so often associated with
crusading fervour. There were indeed certain so-called crusades in
which a good many English knights took part in Richard II's day, but
they were crusades in name only. The Great Schism in the church
made it possible for Despenser's expedition to Flanders in 1383 and
Gaunt's attempt to conquer Castile in 1386–7 to rank technically as
crusades, in that the Roman Pope granted indulgences to those who
served in these two campaigns against people whom he regarded as
schismatic because they obeyed the Pope of Avignon. The preaching
of these pseudo-crusades and the sale of indulgences to help pay for
them roused the wordy anger of John Wyclif and his Lollard followers
(and of a number of others too).[2] But it is not with this sort of crusade
that Chaucer's knight is associated in the *Prologue*. His crusades were
true crusades against the infidel, and were fought in the cause which,
according to many historians, was already losing its hold on the commitment of Christian chivalry in the later thirteenth century, in the
age which was witness to the collapse of what was then left of Frankish
dominion in Syria – a century and more before Chaucer wrote.

That is what troubled me, and explains why my question originally
arose. Is one to conclude, I asked, that Chaucer in his *Prologue* introduced with the Knight a figure more stylised than the others, embodying values that already looked antique? Because Chaucer was an
expert draughtsman from the life, that cannot be a very satisfactory
answer: it would make the knight a very anomalous figure in the
pilgrim group. So the problem for me remained, why is the Knight
drawn in the particular way that he is? I have found since that I am
by no means the only one troubled by it. It has so troubled Mr Terry
Jones that he has recently written a remarkable book, *Chaucer's*

2. J. Wyclif, *Polemical Works*, ed. R. Buddensieg (Wyclif Society, London, 1883), II,
579–632.

Knight, the portrait of a medieval mercenary, suggesting that the difficulties arise from the fact that the traditional view, that the Knight has been portrayed as an ideal figure, is wholly mistaken.[3] Chaucer's intention, he thinks, was not to paint a picture of a knight who was truly 'parfit' and 'gentil', but to indict in a biting satire the kind of professional mercenary who sought to give himself the airs of knighthood while breaking every rule of chivalry. The Knight's far-flung military experience is not, in Mr Jones' view, a sign of genuine dedication to the crusade; it is a sign that he represents one of those ruthless and rootless men whose swords were at the disposal of any who could offer them prospects of pay or plunder, and who were more likely to be found in the service of foreign masters in strange lands than in that of their native liege lord. For a number of reasons, some of which will I hope become apparent, I do not myself believe that this view of the Knight will stand up to scrutiny. I do however think that it does have one great virtue, that it underscores the need to relate Chaucer's Knight to the contemporary scene of Chaucer's lifetime. Chaucer was at once too good an artist and too shrewd an observer to have distorted his picture of the Canterbury pilgrims by throwing into their company a type figure symbolising an outdated ideal.

Rather than agreeing with Mr Jones, I believe for myself that we need to view the Knight in terms similar to those in which we must view the Parson and the Plowman of the *Prologue*, figures drawn very definitely from the contemporary scene whose lives indicate patterns of virtuous living that are not outmoded, but which too few, in Chaucer's opinion, made a sufficiently serious effort to follow. This is a view which has a clear historical implication with regard to the Knight. If it is right, then crusading as a practical ideal must have stirred a somewhat more lively interest, and experience of it must have been a little less uncommon than it is usually taken to have been in the age of Chaucer. Since I am an historian and not a Chaucer critic, this implication is more important to me than the question of what Chaucer's real intention was, a question which I am sure I am wiser to leave to the professionals. What I want to investigate is, therefore, what evidence there is that crusading really was a live issue, an ideal to which English knighthood really did pay more than lip service, in the latter half of the fourteenth century.

Given this objective, there is one point that is worth making while Chaucer's knight is still in the forefront of our minds. Let us note not only that he fought against the heathen, but where he fought against

3. T. Jones, *Chaucer's Knight, the portrait of a medieval mercenary* (London, 1980).

them. He was in Granada and at the siege of Algeciras, fighting the Moors in Spain. He was at Satalia, and at Alexandria when it was taken by King Peter de Lusignan of Cyprus in 1365. He had also been in Prussia and Lithuania fighting the pagans there, and that more than once:

> Ful ofte tyme he hadde the bord bigonne
> Aboven alle nacions in Pruce.[4]

Here are three different areas of crusading enterprise, Spain, the eastern Mediterranean, and Prussia; and the nature of crusading enterprise was of course a little different in each one of them, not only in terms of crusading objectives, but also from the point of view of the problems confronting the would-be crusader. One limiting factor affecting participation in crusades to the Orient in the fourteenth century was that there were not very many major expeditions, and that little continuous fighting was conducted against the infidel in the eastern Mediterranean. When I speak of continuous fighting I am thinking of the kind of campaigning in which a knight could take an occasional part as a pilgrim visitor, in the way that so many had done in the days when there was a Frankish kingdom in Syria. So with regard to this sphere of operations it is reasonable to concentrate attention on the English contribution to the major expeditions which are well chronicled: the Alexandrian crusade of 1365; the duke of Bourbon's crusade to Tunis in 1390; and the great French expedition against the Turk which came to grief at Nicopolis in 1396. No doubt there were other Englishmen besides those who joined these crusades who saw service in the east in the company of the Knights Hospitaller, joining them perhaps for some minor campaign in the course of making the popular pilgrimage to the Holy Places, but the names of such are not easy to recover. In Spain likewise, crusading activity was intermittent, and there was not sufficiently continuous fighting to offer standing and sure opportunity to the casual crusader, intent on fulfilling an individual commitment to Christian martial endeavour. Henry of Grosmont, earl of Derby, and William Montagu, earl of Salisbury, distinguished themselves in 1343–4 in Alfonso XI's crusade which culminated in the taking of Algeciras.[5] But the next reign in Castile saw the beginnings of the internal strife in which Pedro the Cruel, in spite of English backing, ultimately lost his throne to his francophile and bastard half brother Henry of Trastamara, and in their struggles the fight against the infidel was largely forgotten. Plenty of Englishmen went to Spain, but most went to do battle not

---

4. *Canterbury Tales*, General Prologue, 52–3.
5. K. Fowler, *The King's Lieutenant* (London, 1969), 45–7; *Cronica del Rey don Alfonso XI* (Biblioteca de Autores Españoles lxvi, Madrid, 1875), 360–70.

with the Moors but with Christian Spaniards (though there is some evidence that those who joined Du Guesclin on his first expedition to Spain expected, once they had settled Pedro's hash, to be led against the Moors; they included a number of Englishmen).[6] The conditions of war in the third area of confrontation with the enemies of the Cross were markedly different. The wars of the Teutonic Knights against the pagans of Lithuania were much more continuous, and they had an objective that had been lost sight of for more than a century in the Orient, the settlement – and the protection of the settlement – of newly conquered lands. Whenever there were sufficient martial pilgrims in his lands the Grand Master or his Marshal would lead them out on a *reise*, an expedition into the lands of the pagans. This activity reached its climax during the long mastership of Winrich von Kniprode in the second half of the fourteenth century, and in that time 'Pruce' and 'Lettowe' were the principal areas of crusading activity for the Christian knighthood of western Europe.[7]

I cannot claim to have sifted exhaustively all the sources which might throw light on English participation in crusading warfare in these three areas. One particular source I have however looked at quite carefully, the records of three great armorial disputes tried before the Court of Chivalry – the court, that is, of the Constable of England and the Earl Marshal, which was the highest military tribunal of the realm, and had (as indeed it still has) jurisdiction over all pleas concerning armorial bearings. The record of one of these cases, that between Sir Richard Le Scrope and Sir Robert Grosvenor, who in 1385 both claimed the right to the arms *azur a bend or*, has long been in print.[8] Records of two other armorial cases tried before this same court survive in full in manuscripts. These are the cases of Lovell v. Morley over the right to bear the arms *argent a lion rampant sable corone et enarme or*, and of Grey v. Hastings over the right to the arms *or a manche gules*.[9] In all three cases there was a tremendous

6. Cuvelier, *Chronique de Bertrand du Guesclin*, ed. E. Charrière (Paris, 1839), i, 270, 320–2, 349–50.

7. E. Christiansen, *The Northern Crusades* (London, 1980), provides an excellent survey of the wars in this area; see especially Chapter 6 for the significance of the mastership of Winrich von Kniprode.

8. N. H. Nicolas, *The Controversy between Sir Richard Scrope and Sir Robert Grosvenor in the Court of Chivalry* (London, 1832), quoted henceforward as *Scrope and Grosvenor*.

9. PRO, C47/6/1 (Lovell v. Morley); College of Arms MS *Processus in Curia Marescalli*, I–II, (Grey v. Hastings). This latter is a seventeenth-century transcript of the proceedings in the case; the same volumes also contain a transcript of proceedings in Lovell v. Morley. On the history of the MS see A. R. Wagner, 'A fifteenth-century description of the brass of Sir Hugh Hastings at Elsing, Norfolk', *Antiq. Jour.*, xix (1939), 421–2, and R. I. Jack, 'Entail and Descent: the Hastings Inheritance, 1370 to 1436', *BIHR*, xxxviii (1965), 14 n.l. I am deeply indebted to Mr Theobald Mathew, Windsor Herald, and to the Officers of Arms for permitting me to consult this MS.

effort to bring all the evidence that could be uncovered before the
court; and commissioners were sent about the land to view muniments,
to inspect sepulchral monuments and armorial glass in churches of
which the parties or their ancestors had been benefactors, and above
all to gather the evidence of knights and men-at-arms – *generosi* –
about the occasions on which the parties and their kinsmen and ancestors had used the arms to which they laid claim in war and at tournies.
The testimony of these witnesses (and in all three cases they were
very numerous) is a gold-mine of military biographical detail for the
period from approximately 1330 to the end of the fourteenth century.
The case of Scrope v. Grosvenor has in addition a particular interest
in the present context, since Chaucer himself was called as a witness
for the Scropes and gave substantial testimony. It therefore presents
to us Chaucer in the company of the knighthood of his time, speaking
in *propria persona* not as poet or diplomat or controller of the customs
but as one who had seen honourable war service and could recall what
old knights and esquires worthy of credence in points of chivalry had
retailed in his hearing.[10]

The reason why the records of these three Court of Chivalry cases
is useful for my present purpose is simple, and it is also rather striking:
it is that no less than four out of the six families involved as principals
in them prove to have had contemporary or near enough to contemporary crusading experience. Robert Morley, ancestor of the Lord Morley who in Richard II's reign was challenging the right of Lord Lovell
to the arms *argent a lion rampant sable etc.*, had died in Prussia.
William Grey, parson of Reydon, deposed that he had been told by one
of his ancestors, who had been there, that he had seen in Prussia a
glass window depicting a knight in those same arms. He knew (and
the testimony of others supported this) that Robert Morley's faithful
men had brought back his heart, and had buried it in the church of
Reydon – the body lay in Prussia, where he fell. As far as crusading
went, though, the Lovells were more than even with the Morleys.
John Breux, knight, saw Lord Lovell armed in Prussia – though not
in the arms claimed, which had then not yet come to him from the
Burnells (or so Lovell asserted). Breux had also seen Lovell armed in
his arms beyond the Great Sea – that is to say, in the eastern Mediterranean.[11] Hugh Hastings, father of Edward Hastings who in the
reign of Henry IV claimed the arms *or a manche gules* against Lord
Grey of Ruthyn, was another crusader. Robert Fishlake had been with
him when he travelled to the east, and saw Sir Hugh hang an escutcheon of his arms in the *Maison d'Honneur* of the Hospitallers at Rhodes:

10. *Scrope and Grosvenor*, i, 178–9.
11. PRO, C47/6/1, Morley witnesses nos. cli, clii, and (Breux) cii. The evidence of Sir
John Breux (no. cii) has been misplaced, and appears out of order on the roll.

wherever he was armed on his travels, said Robert, Hugh left an escutcheon of his arms.[12] Either this Sir Hugh or his father, it would seem, was also in Prussia, for Sir Thomas Erpingham, when he went on the *reise* in the company of Henry Bolingbroke, saw the arms hung in the *Maison de Dome* (? the Marienkirche) at Konigsberg, as the arms of Hastings (with a label, for a mark of cadency).[13] John Parker, who had served in France in 1359 with Hugh the elder (Edward Hastings' grandfather), had always heard, he said, that Hugh Hastings 'had first raised his banner of the said arms in battle against the Saracen'.[14] There is no record, as far as I can make out, of any of the Greys of Ruthyn, Hastings' rivals, playing any part in a crusade in the fourteenth century. But the record of the other three families – Hastings, Lovell and Morley – is impressive. So is the way in which they and those associated with them seem to have looked upon their part in the crusade. The heart brought back from Prussia, the memorials left in Konigsberg and at Rhodes to remind Englishmen who might come after that a Morley or a Hastings had been there in arms, these are expressive of the esteem set upon this kind of enterprise.

I do not know of any evidence that any of the Grosvenors went on crusade. They were a Cheshire family, not yet of any great distinction in 1386 when the dispute between Robert Grosvenor and Richard Le Scrope was heard in the Court of Chivalry, and their military experience seems largely to have been in Gascony and in the Scottish border wars. The Scropes, in contrast, had a crusading record beside which those of Morley, Lovell and Hastings alike pale into insignificance. The Scropes were an old Yorkshire family but the men who really put their fortunes on the map were two brothers, both distinguished lawyers of the early fourteenth century.[15] Henry, the elder and from whom the line of the Scropes of Bolton descended, was chief baron of the Exchequer from 1330 to 1336; Geoffrey, the cadet and ancestor of the Scropes of Masham, was Chief Justice of the King's Bench from 1324 to 1340. Richard Le Scrope, the plaintiff of 1386, was Sir Henry's son. He himself never went on crusade, as far as I know, though he was a warrior of note in France. But his son William, who was to rise to be earl of Wiltshire under Richard II, served in Prussia and it is possible that his third son Stephen did also.[16] The Scropes of Masham had a still more impressive record. Henry, the son of Chief Justice Geoffrey, seems to have no holy war campaign ribbon, but his brother William

---

12. College of Arms MS, *Processus*, i, 432–3; see also 462.
13. Ibid., i, 441.
14. Ibid., i, 534.
15. On Sir Henry and Sir Geoffrey Le Scrope see E.L.G. Stones, 'Sir Geoffrey le Scrope, Chief Justice of the King's Bench', *EHR*, lxix (1954), 1–17.
16. *Scrope and Grosvenor*, i, 172; *Die Chronik Wigands von Marburg*, ed. T. Hirsch, M. Töppen and E. Strehlke (Scriptores Rerum Prussicarum II, Leipzig, 1863), 653.

certainly went on crusade to the east, and was in the company of the earl of Hereford at Satalia.[17] Henry's eldest son, another Geoffrey, died on crusade in Prussia in 1362.[18] Stephen, who ultimately succeeded as Lord of Masham, served like his brother in France and after 1360 followed his crusading example. He joined the army of Peter of Cyprus, and at the taking of Alexandria he was knighted by the king himself; later he was to serve in Prussia too.[19] Another and a younger brother of these two, Henry Le Scrope, seems to have died on crusade in the east.[20] Thus, if one puts the Scropes alongside Chaucer's Knight, one will find a Scrope at 'Satalye', 'at Alisaundre . . . whan it was wonne', and a group of young Scropes playing their part in a whole series of ventures in 'Lettow' and 'Pruce'. As the Chaucerian scholar Manly long ago pointed out, their collective experience could have served Chaucer as a model.[21] Chaucer knew of them, and testified in 1386 that from the time that he was first armed in 1359 it had always been the report that he had heard that the arms *azur a bend or* had belonged to the Scropes from time immemorial.

It is worth mentioning also some of the witnesses whose testimony gives us the evidence that the Scropes were crusaders (and who were therefore themselves crusaders too, having seen the arms displayed against the infidel). They were not all connections of the Scropes and they were by no means all northerners as the Scropes were. Sir Richard Waldegrave told the Court of Chivalry of how 'beyond the Great Sea he saw Sir William Le Scrope armed in the said arms with a label, in the company of the earl of Hereford at Satalia, at a parley that was held between the King of Cyprus and Takka Lord of Satalia'. Waldegrave, who in Hereford's retinue had seen service in Prussia as well as in the east, was a Suffolk knight: he sat for the county many times in Parliament and was Speaker of the Commons in 1381.[22]

17. *Scrope and Grosvenor*, i, 166.

18. Ibid., i, 123, 146, 188.

19. Ibid., i, 124–5; *Chronik Wigands von Marburg*, 653. It is not clear whether Wigand refers to Stephen of Bolton or Stephen of Masham, but I am inclined to think the latter.

20. *Scrope and Grosvenor*, i, 125. It seems almost certain that young Henry Le Scrope of Masham was the Scrope whose tomb Nicholas Sabraham, the witness here testifying, saw at Messembria in a church. He describes the arms on the tomb as those of Scrope, differenced with a label of three points argent charged with as many besants, gules; in *A Roll of Arms of the reign of Richard II*, ed. T. Willement (London, 1834), 16, Henry Le Scrope appears at no. 146 with the arms of Scrope differenced with a label of three points argent, charged with as many bars gules. The visual difference is very slight and Sabraham was in any case relying on memory; the identification is the more plausible since all are agreed that Henry, of whom very little is known, must have died young, and this would account for him. I must acknowledge gratefully the advice of Mr Michael Maclagan, Richmond Herald, about the heraldic evidence in this case.

21. *Canterbury Tales*, ed. J. M. Manly (London, n.d.), 500.

22. *Scrope and Grosvenor*, i, 166. On Waldegrave's career see further J. S. Roskell, 'Sir Richard de Waldegrave of Bures St. Mary', *Proceedings of the Suffolk Institute of Archaeology*, xxvii, part 3 (1957), 154–75.

Alexander Goldingham, esquire, who also saw William Le Scrope in Hereford's company, was lord of the manor of Chigwell in Essex.[23] William de Lucy, who had seen the arms of Scrope displayed both in Prussia and in the east, was a Dorset man.[24] Thomas FitzHenry, who saw young Geoffrey Le Scrope buried in Prussia in the family arms, came from Lincolnshire.[25] Here is evidence that crusading experience was spread through knightly society in widely different parts of the country. The background of the crusaders is also interesting. Some were of good genteel stock like Waldegrave: others were much poorer, more or less professional fighting esquires. Nicholas Sabraham, who was present when Peter of Cyprus knighted Stephen Le Scrope before Alexandria, seems to have been a real professional soldier: he had first seen service under Edward de Balliol in Scotland, probably about 1340; he had been at Crécy, at the siege of Calais, and had fought both in Brittany and Spain; besides that, he told the Court of Chivalry, 'he had been armed in Prussia, in Hungary, at Constantinople, at the Bras de St. Jorge, and at Messembria'; and one of the Scropes, he knew, was buried at Messembria – it must, I think, have been young Henry Le Scrope of the Masham line. This splendid old soldier, after something like thirty years service in arms, had at the time of the Scrope v. Grosvenor case settled down as the husband of a Northumbrian heiress of moderate fortune.[26] Another more or less professional warrior who had seen crusading service (Prussian in this case) was Henry Ferrers, a bastard son of lord Ferrers of Groby, last heard of before the Scrope v. Grosvenor case as a captain under bishop Despenser in Flanders who had sold his fortress to the advancing French for a price a little too good to be respectable.[27] And among the poorer I must not forget faithful John Ryther, Geoffrey Le Scrope the younger's esquire, who buried his master's body when he died before Piskre in 1362 and stayed in Konigsberg at the end of the *reise* to see to the placing of a glass panel of the arms of Scrope in the church there.[28] Research has (as far as I know) failed to trace precisely what John Ryther esquire of Yorkshire's parentage and connections were, but from the references to him in the testimony of other witnesses in the case it is clear that he was in his day a figure well enough known among the soldiers, squires and aristocrats of the north country, not for his wealth or power but as one respected for his long and varied martial career.

I have not mentioned by any means all those who, by their testimony

23. *Scrope and Grosvenor*, i, 70; ii, 227.
24. Ibid., i, 77; 261.
25. Ibid., i, 123; ii, 320–1.
26. Ibid., i, 124–5; ii, 323–5.
27. Ibid., i, 188; ii, 443–5.
28. Ibid., i, 146; ii, 351–2.

in the Scrope v. Grosvenor controversy of 1386, revealed their crusading experience. I hope, however, that I have mentioned just enough to give an impression of what a varied group they form, in terms of influence, experience, ancestry and local background. The military careers of a number of them also suggest that, among those who had once gone on crusade, a quite wide, if haphazard, crusading experience was not uncommon. A man like Sabraham, having once been on a crusading expedition, might think of going on another. The same sort of pattern is illustrated in family terms in the experience both of the Scropes and of the Hastings of Elsyng. Other sources give further evidence of what looks like a crusading tradition in some families. Two particularly notable examples are the Uffords of Suffolk and the Beauchamps of Warwick. The Warwick pageant, commemorating Richard de Beauchamp, the earl who served Henry V so well in France and who died in 1439, tells how as a young man he took his way to 'Russy, Lettowe, Poleyn and Spruse Westvale and other coostes of Almayn toward Englond by such coostes as his auncestry hadde labored in, and specially earl Thomas his grauntfadre that in warre had taken the Kynges son of Lettowe and brought hym into Englond and cristened hym at London namyng hym after hymself Thomas.'[29] It would seem that the reference must be to an expedition either of 1361 or of 1365. Certainly this same earl Thomas set out to join Peter of Cyprus in 1364, when we hear of him tourneying at Venice while waiting for the host to assemble. He does not in fact seem to have gone to Alexandria, though, but to have gone to Prussia instead.[30] Three years later his son and earl Richard's father, another Thomas, was bound in the same direction, having leave to pass from Dover on his way to Prussia, together with his brothers William and Roger and in their company nine esquires and twenty yeomen.[31] The record of the Uffords is a little less detailed, but equally impressive. One of the Uffords, a son of the later earl of Suffolk, was in Prussia in 1331.[32] Thomas Ufford was leading a company of Englishmen there in 1348, and was back in 1362 and in 1365 (like Warwick, he had set out to

29. *Pageant of the birth, life and death of Richard Beauchamp, Earl of Warwick 1389–1439*, ed. Viscount Dillon and W. St John Hope (London, 1914), 44.

30. N. Jorga, *Philippe de Mézières et la Croisade au XIVe siècle* (Bibliothèque de l'École des Hautes Études, cx, Paris, 1896), 205, 243, 254; *Chronik Wigands von Marburg*, 549, 551.

31. *CPR.* (1367–70), 56. There are a good many references in the *CPR* to individuals proposing to make the journey to 'Pruce', to the numbers in their company and the sums that they carried for expenses, including *CPR*, (1361–4), 251–2 (Robert Howard); *CPR*, (1367–70), 57 (Ivo Fitzwarin); 58 (Hugh Despenser); 65 (Thomas de Boynton); 72 (William de Furnival); 127 (Robert Urswyk); *CPR*, (1381–5), 274 (Hugh Despenser); *CPR*, (1388–92), 413 (Lord Despenser). Thomas Beauchamp, William and Roger 'le fitz chivaler' travelled with 9 esquires, 20 yeomen and 30 horses, and with 1000 marks for their expenses.

32. *Chronik Wigands von Marburg*, 479.

join Peter of Cyprus but had found preparations going too slowly for his patience, or perhaps his pocket).[33] If anyone had ever challenged the arms of Ufford or of Beauchamp in the Court of Chivalry, it looks as if they would have brought to light a body of testimony with crusading experience even more eloquent than that which the challenge to the Scropes elicited.

The Beauchamps and the Uffords were families of older blood, richer and of more moment than the Scropes, mere barons whose family had made its way rapidly forward by good marriages and solid service in the professions of law and arms. The crusading record in the fourteenth century of some other comital families will also repay examination. There are some which have no crusading experience in the period that I can uncover; those of Stafford, March, and Arundel for instance.[34] But a very high proportion of comital families do prove to have a crusading veteran somewhere in their ranks. Humphrey de Bohun, earl of Hereford, saw service in Prussia, and was at Satalia and at the taking of Alexandria.[35] Edward Courtenay, the earl's son of Devonshire, was setting out for Prussia together with two brothers in 1368.[36] William Montagu, whom Edward III made earl of Salisbury, was at the siege of Algeciras, and his descendant John Montagu, Richard II's earl, fought in Prussia.[37] Thomas Holland, earl of Kent in right of his marriage to Joan of Kent, Richard II's mother, was another Prussian veteran, and earned there the love and respect of the French lords who were his companions on the *reise*.[38] Hotspur, the famous son of the first earl of Northumberland, was in Prussia in 1383.[39] His uncle Sir Thomas Percy seems to have served there in 1391,[40] and five years later his younger brother Sir Ralph joined the ill-fated crusading host that was overwhelmed by Sultan Bajazeth at Nicopolis.[41] One at least of the Nevilles, the Percy's great rivals, joined Bourbon's crusade to Tunis.[42] I am talking here of men who, if they went on crusade, did not go alone. They were captains by birth and their families were those that set the tone of aristocratic *mores*. Crusading could not look outdated (or disreputable, as Mr Terry Jones hints) as long as their

33. Ibid., 514, 551; Jorga, op. cit., 269; *CPR*, (1361–64), 251–2.
34. Thomas, earl of Stafford did however embark for Prussia with Gloucester in 1391, but both were turned back by storms in the North Sea; see A. Goodman, *The Loyal Conspiracy* (London, 1971), 57–8.
35. Jorga, op. cit., 364–6; A. S. Atiya, *The Crusade in the later Middle Ages* (London, 1938), 518.
36. *CPR*, (1367–70), 128.
37. For William, see *ante*, n. 5; for John, K. B. McFarlane, *Lancastrian Kings and Lollard Knights* (Oxford, 1972), 178.
38. *Oeuvres de Froissart*, ed. de Lettenhove, iv, 406, 411.
39. Ibid., x, 243.
40. *Chronik Wigands von Marburg*, 646, 648.
41. J. J. N. Palmer, *England, France and Christendom, 1377–99* (London, 1972), 240.
42. Atiya, op. cit., 408 n. 3, 522.

involvement in the enterprise was as active as the record shows it to have been in the fifty or so years that separate the siege of Algeciras in 1343 from the battle of Nicopolis in 1396.

It is true that neither Edward III nor any of his sons ever fought the infidel. When Peter of Cyprus came to England to recruit support for his crusade of 1364–5, Edward listened to him but declared he was too old to go on crusade and referred the visitor to his children; they did not respond.[43] Among Edward's sons, Thomas of Woodstock was the one who came nearest to being armed against the pagans; he embarked for Prussia in 1391, but was driven home by the storms of the North Sea.[44] But the crusading tradition was important in the royal circle. Henry of Grosmont, first duke of Lancaster, was Edward III's kinsman, and his daughter and heiress Blanche married the King's son John of Gaunt; he was twice a crusader, at Algeciras in 1343–4 and in Prussia in 1355.[45] Gaunt's son, Henry Bolingbroke, went to Prussia, as we have seen, in 1390, and he returned there again in 1392, though on this second occasion he saw no fighting. The men who served with him in Prussia, such as Thomas Erpingham, John Norbury, and John Waterton, were among the inner group of his familiars who made the coup of 1399 work and on whom he relied heavily in his early years of kingship.[46] And Gaunt's eldest illegitimate son by his mistress Katherine Swynford, John Beaufort, first earl of Somerset, was a noted crusader. In 1390 he joined the duke of Bourbon's crusade to Tunis: in 1391 he was in Prussia; in 1396 he was at Nicopolis, and he was one of the fortunate few who came home.[47]

If things had gone differently in that great battle, the tale might be more impressive still. The expedition that came to grief there had been thought of as the vanguard of a larger expedition, to be organised by the kings of France and England together. The rapprochement and the long truce which they agreed upon in 1395 came as the climax to a sustained diplomatic effort which had long had in view as one of its prime objectives a combined Anglo-French expedition against the Turk.[48] Richard II had accepted gracefully the elaborate allegorical letter, urging the need for peace between France and England in the interest of Christendom and the crusade, that Philippe de Mézières

43. *Oeuvres de Froissart*, vi, 380–1; and compare T. Johnes' translation of Froissart's *Chronicles* from the Hafod MS, (London, 1842), i, 306.

44. On Gloucester's crusading plans see Palmer, op.cit., 198, and Goodman, *The Loyal Conspiracy*, 57–8, 78, 92.

45. See *ante*, n. 5, and Fowler, *The King's Lieutenant*, 104–6.

46. L. Toulmin Smith, *Expeditions to Prussia and the Holy Land made by Henry Earl of Derby* (Camden Society, New Series, lii, London, 1894); F. R. H. Du Boulay, 'Henry of Derby's expeditions to Prussia 1390–1 and 1392', in F. R. H. Du Boulay and C. M. Barron (eds.), *The Reign of Richard II*, (London, 1971), 153–72.

47. Atiya, op. cit., 408 n. 3, 519; Palmer, op. cit., 184–5, 239–40.

48. Palmer, op. cit., chapter 11, 180–210.

had written for him – de Mézières was the ex-chancellor of Peter of Cyprus, ex-councillor of Charles V and ex-tutor of Charles VI, and the chief literary propagandist of the crusade in the Latin West. Richard II's uncles of Lancaster, York and Gloucester all enrolled as associates of de Mézières' Order of the Passion, the new crusading order that he described in his letter to Richard as 'une nouvelle chevalerie du crucefix qui doit estre mandee oultremer'.[49] Some of the names of other Englishmen who enrolled in this order at the same time are also striking. They include a number of Richard's close and courtly intimates, like his cousin Rutland, Mowbray the Earl Marshal and Lord Despenser, together with a number of chamber knights like Richard Adderbury and Lewis Clifford – the last named being also, incidentally, a friend of Chaucer and a fellow poet.[50] They also include a number of men whose names I have already mentioned as genuine ex-crusaders, like Ralph Percy and Thomas Erpingham. The crusade was very much in men's minds in England, and was a live issue in political society, among the highest and most influential in the realm, in the late 1380s and the 1390s, which was the very period, as it happens, when Chaucer was writing his *Canterbury Tales*.

The first conclusion that stems from the evidence that has accumulated thus far seems to me quite clear. Chaucer may have credited to his Knight a wider and longer crusading experience than any known individual of his time could boast, but there is nothing to occasion surprise in his emphasis on the part his Knight had taken in wars against the heathen. To go on crusading expeditions was, it is true, the exception to the common rule of his day – there are many more witnesses in the great armorial disputes whose military experience is limited to the Anglo-French war than there are men who had been further afield – but it was a not uncommon exception. The ideal of the crusade clearly remained a strong one; the question of the organisation of large-scale expeditions remained a live issue as a practical political objective; and a very substantial number of men showed their individual commitment to crusading by taking part in expeditions at their own risk, at their own cost, and on their own initiative. That is one reason why I continue to believe that what Chaucer was trying to portray in his *Prologue* was the best kind of knight of his time, one who had expressed his love of 'honour' and 'chivalrie' by his dedication to the noblest activity for a knight; a figure idealised somewhat, perhaps, but by no means antiquated in his outlook or remote, in his described life-style and ideals, from the English aristocrats and

49. P. de Mézières, *Letter to King Richard II*, ed. G. W. Coopland (Liverpool, 1975), 103; M. V. Clarke, *Fourteenth Century Studies* (Oxford, 1937), 286.

50. A. Molinier, 'Description de deux manuscrits contenant la règle de la *Militia Passionis Jhesu Christi* de Philippe de Mézières', *Archives de l'Orient Latin*, i (1881), 363; G. L. Kittredge, 'Chaucer and some of his friends', *Mod.Phil.* i (1903), 6–13.

knights whom Chaucer knew personally about the court of Richard II. The crusaders and would-be crusaders with whom he would have had most contact there and elsewhere belonged, moreover, to the true gentility, not to the mercenary riff-raff of the free companies with whom Terry Jones would like to associate Chaucer's Knight.

Plenty of men went on crusade: that in itself does not of course define just why they did, and I am sure Mr Jones is right to approach that question at any rate with some scepticism. It is not easy to believe that an experienced and thoroughly unscrupulous politician like Henry Bolingbroke or a captain like Henry Ferrers with an eye open for dubiously legitimate war profits was actuated by simple and single-minded zeal for the cause of the cross. The pressures of conformism, to fall in with the demands of accepted ideals, together with the quest for reputation and perhaps the lure of adventure, were more likely the mainsprings of their enterprise. The case of a man like, say, Bolingbroke's grandfather Henry of Grosmont, is a little different, though. One imagines that the religious significance of holy war – of the 'blessed viage' as it was often called – may have meant rather more to this great captain and diplomat whom we find, in his *Livre de Seyntz Medicines*, castigating his personal sins, the blood that he has shed, his love of glory, and the lust that drove him in youth to take more joy in prostitutes than in honest women.[51] Whether one is looking at a Henry of Grosmont or a Henry Bolingbroke, however, one point is abundantly clear. That is that the motive for crusading in this period had very little to do with the quest for gains of war, for plunder and ransoms, which is the motive that has been so strongly stressed over the last twenty years with regard to English knightly involvement in the Hundred Years War. The lure of crusading had very little indeed to do with that sort of material advantage.

In fortunate circumstances there could of course be windfalls. There was a vast booty taken at the capture of Alexandria. The determination of the leaders of the substantial English contingent in the army there to get more than their share of swag seems to have been one of the reasons why the success was not followed up. In contrast, neither Bourbon's expedition nor the Nicopolis crusade brought anyone much profit. More men, moreover, went over the years to Prussia than ever went to the east, and he would have been an ignorant man indeed who went to Prussia in the hope of making a fortune out of winnings of war. The Wilderness was the name men gave to the land of the Samogitians, beyond the river Memel, which was the scene of most of the fighting in which Englishmen took part in the fourteenth century. The terrain here was appalling for campaign purposes, utterly unlike

---

51. Henry of Lancaster, *Le Livre de Seyntz Medicines*, ed, E. J. Arnould (*ANTS*, II, Oxford, 1940), 12, 17, 43; 9, 10, 16; 22, 52, 179.

sunny France where men made themselves rich through spoils. Effectively it could only be traversed by cavalry in conditions either of drought or deep frost. The great rivers had to be crossed by ferry, and in the winter floods the perils could be great. If rain or a thaw set in in mid-campaign, horses' hooves would sink too deep in the morasses to carry their riders forward. The villages and forts of the pagans seldom offered rich takings in *specie*. The land could be made rich, but it was the German settlers with whom the Teutonic Order colonised its conquests that made it so, once it was secure. In the meantime, country at the edge of the fighting frontier was often reduced to near desert – it was part of the policy of the Knights to clear a no man's land beyond the fringe of their settlements. The Teutonic knights had indeed material gains to win from the wars, for the land securely taken would be theirs, and so would be the labour of those that they subdued, converted forcibly to Christianity and resettled as cultivators. But there was no comparable advantage on the material side for the pilgrim in arms who came to Prussia and experienced the adventure and the risks of a *reise*.

The aid of the westerners was of course invaluable to the Teutonic Knights, and the manner in which they encouraged pilgrims to their wars is significant, and revealing with regard to crusading motives in the fourteenth century. They did not usually offer wages of war, but they did spend money on their visitors, making sure that they were entertained in a manner worthy of heroes, feasting them and taking them hunting for unfamiliar beasts, for elk and bear. They encouraged them to leave a memorial of themselves and their achievement: to judge by the testimony given in the Scrope v. Grosvenor dispute, there must have been a time when a whole history of foreign crusading enterprise could be read in the armorial glass and blazoned memorials of the Marienkirche of Konigsberg. At the beginning sometimes but more often at the end of a *reise* a great feast was given for the leaders of visiting contingents, called the *Eretisch*. At a high table places of honour were reserved for those knights who had, by general estimation, performed the most noble and notable deeds of arms. The chronicler d'Oronville gives a vivid picture of one of the brothers of the Teutonic order distributing to these chosen ones at the end of the feast special badges bearing the motto '*Honneur vainc tout!*'.[52] Thus a cult of the *reise* was propagated and began to acquire a mystique of its own, and we can see this sort of mystique acquiring impact outside Prussia, as well as in the lands of the Order. The statutes of a southern French order of chivalry called the Tiercelet for instance permitted

---

52. *Chronique du Bon Duc Loys de Bourbon*, ed. A.-M. Chazaud (Société de l'Histoire de France, Paris, 1876), 65–6; and see A. S. Cook, 'Beginning the Board in Prussia', *JEGP*, xiv (1915), 375–88.

any member who had been on a *reise* to wear its insignia with a special difference, to show that he had taken part in a very special enterprise.[53] There is no parallel provision in the statutes of the one great English order of chivalry of this period, the Garter, but the way that the Warwick pageant looks back to the ancestral achievement of the Beauchamps in the 'coostes of Almayn' makes it quite clear that in England too experience of the *reise* had acquired a very special significance in the knightly world.

The continuing force of the ideal of chivalry and the appeal of its mystique were clearly key factors in keeping crusading enthusiasm alive. Here we must remember what chivalry, the order of knighthood, was, that is to say an ethic that was at once Christian and martial and aristocratic. Its elitist social and martial overtones undoubtedly contributed much to its enduring force, at least as much as the Christian sanction that it had acquired in an earlier age. That is what I am getting at when I say that in many cases conformist acceptance of established ideals, together with the prospect of winning repute and the lure of adventure, were probably the mainsprings of crusading motivation. But it is not really my purpose to diagnose just what it was that kept crusading enthusiasm alive in the time of Chaucer, but more simply to show that it did remain alive, that knights did still respond to its promptings and risk body and fortune by so doing, and that it was still widely respected as the highest expression of chivalrous dedication. Whatever Chaucer intended by his description of the Knight in the *General Prologue*, there seems to me no doubt, in the light of the English response to the call of the crusade, that in his day the knight who was not only worthy in his 'lordes werre' but had also fought far afield for the faith could be held up to the secular aristocracy as a model of virtuous activity in his estate. Certainly that was so on the continent, as the careful record of the crusading exploits of such as Marshal Boucicaut reminds us,[54] together with comments such as that of the Soldich de la Trau, that he held to have been present at Bourbon's siege of Tunis, inconclusive as it was, more honourable than to have been at three mortal battles in the field in ordinary war.[55] Still more significant in the present context are the *lobdichten* of Guelders Herald, his poetic praises of named and actual knights whom he held to have been in his day of the highest prowess. His litanies of the campaigns of such men as the duke of Juliers, Rutger Raets and Adam von Moppertingen emphasise their deeds in Prussia and beyond

53. M. G. A. Vale, 'A Fourteenth-Century Order of Chivalry: the *Tiercelet, EHR*, lxxxii (1967), 340.

54. *Le Livre des faicts du bon Messire Jean Le Maingre, dit Boucicaut*, ed. M. Petitot (Collection des Mémoires relatifs à l'Histoire de France, VI, Paris 1825), chapters 12, 18, 22–8.

55. *Chronique du Bon Duc Loys de Bourbon*, 248.

the 'great sea' in a manner that is not so very distantly reminiscent of Chaucer's record of his own Knight's achievements in the *General Prologue*.[56]

In another essay in this volume Richard Green reminds us that in the late middle ages he who would be a courtier had to learn also to be a lover, and of the instructions that little Jehan de Saintré received under that head. Later in the same story Anthoine de la Sale describes, with the loving attention to detail of one versed in heraldic lore, the feats of his hero in the lists that did honour to his lady. After that, Saintré's next great exploit was to lead a glorious crusade in Prussia, which was the climax of his career in knighthood.[57] Of course a knight is not quite the same thing as a courtier, but the story of Saintré reminds us that at the end of the fourteenth century the two ideas were still close to one another. In the days of King Richard II a great many courtiers were knights, and courtesy – the manners fitting to a court – was an essential quality of good knighthood. Richard's court may not have been a centre of the patronage of cultural activity in the most usual sense of the term, but the king was a generous patron to cultured knights like him whom Deschamps hailed as 'the amorous Clifford', – a man who knew how to play the game of courtly love but who had also seen service in the wars, and was a member of the crusading Order of the Passion.[58] The Black Prince's influence no doubt had much to do with the strong martial element among the men close to the King. The jousts of St Inglevert are perhaps not quite part of the history of English court culture, but the great Smithfield tournament where Richard's badge of the White Hart was first displayed was a similar occasion, and much nearer to it;[59] and if John Palmer is right about the Wilton Diptych – and I think he is – it finds its context in plans for a great chivalrous enterprise, the crusade against the Turk.[60] If the history of the crusading interests and experience of the English aristocracy of Chaucer's day is not strictly court history, it does, I think, tell us a good deal about the atmosphere and preoccupations of the actual court of Richard II.

56. *Wapenboek ou Armorial de 1334 à 1372, par Gelre Héraut d'Armes*, ed. V. Bouton (Paris, 1881), i, 41, 90–1, 101.

57. A. de la Sale, *Le petit Jehan de Saintré* (London and Paris, 1911), chapters 18–43, 58–63.

58. *Oeuvres Complètes de Eustache Deschamps*, ed. Marquis de Queux de Saint-Hilaire and G. Raynaud (Paris, 1878-1903), iii, 375–6.

59. *Historia vitae et regni Ricardi II ... a monacho quodam de Evesham*, ed. T. Hearne (Oxford, 1729), 122.

60. Palmer, op. cit., 242–4.

I must most gratefully acknowledge my debt to Miss J. Bateson of St Anne's College, Oxford, who helped me with the correction of the proofs, and ironed out a number of inaccuracies. Those that remain are my mistakes.

4

The Education of the Courtier

Nicholas Orme

'The king's household is the chief academy for the nobility of England. It provides schooling in athletics, moral integrity and good manners, through which the kingdom flourishes, acquires honour and is protected against invaders.' The words are those of Sir John Fortescue in the 1460s,[1] but they could equally well have been written one or two hundred years earlier. Throughout the later middle ages, the court and household of the kings of England were important centres of education and of educated people. First, the king's household and the ancillary establishments of the queen and the royal children were in part schools for the training of young aristocratic men and women. The royal children were brought up there; so were many orphan heirs in the king's wardship, and so were other noble children sent or gathered for the purpose. Secondly, the king's court was a meeting place of adult noblemen and women, educated in other great households, schools and universities. The manners and accomplishments which children learnt and adults practised at court made up a code of behaviour, 'courtesy', which formed a model for the aristocracy as a whole. In the following pages we shall attempt to reconstruct the education of the lay aristocracy of later medieval England: the dominant group among both those who staffed the royal household and those who visited the king's court. By 'aristocracy' we mean the whole of the medieval 'second estate' of society: the royal family, peers and great magnates, knights, esquires and ordinary gentlemen, both male

---

1. 'In ea [domus regia] gignasium supremum sit nobilitatis regni, scola quoque strenuitatis probitatis et morum quibus regnum honoratur et florebit, ac contra irruentes securatur': Sir John Fortescue, *De Laudibus Legum Anglie*, ed. S. B. Chrimes (Cambridge, 1942), 110–11.

and female. It was the education of this estate which came nearest to embodying courtly education in England during the period.

Few laws prescribed how medieval boys and girls should be educated. The command of the church that everyone must be baptised, confirmed and taught to pray, constituted the only major directive about the matter.[2] There was no attempt in medieval England, as there was in Scotland in 1496, to impose a statutory obligation upon the aristocracy to send their sons to school.[3] Yet if stated laws were few, many other invisible forces shaped the form which aristocratic education took. The church again, by preaching a code of belief, worship and behaviour, stimulated the teaching of children in prayer and confession, deportment in church, and Christian ethics. Law and custom, which required the male aristocracy to govern and defend the realm, necessitated boys being taught to read, in order to understand administrative and legal documents, and to be trained in military techniques. Aristocratic wealth and possessions indicated the preparation of boys and girls for adult life of a certain style. Future knights and ladies needed to learn how to behave to one another and how to follow the occupations of civilised life: music, embroidery, dancing, and exercises such as archery and hunting. The emphasis placed on these different elements may have differed from household to household, but there is unlikely to have been wide variation. Aristocratic families were interrelated, and the standards of one were influenced and regulated by others. The institution of feudal wardship took fatherless children away from their mothers to be educated in the households of their superior lords. Travel and social intercourse, most notably through attending the court itself, also diffused a common code of values and accomplishments. Medieval England was a nation, not a group of tribes, and the education of aristocratic boys and girls is likely to have aimed at similar objectives in most places.

Literature was another shaping force. Throughout the later middle ages, many writings circulated among the aristocracy and their servants which helped to establish common standards and techniques in education. First, there was the great corpus of religious and moral literature which gave knowledge of God, narrated Christian history, taught virtues and censored sins. Most of it was addressed to mankind as a whole, rather than to children in particular, but by moulding the attitudes of parents and teachers it reached the young as well, albeit indirectly. A second genre of literature, related to the first, consisted of works of advice to kings and princes specifically, on how to govern

2. *Manuale ad Vsum Sarisburiensis*, ed. A. Jefferies Collins (Henry Bradshaw Soc., XCI, 1958), 32, 37–8.

3. *The Acts of the Parliaments of Scotland, 1124–1707*, ed. T. Thomson & others, 12 vols. (Edinburgh, 1814–75), II, 238.

themselves and their subjects. Historians have called such writings 'mirrors of princes'. One of the most famous, the *Secretum Secretorum*, was the translation of an Arabic text allegedly containing the counsel of Aristotle to Alexander the Great.[4] Others were original works by French and English scholars and poets, of which a long series was produced from the twelfth century onwards, including (in England) Hoccleve's *Regement of Princes*, Fortescue's *De Laudibus Legum Anglie* and Skelton's *Speculum Principis*.[5] Both the *Secretum* and several others of the 'mirrors' circulated in later medieval England in Latin, French and English versions, and though written primarily for kings or their sons, they are frequently to be found in the possession of the nobility. This shows that the aristocracy shared the interest of their rulers in statecraft, and suggests that the 'mirrors' in consequence may also have influenced the education of aristocratic children. A third supply of educational ideas came from imaginative secular literature: romances and chansons de geste. These works, even at their most sensational, were not wholly confined to fictional happenings but portrayed knights and ladies who typified the virtues of real society and set standards of behaviour which their readers could imitate. Many stories went further than this, since they began by describing how their heroes and heroines were brought up, thus providing models for the educational process itself. Medieval parents and children must have absorbed something about standards and techniques in education as they read about the ideal upbringings of Guy of Warwick and Felise, Paris and Vienne, Chaucer's Squire, and Virginia in his 'Physician's Tale'.[6]

The concern of most medieval literature with the education of children, however, can only be rated as secondary. Generally, the educational message was addressed to mankind as a whole; often, as in works of fiction, it competed with the aim to entertain. Medieval England was short of books which discussed the education of young people as a primary theme. There was nothing so relevant or so widely diffused as *The Governor* by Sir Thomas Elyot or Henry Peacham's *Compleat Gentleman* in the sixteenth and seventeenth centuries. The absence of texts does not mean that education was not practised among the medieval aristocracy; many records prove the contrary, as we shall

4. *Secretum Secretorum: Nine English Versions*, ed. M. A. Manzalaoui, I: Text, *EETS* OS 276 (1977); George Cary, *The Medieval Alexander*, ed. D. J. A. Ross (Cambridge, 1956), especially 105–10, 250–1, 287–90, 344–5.
5. For a good recent survey of the genre see *Four English Political Tracts of the Later Middle Ages*, ed. J.-P. Genet, Camden Society, fourth series, XVIII (1977), ix–xix.
6. *The Romance of Guy of Warwick*, ed. J. Zupitza, *EETS* ES 25–6 (1875–6), 3–5; ibid., 42 (1883), 6–7; *Paris and Vienne*, ed. M. Leach, *EETS* OS 234 (1957), 1–2; *Canterbury Tales*, ed. Robinson, General Prologue, lines 79–100; Physician's Tale, lines 30–66.

see. The lack was one of educational consciousness. Most medieval
thinkers and writers failed to distinguish children as a separate group,
or education as a process separate from human life in general. Works
which discussed the training of the young were few, and most of them
dealt with the subject as part of wider studies of mankind, rather than
in its own right. The principal discussions of children's education
which circulated in medieval England owed their birth or their popularity to the rise of the universities and the friars in the thirteenth
century. First, there was Aristotle's *Politics*, the seventh and eighth
books of which contain an extended discussion of the training proper
to the aristocracy. It has not yet been ascertained that any noble
household contained a copy of the *Politics*, either in Latin or in the
fourteenth-century French translation by Nicholas Oresme, but the
work was studied in the English universities and must have been
known to the graduate friars and secular clergy who mingled with the
aristocracy and advised them.[7] Next should be mentioned the encyclo-
paedia of the English Franciscan scholar, Bartholomew Glanville, *De
Proprietatibus Rerum*, compiled in the mid-thirteenth century. This
work includes several chapters, descriptive rather than instructive,
about the duties of parents and nurses and the care of young children
from birth until the age of seven. It circulated widely in medieval
England in the original Latin, was translated into French in 1372 and
into English by John Trevisa in 1398.[8] Thirdly, there was the great
work of the Italian Augustinian friar, Giles of Rome, *De Regimine
Principum*, composed for the young Philip the Fair of France in the
1270s. This treatise, as well as providing one of the most complete and
coherent accounts of the duties of kings, contained a section of
twenty-one chapters on the education of aristocratic boys and girls. It
was well-known in late-medieval England in Latin; several of the
aristocracy are known to have possessed French translations, and a
single copy even survives of an English version, made in about 1400.[9]

7. On the knowledge of Aristotle's *Politics* in later medieval England see S. H.
Thomson, 'Walter Burley's commentary on the *Politics* of Aristotle', *Mélanges Auguste
Pelzer* (Louvain, 1947), 557–78.

8. On the author see A. B. Emden, *A Biographical Register of the University of Oxford
to A.D. 1500*, 3 vols (Oxford, 1957–9), II, 771–72, and on the French translation,
Dictionnaire des Lettres Françaises, I: *Le Moyen Age*, ed. R. Bossuat & others (Paris,
1964), 57–8. The English translation has been edited: *On the Properties of Things. John
Trevisa's Translation of Bartholomaeus Anglicus De Proprietatibus Rerum*, ed. M. C.
Seymour & others, 2 vols. (Oxford, 1975).

9. The only available modern edition is of the 13th-century French translation by
Henri de Gauchy: Giles of Rome, *Li Livres du Gouvernement des Rois*, ed. S. P. Molenaer
(New York & London, 1899). The English translation, possibly by John Trevisa, is
discussed in John Trevisa, *Dialogus inter Militem et Clericum*, ed. A. J. Perry, *EETS*
OS 167 (1925), xcviii–c. For some references to the work's popularity in later medieval
England see R. H. Jones, *The Royal Policy of Richard II: Absolutism in the Later Middle
Ages* (Oxford, 1968), 154–63.

The translations of Bartholomew and Giles have a particular interest for the historian of education. They show that the works concerned, though academic in nature, were coming to attract the interest of the lay aristocracy as well: the owners and readers of books in French and English. Among the many matters that the treatises contained, their noble readers must have learnt something about education and its theory. This learning had a sequel, since a few of the medieval aristocracy were moved to write about the subject themselves. As early as the mid thirteenth century, Walter of Bibbesworth, a knight of Essex, wrote a treatise which explained, *inter alia*, how to bring up babies and how to teach noble boys the French vocabulary they would need in adult life to organise the husbandry of their estates.[10] A century later Geoffroy de la Tour Landry, a knight of Anjou, compiled the *Book of the Knight of the Tower* in the 1370s. This was a prose collection of moral stories and observations in French, intended to educate his daughters in the absence (through death) of their mother. It reached England in French during the fifteenth century and two English translations were made, one of them by Caxton who also printed it.[11] Notable too is Peter Idley, lord of the manor of Drayton in Oxfordshire and controller of the king's works under Henry VI, who produced in about the 1450s, a long verse treatise of 'Instructions' for his son. The work, adapted and translated from various earlier moral works by Albertano da Brescia, Robert Mannyng and John Lydgate, achieved a modest circulation and survives in seven manuscripts.[12] None of these authors can be rated highly as educational theorists. The works of Idley and La Tour Landry in particular draw heavily on other authors; they are not very orderly, and their models are literary rather than academic. Nevertheless they all possess a very great importance in the social history of education. Like the translations of Bartholomew and Giles, their writings show that educational literature had ceased to be the preserve of clerical intellectuals. It was becoming a matter of interest to the lay aristocracy.

The educational writers of the middle ages all agreed that the basic responsibility for bringing up children belonged to their fathers and mothers. 'A man loueth his childe,' declares John Trevisa in his translation of Bartholomew in 1398,

and fedith and noriscith him, and settith him at his owne bord whenne he is i-wenyed, and techith him in his youth with speche and with

10. *Le Traité de Walter de Bibbesworth sur la langue française*, ed. A. Owen (Paris, 1929), especially 43–70.
11. *The Book of the Knight of the Tower*, ed. M. Y. Offord, *EETS* SS2 (1971).
12 *Peter Idley's Instructions to his Son*, ed. Charlotte D'Evelyn (Boston and London, Modern Language Association of America, Monograph Series, VI, 1935), especially 1–35.

wordis, and chastith him with beting, and settith and puttith him to lore vndir warde and kepinge of wardeynes and tutours. And the fadir schewith him no glad chere lest he worthe proude. And a . . . yeueth to his childeren clothinge and mete and drinke as here age askith, and purchasith lond and heritage for his children alwey and maketh it more and more.[13]

This admirably summarises the duties which the noble father was expected to bear in mind. He should maintain the child with food, drink and clothing. He should teach the child, or appoint tutors to do so instead. Finally, he should provide the child with an endowment or career. The ethic of parental responsibility can also be traced in practice. The household accounts of noble and gentle families record expenditure on children's food and clothes, and sometimes indicate the presence of nurses, guardians and schoolmasters. Wills, enfeoffments and marriage contracts reveal the disposition of property by parents to support their offspring. By the second half of the fifteenth century, letter collections like those of the Pastons, the Plumptons and the Stonors record some of the personal relationships within the families of the lesser aristocracy. The letters have a special value in illuminating the role of women in the educational process. Mothers emerge as powerful auxiliaries during their husbands' lifetimes and as substitutes for them after they died. Agnes, the widow of William Paston I, held sway over her children following his death in 1444. She wrote to her son Edmund, a student at the inns of court, that he should think each day of his father's injunction to learn the law; she bullied her daughter Elizabeth until she was married, and urged the tutor of her youngest son Clement, then aged sixteen, that he 'trewly belash him' if he had not done well.[14] Margaret, the wife of John Paston I and a milder woman, interceded for her eldest son John II when he displeased his father, but broke into fury when her daughter Margery fell in love with the family's bailiff, Richard Calle, and ended by forbidding her the house.[15] Parental interventions could be dramatic; as in Margery's case, they were not always effective.

The responsibilities of aristocratic parents for their offspring, however, were not discharged in person all the time. Parental dignity and business made it necessary to entrust at least part of the everyday care and training of the children to others, who had more time or expertise for the purpose. This process began at birth, since it was common if not universal for aristocratic mothers to depute the feeding of their babies to a wet nurse possessing, in the opinion of Giles of

13. *On the Properties of Things*, book VI, chapter 14.
14. *Paston Letters and Papers of the Fifteenth Century*, ed. N. Davis, 2 vols. (Oxford, 1971–6), I, 27, 41; II, 32.
15. Ibid., I, 289–90, 293, 341–3.

Rome, as many as possible of their own physical characteristics.[16] The nurse's duties are described by Bartholomew.[17] She suckles the baby, kisses, cleans and washes it, gives it medicines and dances it up and down. She whistles or sings the child to sleep, swathes it in sheets and clouts, and stretches out its limbs with cradle bonds lest they should grow awry. At a later stage she weans the child by feeding it food chewed in her own mouth, and teaches it words by saying them over and over, in a gentle voice. The social status of those employed as nurses is not clear, but we may guess them to have been the wives of yeomen, grooms or other men of free status in their masters' service. Their breast-feeding duties lasted for about two years, after which they may have remained with their charges as servants. The best-recorded nurses, those of the royal children, were well paid for their work with grants and annuities, and in one or two cases the benefits were redoubled at a later date when the former baby ascended the throne as king.[18]

Medieval theorists divided childhood into three parts: *infancia* from birth to the age of seven, *puericia* from seven to fourteen, and *adolescencia* from fourteen to twenty-one or later.[19] Both Aristotle and Giles regarded *infancia* as a period in which food, play and exercise should take precedence over formal training, though Aristotle proposed that boys should become onlookers at the training of their elders when they were five.[20] Most aristocratic children of both sexes apparently remained under the government of women when they left their wet-nurses, until they were seven. Among the lesser aristocracy they were probably supervised by their mother and her household women, but in the families of the king and of some great magnates, where the mother was not available for this duty, we find the care of the young children being deputed to a mistress of the nursery. Unlike the nurse, the mistress was a noble- or gentlewoman. Her tasks would have been to supervise the nurse and the children's other servants, to provide the nursery with food and clothes, and probably also to help the children to speak and to learn good manners. We find Elizabeth of St Omer acting as mistress of the four year-old Black Prince and his younger sisters in 1334,[21] and Maria Hervy of the six year-old Henry

16. Giles of Rome, *De Regimine Principum* book II, part II, chapter 15.

17. *On the Properties of Things*, book VI, chapter 9.

18. There are references to royal nurses throughout the *Calendars of Patent Rolls, 1216–1509* (London, 1891–1916).

19. *On the Properties of Things*, book VI, chapter 1.

20. Aristotle, *Politics*, book VII, chapter 17; Giles of Rome, *De Regimine Principum*, book II, part II, chapter 15.

21. T. F. Tout, *Chapters in the Administrative History of Mediaeval England* (Manchester, 1920–33), V, 319–20.

V and his younger brothers and sister in 1393.[22] Lady Alice Butler, who was appointed to teach courtesy and 'nurture' to the two year-old Henry VI in 1424, doubtless fulfilled a similar role.[23] Some light is thrown on the duties of these ladies by an indenture of 1502 between Robert Turberville, treasurer of the household of Edward Stafford, duke of Buckingham, and Margaret Hexstall, gentlewoman.[24] It arranged for Margaret to attend on the duke's heir, the nine month-old Lord Henry Stafford and his elder sisters, in the ducal manor of Blechingley. She was not to remove the children without the permission of one of the duke's councillors, and was to provide food for her charges and their servants, to a total number of seventeen. Finally, she was to choose the menus and see that the children were served each day with four or five dishes of flesh and fish. The indenture does not mention educational duties, but these may well have been taken for granted.

In the seventh year, or at the age of seven, the training of boys and girls began to diverge. According to the theorists, boys of this age were ready to undergo instruction and discipline from men, or, as John Trevisa expressed it, to be 'put and sette to lore vndir tutours and compelled to fonge [i.e. undergo] lore and chastisinge'.[25] So too in practice Henry VI, discharging the mistress of his six and a half year-old son Edward in 1460, explained that he was sufficiently grown 'to be committed to the rules and teachings of wise and strenuous men, and to understand the arts and manners of a man, rather than to stay further under the keeping and governance of women'.[26] The arrangements for providing the tutors of aristocratic boys are difficult to reconstruct, since they are badly recorded and may have varied from family to family according to wealth and status. In the best-known cases, those of the heirs to the throne, the boy was entrusted to a senior knight or nobleman who was entitled his master (*magister*) or tutor (*pedagogus*).[27] Edward I was tutored by Sir Hugh Giffard, Henry VI by the earl of Warwick, and Edward V by Earl Rivers. Richard II had three such masters: Sir Richard Abberbury, Sir Guiscard D'Angle and Sir Simon Burley. The knightly tutor probably exercised a general oversight of his royal pupil, saw to his manners, taught him to ride, and supervised his training in arms when he grew older. Literary

22. PRO, Duchy of Lancaster, Accounts Various, DL 28/1/4–5; J. H. Wylie, *History of England under Henry the Fourth*, 4 vols. (London, 1884–98), IV, 163, 171.
23. *Proceedings and Ordinances of the Privy Council*, ed. N. H. Nicolas, 7 vols, (London, Record Commission, 1834–7), III, 143.
24. *A Relation . . . of the Island of England, 1500*, ed. Charlotte A. Sneyd, Camden Soc., XXXVII (1847), 75–6.
25. *On the Properties of Things*, book VI, chapter 5.
26. *CPR, 1452–61*, 567.
27. Nicholas Orme, *English Schools in the Middle Ages* (London, 1973), 22 and note 5.

studies were entrusted to a separate clerk or schoolmaster, Edward III being taught by John Peynel, Henry VI by John Somerset, and Edward V by John Giles.[28] It is possible that this diarchy of knightly tutor and clerical schoolmaster was also imposed on the younger sons of the king and the sons of the great magnates, though the evidence for it is difficult to find. Among the lesser baronial and knightly families, however, where unoccupied knights were harder to come by, a cleric may have acted alone as tutor, giving general supervision as well as literary instruction. During the 1430s and 40s Robert Hungerford and John Tiptoft, both heirs to baronies, each spent some time at Oxford under the care of a graduate cleric,[29] and Edmund and Jasper Tudor are said to have been entrusted to virtuous priests for teaching and for guidance in good living and behaviour.[30] Sometimes a domestic chaplain may have undertaken this task, as John Still appears to have done in the Paston family in 1468.[31] The appointment of a cleric alone as tutor need not have meant that military and athletic training was absolutely neglected. Most medieval clergy were used to riding, some were only too fond of hunting, and others had been present at battles and knew something about fighting. It was not a knight but a precentor of Salisbury Cathedral, Nicholas Upton, who wrote the chief English treatise of the fifteenth century on heraldry and the laws of war.[32]

Aristocratic girls, unlike their brothers, remained under female supervision throughout the periods of *puericia* and *adolescencia*, until they became married. The system by which they were governed was also subject to variations, depending on the importance and wealth of their families. Among the lesser aristocracy, the care of the older girls like that of the nursery children probably fell to the lot of their mother. Life in a small household brought mothers and daughters closely together, while resources for paying a special governess were limited. Most mothers must have been capable of teaching behaviour, deportment, dancing, embroidery and even language and reading.[33] What they lacked in religious and literary expertise could be easily supplied by a chaplain or friar. In the families of the king and the greater magnates, however, where mothers and daughters spent more of their lives apart, there developed during the later middle ages the office of mistress, the female equivalent of the boys' master or tutor. Like the mistress of the nursery, the mistress of the royal or noble girl was

28. *CCR, 1327–30*, 573; *CPR, 1429–36*, 241; ibid., *1467–77*, 592.
29. Emden, II, 985; III, 1877.
30. *Henry the Sixth: a Reprint of John Blacman's Memoir*, ed. M. R. James (Cambridge, 1919), 8–9, 30–1.
31. *Paston Letters*, ed. Davis, I, 540.
32. Emden, III, 1933–4.
33. On mothers as teachers see *The Book of the Knight of the Tower*, 3–4, 13.

herself a lady of aristocratic rank. The best known of them all, Katherine Swynford, mistress of the daughters of John of Gaunt in the 1370s (and also to Gaunt himself), was a knight's daughter married to a knight in her master's retinue.[34] Katherine Waterton, mistress of Henry IV's daughter Philippa in the first decade of the fifteenth century, was also the wife of a knight in her lord's service.[35] The existence of mistresses in the households of the great magnates was sufficiently common at the end of the fourteenth century to attract the attention of Chaucer himself. In his 'Physician's Tale', which opens with an evocation of the virtues of Virginia, a noble girl of ideal qualities, Chaucer breaks into the narrative with an exhortation to 'maistresses . . . that lordes doghtres han in governaunce'.[36] He asserts that they fall into two kinds: those who are well known for their honesty and those who, though they have fallen into frailty (evidently of a sexual kind), have reformed themselves and gained a reputation for experience. He ends by urging them to keep a close guard on their charges and not to slacken in teaching them virtuous things. Like the mothers and the tutor, the mistress probably taught a wide range of accomplishments in an informal way, presumably helped when necessary by a cleric in the spheres of religious and literary studies.

In what has already been said, we have assumed that aristocratic children were brought up in the households of their own parents. This is not wholly true. Their education began at home, indeed, and involved the arrangements that have been described, but it is probable that most of them also left home during the course of their childhood and got part of their training elsewhere. Departure from home could take place at any time, and by accident as well as by design. In the first case a father might die or fall into disfavour, causing his children to be removed into the wardship of his feudal superior or that of the king. Alternatively, parents might lay deliberate plans for their children to spend their *puericia* or *adolescencia* in the household of a greater magnate, or in a specialised institution such as a school or university. There were good reasons for such a move. Boys and girls alike stood to benefit from widening their experience of life in another environment, and could gain useful patronage from the lords and ladies with whom they were boarded, leading to service or marriage in adult life. Boys who aimed at careers involving special skills were likely to gain a better understanding of fighting by living with a famous knight, religion with a prelate, or scholarship in a university. Educationists approved the sending of children away from home. William Worcester

---

34. *John of Gaunt's Register, 1379–83*, ed. Eleanor C. Lodge & R. Somerville, vol. II, Camden Society, third series, LVII (1937), 302–3, 93.
35. Wylie, *England under Henry the Fourth*, IV, 222, 241.
36. Ed. Robinson, lines 72–82.

and Sir John Fortescue, writing in the third quarter of the fifteenth century, both praised the placing of youths in the households of the king and the magnates, as a means by which they would receive more expert and disinterested supervision and become more proficient in arms and noble behaviour.[37] Some commentators believed that parents, in contrast, were too indulgent. The children of most rich men 'be loste nowadais in ther youghe at home, and that with ther fathers and mothers'. So wrote the author of a set of school exercises at Magdalen College, Oxford, in about 1500.[38] He went on to censure mothers for playing with their children as if they were dolls, allowing them to use bad language, and being unwilling to put them to any discipline. When the children arrived at adulthood, he asserted, they had no shame, were bold to do evil, and showed every probability of ending their lives on the block or on the gallows.

There is no need to quarrel with Fortescue's view that the pre-eminent place to which aristocratic children could be sent in the later middle ages was the royal household. Here, in the household itself, or in those of the queen and the royal children, could be found orphan sons of the tenants-in-chief, some of them heirs to earldoms and baronies. Here too were sons with fathers still alive, who were important enough to gain the privilege of court attendance during their youth or early manhood. Already by 1318, the date of the Household Ordinance of York, 'the children who lie in the king's ward' were a regular charge on the household, taking wages and liveries after their degree.[39] The heirs to the throne were often brought up alongside these wards, in less seclusion than their Hanoverian and Victorian successors. In 1301 the future Edward II, then aged sixteen, was accompanied by ten wards in his household, including Gilbert de Clare later earl of Gloucester and the notorious Piers Gaveston.[40] Every boy except Gaveston had his own master with him. In 1425 the privy council of the four year-old Henry VI commanded that all the heirs of baronies in the king's wardship, the keeping of whom had apparently become dispersed, should return to dwell in the royal household, each with at least one master to be paid for at the king's expense.[41] During the course of the fifteenth century the educational arrangements in the king's household became increasingly formalised. By about 1449 there

---

37. *The Boke of Noblesse*, ed. J. G. Nichols (London, Roxburghe Club, 1860), 76–7; Fortescue, *De Laudibus Legum Anglie*, ed. Chrimes, 110–11.

38. *A Fifteenth Century School Book*, ed. W. Nelson (Oxford, 1956), 13–14. Compare Edmund Dudley, *The Tree of the Commonwealth*, ed. D. M. Brodie (Cambridge, 1948), 45, 68.

39. T. F. Tout, *The Place of the Reign of Edward II in English History* (Manchester, 1914), 280.

40. Tout, *Chapters*, II, 172.

41. *Proceedings and Ordinances of the Privy Council*, ed. Nicolas, III, 170.

was a grammar master to teach 'the noble boys brought up in the king's household', an office which continued on a regular basis during the following hundred years.[42] By the reign of Edward IV the 'Black Book of the Household', compiled between 1467 and 1477, mentions not only the king's wards but a separate category of noble youths called 'henchmen', six in number or more 'as hit shall please the king'.[43] The henchmen were sometimes wards and sometimes not. It was recorded on the tomb of Thomas Howard, second duke of Norfolk who died in 1524, that he was henchman to Edward IV: at a time when his father, Sir John Howard, was still alive.[44] The henchmen, and perhaps the wards as well, were under the supervision of a 'master of the henchmen' with the rank of a squire, who was charged with teaching them courtesy, languages, music, riding and feats of arms.[45] Instruction in grammar was given by the grammar master.[46] The assembly of noble youths in the household thus evolved into an organised school with a defined curriculum and professional teachers. But not all court education was so formal. It was also possible for a young man to be sent to court and to stay there at his father's expense on the peripheries, awaiting recognition and a permanent place, like the nineteen year-old John Paston II, reputedly too shy in 1461 'to put forthe hym-selfe' and gain advancement.[47] This kind of attendance could also be educative, bringing as it did a young squire into contact with great men, formal life, and the latest fashions in cultural accomplishments.

The educational function of the king's household was paralleled in those of the great lay magnates. Here too we find frequent references to boys, and also girls, as wards, pages and paying guests, formally or informally undergoing education. The best-known example of a page is that of Chaucer himself, son of a London merchant and vintner, who first appears in historical records in the household of the countess of Ulster in 1357, when he was in his teens.[48] Education through wardship is typified by the future Henry VII, born earl of Richmond in 1457, but deprived of his title by Edward IV five years later. He spent the next seven years of his life as a ward in the household of William Lord Herbert at various places in Wales, including Raglan.[49] Since Edward Haseley, dean of Warwick, is described in 1495 as

42. *Liber Regie Capelle*, ed. W. Ullmann, Henry Bradshaw Soc., XCII 1961), 57; Orme, *English Schools in the Middle Ages*, 218–19.

43. A. R. Myers, *The Household of Edward IV* (Manchester, 1959), 126.

44. J. Weever, *Ancient Funerall Monuments* (London, 1631), 834; (London, 1767), 554.

45. Myers, *Household of Edward IV*, 126.

46. Ibid., 137–8.

47. *Paston Letters*, ed. Davis, I, 199–200.

48. *Chaucer Life-Records*, ed. M. M. Crow & C. C. Olson (Oxford, 1966), 13–18.

49. S. B. Chrimes, *Henry VII* (London, 1972), 14–17.

'instructor to the king in his tender age', it looks as though the amenities of the Herbert household included a schoolmaster.[50] Certainly by the early sixteenth century, several great magnates had come to institute bodies of henchmen, wards and grammar masters in their households, on the lines of the royal ones.[51] The sending away of girls in a similar manner is well illustrated in the Paston Letters. Elizabeth, daughter of William Paston I, was boarding with Lady Pole in 1458 when her mother sent her some money and urged her to accustom herself to work readily like other gentlewomen.[52] A decade later John I's wife Margaret did her best to place their elder daughter Margery with Lady Oxford or Lady Bedford in 1469, to forestall her love affair with the bailiff.[53] Anne, the younger daughter, also lived away from home with the wife of Sir William Calthrop until about 1470 when Sir William asked for her removal, on the grounds that he had to reduce his household.[54] A mother who sent her own daughters to board elsewhere might equally well receive strange girls herself. Margaret's cousin, Sir John Hevingham thought so in the early 1460s, at any rate, when he asked her to take in a girl called Agnes Loveday at his own expense. She was not at her ease in her present situation, he said, and all his efforts to place her with another family had failed.[55]

The education of the aristocracy was not confined to secular households; many examples occur of boys and girls being trained in those of the clergy. There was, of course, much in common between the establishment of a prelate and that of a lay magnate. Each provided similar opportunities to gain patronage, meet other people, acquire good manners and be trained in special techniques. We find William, son and heir of James Lord Berkeley, in the household of Cardinal Beaufort in 1437–8 at the age of twelve;[56] Thomas More, son of Sir William More, in that of Cardinal Morton in about 1491, when he was thirteen;[57] and Henry Percy, son and heir of the earl of Northumberland, in that of Cardinal Wolsey in 1522, at the age of twenty.[58] Recourse could also be had to a religious house for the same purpose. In the case of male foundations, this meant joining the abbot's retinue and staying in his private lodging, rather than dwelling among the

50. *CPR, 1485–94*, 332.
51. For examples and references see Orme, *English Schools in the Middle Ages*, 321–2.
52. *Paston Letters*, ed. Davis, I, 42.
53. Ibid., 339.
54. Ibid., 339, 348.
55. Ibid., 350–1.
56. J. Smyth, *The Lives of the Berkeleys*, ed. Sir J. Maclean, 2 vols (Gloucester, 1883), II, 100.
57. Emden, II, 1305–6.
58. George Cavendish, *The Life and Death of Cardinal Wolsey*, ed. R. S. Sylvester, *EETS* OS 243 (1959), 29–30.

monks themselves. John Hertford, abbot of St Albans (1235–63), was remembered long afterwards as a man to whom the nobility of England had sent their children to be educated.[59] The abbot of Hyde at Winchester had eight noble boys lodging with him in order to study in about 1450,[60] and Woburn Abbey, in the 1530s, housed three young gentlemen commoners and their own schoolmaster.[61] Nunneries, on the other hand, opened themselves fully for the reception and training of children, to an extent well beyond that of the orders of men.[62] It is significant that Chaucer, when he described the Prioress, sketched a portrait of which nearly half was a list of educational accomplishments, such as a nun might teach or a girl absorb: French of the Anglo-Norman dialect, deportment, careful speech and good table manners.[63] Bishops visiting nunneries throughout the later middle ages found them boarding children on a large scale, of both sexes and of all ages, some of them sleeping in the nuns' own dormitories. Rules were often laid down to control these practices. Children were ordered to be banished from the dormitories; nuns were to receive only one child each, or only children licenced by the bishop; boys were not to remain after a certain age, variously fixed from five to eleven, or girls after twelve to fourteen. The need for regulation testifies to the great popularity of nunneries as centres of education.

There remains one other group of institutions to which aristocratic boys were sent to be trained. These were the specialised centres of education: schools and universities, joined in the fifteenth century by the inns of court. Throughout the later middle ages sons of the nobility and gentry went away from home to one or other of these institutions in order to gain specialised knowledge which the household could not provide: advanced grammar, the liberal arts, theology, and the various kinds of law. Until about 1400, however, departure to school or university was probably mainly confined to aristocratic boys intended for ecclesiastical careers. Those who anticipated remaining in secular life could learn enough grammar for their needs in the household, though some of the lesser aristocracy who had no tutor at hand may have sent such boys to a local school instead. There was always the possibility, of course, that ecclesiastical trainees might revert to secular life in adulthood, either through lack of vocation or the unforeseen inherit-

59. *Gesta Abbatum Monasterii Sancti Albani*, ed. H. T. Riley, 3 vols (London, Rolls Series, 1867–9), I, 397.

60. T. Warton, *History of English Poetry*, ed. W. C. Hazlitt, 4 vols (London, 1871), IV, 9.

61. *Calendar of Letters and Papers, Foreign and Domestic, Henry VIII*, XIII, part I, 361.

62. On education in nunneries see Eileen Power, *Medieval English Nunneries, c. 1275–1535* (Cambridge, 1922), 237–84, 568–81.

63. *Canterbury Tales*, General Prologue, lines 118–41.

ance of family property. John Balliol, a fourth son who was at school at Durham in the 1260s, survived to inherit the Balliol lands and become king of Scotland.[64] William Beauchamp, another fourth son, began to study at Oxford in 1358–61, when the death of his elder brothers caused his diversion into a military and political career which ended in his elevation to a barony in 1392.[65] By the early fifteenth century, however, the sending of boys away to school or university was becoming extended from those who would or might become ecclesiastics to those who were definitely intended to remain seculars. We have already mentioned the nine year-old Robert Hungerford, who stayed for three terms in University College, Oxford, in 1437–8, and John Tiptoft who spent a longer period of three or four years in the same college in 1440–4, during his early teens.[66] Cambridge likewise reveals Henry Holland, son of the earl of Huntingdon, as a commoner of the King's Hall in 1440–2,[67] and the less exalted John Paston I at Trinity Hall and Peterhouse at about the same time.[68] All four youths were the eldest sons and heirs of their families, and there can be no doubt that their presence in university towns were aimed at enhancing their adult careers as landowners and men of affairs, rather than training them to enter the Church. It is an interesting development, but it should not be overestimated. The boys concerned need not have studied more than grammar and elementary logic, and they were not apparently followed by many others of their kind during the fifteenth century. Visiting heirs of the aristocracy could easily escape record, but it still seems true to say that the universities did not become widely popular as training centres for such youths until the second half of the sixteenth century.[69]

More important much earlier was the role of the inns of court and chancery in London. Here too institutions originally concerned with training professionals were infiltrated by nobility and gentry merely intent on acquiring a general education for aristocratic life. But whereas comparatively few such boys can be traced at the late-medieval universities, the inns were already attracting significant numbers by the second half of the fifteenth century. Fortescue's famous account of English legal education, written between 1468 and 1471, states that knights, barons and other magnates and noblemen were placing their

64. *Historiae Dunelmensis Scriptores Tres*, ed. J. Raine, London & Edinburgh, Surtees Soc., IX, (1839), 74.

65. Emden, I, 138–9.

66. Above, note 29.

67. A. B. Emden, *A Biographical Register of the University of Cambridge to 1500* (Cambridge, 1963), 321.

68. *Paston Letters*, ed. Davis, I, 215; II, 21.

69. A. B. Emden, *A Biographical Register of the University of Oxford A.D. 1501–1540* (Oxford, 1974), xxiii–xxiv.

sons at the inns not in order be trained as lawyers, nor in order to practise law for a living, but to prepare them for a life based on independent means.[70] In fact, the surviving registers of the inns before the Reformation do not suggest that many sons of peers entered them to study.[71] Aristocratic admissions are dominated by the sons of knights and gentlemen, for whom the study of law conferred real advantages in running the affairs of a small landed family. Like William Paston I their fathers knew that 'ho so euer schuld dwelle at Paston schulde have nede to conne defende hymselfe'.[72] The practical use of the study of law was one obvious reason for the early popularity of the inns with the aristocracy as against the universities, but there were other reasons too. At a time when facilities for gentlemen commoners in Oxford and Cambridge were still undeveloped, the inns provided accommodation in chambers, sociable meals in hall, and at least a modicum of moral supervision. The early registers of Lincoln's Inn reveal the enforcement of rules against women, dice and cards, which must have been a favourable factor with parents.[73] For those who wished to study there was access to the public law-courts in term time and to the lectures and moots provided by the inns during vacations. For those who did not there were most of the recreations proper to the aristocracy. Fortescue mentions reading, singing, dancing and the playing of games similar to those which were practised in the royal household itself. Here too the inns surpassed the clerical, provincial universities in their closeness to the fashions of court and capital.

The educational system which we have just described seems to have been applied to the individual child with a good deal of flexibility. The practice common in earlier times by which parents vowed a boy or girl at an early age to a life as a monk, friar or nun was unusual after 1300.[74] Parents must have made plans for their sons and daughters to become knights, clerics, wives or nuns in adult life, but these plans were not and could not be decisive absolutely. Deaths among children, and the aptitudes they displayed as they grew up, frequently altered the situation with which each parent had to deal. Many fathers and mothers were careful to keep their options open. When Richard, earl of Arundel made his will in 1393, he thought it likely that his sons Richard and Thomas would both marry, if they lived, but he also provided that a church living should be kept available in case either

70. Fortescue, *De Laudibus Legum Anglie*, ed. Chrimes, 116–21.
71. E.g. *The Records of the Honorable Society of Lincoln's Inn*, I: *Admissions, 1420–1799*, ed. W. P. Baildon (London, 1896), 10–44.
72. *Paston Letters*, ed. Davis, I, 27.
73. *The Records of the Honorable Society of Lincoln's Inn: the Black Books*, I: *1422–1586*, ed. W. P. Baildon (London, 1897), 68, 71, 74, 79, 103.
74. For an example of 1411 see *Calendar of Papal Letters*, VI: *1404–15*, 223–4.

of them wished to become a cleric.[75] So too Margaret Paston, when her teenage son Walter went off to Oxford in the early 1470s, advised him 'that he be not to hasty of takyng of orderes that schuld bynd hym, till that he be of xxiiij yere of agee or more'. She would love him better, she said, as a good secular man than as a lewd priest.[76] It followed that educational specialisation – the separation of some children to be trained as laity and others as clergy – was unwise, at least until the teens, and is unlikely to have been practised inflexibly. Until about fourteen most children probably followed a common curriculum, modified only by sex, and even afterwards a child being trained as a cleric had to bear in mind the possibility of diversion to a secular career. All this goes far to explain the secularism of so many adult clergy. Their inclinations towards hunting, warfare, extravagant clothes, and even the making of love, were not necessarily manifestations of evil natures. They could also have resulted from years of secular education in childhood, which those concerned found hard to shake off when they entered the Church.

The range of studies and pursuits in which aristocratic children were trained was a wide one, including three principal areas: the intellectual, the artistic and the physical. Children begin their intellectual development with the acquisition of language, and for medieval aristocratic children this meant two languages: English and French. Professor Rothwell has recently argued that English was the true vernacular of the aristocracy in England as early as 1150 or 1200, in that it was the language which they absorbed first and naturally from their nurses, household servants, and all the other speakers of English whom they would meet as they grew up.[77] French by the same period, he suggests, was already a taught language which was learnt with a degree of formality from parents, tutors and clergy who knew and used it. John Trevisa in a famous passage of the 1380s noted a decline in the learning of French by the aristocracy:'gentil men habbeth now moche yleft for to teche here childern Frensch'.[78] Notwithstanding this remark, however, it is likely that many and perhaps most aristocratic children went on learning some French throughout the fifteenth century. Despite the increasing use of English for official and literary purposes between 1350 and 1420, French remained the language of most of the books possessed by the aristocracy until Caxton's time in the 1470s, and survived in written and in spoken forms among the common lawyers throughout the century. Concerning the gentry, we

75. *Testamenta Vetusta*, ed. N. H. Nicolas, 2 vols. (London, 1826), I, 131–2.

76. *Paston Letters*, ed. Davis, I, 370.

77. See W. Rothwell, 'The role of French in thirteenth-century England', *Bulletin of the John Rylands University Library of Manchester*, LVIII (1975–6), 445–66.

78. *Polychronicon Ranulphi Higden*, ed. C. Babington & J. R. Lumby, 9 vols. (London, Rolls Series, 1865–86), II, 159.

find it said of Margaret, the four year-old daughter of the Yorkshire esquire William Plumpton in 1463, that she 'speaketh prattely and french, and hath near hand learned her sawter'.[79] In the royal family, Prince Arthur and Henry VIII both had a French master, Giles Dewes, in about 1500,[80] and when Katherine of Aragon was about to leave Spain in 1498 to marry Arthur, she was advised to learn French and be able to converse in it when she reached England.[81] The nature of the French which the English learnt and spoke must always have varied. The children of the great magnates, whose parents and household retainers had travelled in France, could have acquired the French of Paris. Those who lacked such contacts, on the other hand, would have deviated into Anglo-Norman or law French, permeated by English usages. As late as 1535 it was noted that the nuns of Lacock understood a French which was not like the language of France, but resembled that of the English common law.[82]

The teaching of reading and writing was based on a third language: Latin, rather than French or English. Medieval children, when they learnt to read, learnt the alphabet in Latin; when they first practised recognising and pronouncing words, the texts were also in Latin, so that every literate child was a minimal reader and speaker of that language. Literacy, and the elementary knowledge of Latin it involved, were probably universal among the later medieval English aristocracy of both sexes. This is suggested by their involvement in keeping and using written records, in getting and sending letters, in owning books, and in a few cases even in writing them.[83] Learning to read could begin at an early age. Philippa and Blanche, the daughters of Henry IV (then earl of Derby), were three and five respectively when copies of the ABC were bought for them in 1397.[84] Margaret Plumpton, as has been mentioned, was learning the psalter at the age of four in 1463, and Edward V had a schoolmaster when he was five in 1476.[85] Arthur and Henry VIII were being taught at similar ages twenty years later.[86] After assimilating the Latin alphabet, children proceeded to study liturgical texts like the psalter and the antiphonal, learning how to spell the words, how to pronounce them, and how to sing them to the rules of ecclesiastical music. Everyone who reached

79. *Plumpton Correspondence*, ed. T. Stapledon, Camden Soc., IV, (1839), 8.
80. *Dictionary of National Biography*, s.v. Giles Dewes.
81. *Calendar of State Papers, Spanish*, I; *1485–1509*, 156.
82. *Letters & Papers, Foreign & Domestic, Henry VIII*, IX, 47.
83. For recent surveys of aristocratic literacy see M. B. Parkes, 'The literacy of the laity', in *The Medieval World*, ed. D. Daiches & A. K. Thorlby, vol. II, (London, 1973), 555–77; Orme, *English Schools in the Middle Ages*, 21–36; and M. T. Clanchy, *From Memory to Written Record: England 1066–1307* (London, 1979), especially 175–201.
84. PRO, DL 28/1/6 fol. 36.
85. Above, notes 79, 28.
86. Orme, *English Schools in the Middle Ages*, 27–9.

this far, and it seems likely that everyone did, would have been able to pronounce (though not to understand) the words of a Latin text and use a prayer book in church. Furthermore they had acquired knowledge which could serve as the basis for understanding texts in the languages they spoke: English and French.

From this point onwards, the intellectual training of children seems to have diverged according to sex. We do not find much evidence of girls or women practising literary skills beyond those which have just been mentioned, until the early sixteenth century. Many records suggest, on the other hand, that even by the fourteenth century boys usually proceeded to learn grammar: the formations and meanings of Latin words, and the methods of using them in speech, prose writing and verse. Thomas of Woodstock was studying grammar in 1366 at the age of eleven;[87] his great-nephew Henry V had books of grammar bought for him in 1396 when he was eight,[88] and a Donatus or elementary Latin grammar was purchased for Henry's brother John, later duke of Bedford, in 1398.[89] Those of the aristocracy who trained to be clerics and went to university must have become fluent Latinists. The abilities of their brothers who remained as laymen are more difficult to summarise. A few may have achieved the fluency of the clergy. Henry IV was able to spend an afternoon reading in the library of Bardney Abbey in 1406,[90] and Humphrey duke of Gloucester and John Tiptoft earl of Worcester were notable patrons of Latin scholars and collectors of Latin books.[91] Even Peter Idley was able to make his educational translations from the Latin version of Albertano da Brescia.[92] For most such people, however, it seems likely that the use of Latin was confined to practical purposes: the use of prayer books in church and the reading of statutes and legal instruments, most of which followed a regular form. For ease and pleasure, as we know from their books and letters, they preferred to read and write in French or English. True, many noblemen possessed books in Latin, but they also had clerics at hand who could translate and interpret the contents on their behalf.

The learning of language and letters had a religious as well as a literary dimension. The Church's commandment that children should learn the Paternoster, the Ave Maria and the Apostle's Creed[93] was echoed by moralists and educationists. Kings and princes, said Giles

87. F. Devon, *Issues of the Exchequer* (London, 1837), 189.
88. Wylie, *England under Henry the Fourth*, IV, 172.
89. PRO, DL 28/1/6 fol. 42.
90. J. Leland, *Collectanea*, ed. T. Hearne, 2nd ed., 6 vols (Oxford, 1770), VI, 300–1.
91. R. Weiss, *Humanism in England during the Fifteenth Century*, 2nd ed. (Oxford, 1957), 39–70, 112–22.
92. *Peter Idley's Instructions to his Son*, ed. D'Evelyn, 36–8.
93. Above, note 2.

of Rome, should teach their children the articles of the faith, because faith cannot be proved rationally and is especially suitable for the young who do not seek for reason.[94] Reading, as has just been noticed, began with the study of religious texts, and the first pages which a young child had to learn contained the three basic prayers, followed by the psalms, hymns and antiphons of the liturgy. Once literacy had been mastered, a child could read or be read to from adult collections of religious stories and admonitory literature. Every household had its chaplains and friars who could convey this material in oral form as well. Children were also introduced to religious surroundings and observances. The nine year-old Isabella, daughter of Edward III, and her eight year-old sister Joan are both recorded listening to a sermon by a Dominican friar on Palm Sunday 1341.[95] Henry IV took his teenage sons with him to Bardney Abbey in 1406,[96] and the twelve year-old Henry VI prayed at the shrine of St Edmund at Bury when he spent Christmas there in 1433.[97] The familiarity of noble children with religious practices did not ensure, of course, that they all grew into devout or well-behaved adults. Thomas Brinton thought the opposite as true in 1375. When noble children are young and under a master, he said, they attend services, recite litanies, and have a conscience to put away their vices. But when they are lords they sleep until terce (the middle of the morning), and treat divine worship with scorn.[98]

Spiritual and mental improvement was only one side of medieval education. Teaching and upbringing also placed an emphasis on the care and use of the body in a decorous way. The closeness of cleanliness to godliness was recognised even in the middle ages. From the twelfth century onwards there were written guides to personal hygiene and social behaviour, in Latin at first, in French by the thirteenth century, and in English by the fifteenth.[99] They explained such matters as how to keep oneself clean, how to avoid habits unpleasant to others, when and how to speak in public, and the etiquette of waiting at table. Aristocratic youths in great households were expected to do certain symbolic acts of service to their fathers or lords: to carve meat, serve drinks, hold lights, and bring water for washing the hands. When

94. Giles of Rome, *De Regimine Principum*, book II, part II, chapter 5.

95. PRO, Exch. KR, Accounts Various, E 101/389/11.

96. Above, note 90.

97. Sir W. Dugdale, *Monasticon Anglicanum*, ed. J. Caley & others, 6 vols in 8 (London, 1817–30), III, 113.

98. *The Sermons of Thomas Brinton, Bishop of Rochester*, ed. Mary A. Devlin, I, Camden Society, third series, LXXXV (1954), 217.

99. On the genre see S. Gieben, 'Robert Grosseteste and medieval courtesy books', *Vivarium*, V (1967), 47–74; H. Rosamond Parsons, 'Anglo-Norman Books of Courtesy and Nurture', *PMLA*, XLIV (1929), 383–455; and F. J. Furnivall, *Manners and Meals in Olden Time: The Babees Book*, EETS OS 32 (1868).

meals were over, children were encouraged to practise the arts of leisure: music and dancing. Here the sexes were equal. Chaucer not only describes a Squire who knows how to dance, flute, sing and compose songs, but a princess, Canacee, who can dance, and a noble maiden of Troy who has composed a song of love which Antigone, another lady of the city, is able to sing.[100] The sexual equality to which the poet paid tribute really existed. If Henry IV was described by a contemporary as a 'sparkling' musician,[101] his first wife Mary Bohun also had three dozen strings bought for her harp in 1387–8 when she was in her late teens.[102] Likewise, a century later, the young Henry VIII who could dance, set songs, and play the flute and virginals by the time he was nineteen, did not display a male superiority in doing so.[103] His sisters Margaret and Mary also danced well and performed on the lute and the clavichord at similar ages.[104] Indeed, the education of girls had an artistic dimension lacking from that of boys, since they alone were exercised in the decorative arts of tapestry and embroidery. Work of this kind was highly commended by moralists as a means of keeping ladies from idleness and, when it involved the making of vestments for clerics, contributing to the well-being of society.[105] Here too girls were taught an art in childhood which they brought to perfection as women.

The third area of aristocratic education was the physical one. Common sense dictated that all children should be encouraged to take exercise, irrespective of age and sex; both Aristotle and Giles of Rome, as we have seen, urged the need for play and movement up to the age of seven.[106] The peripatetic nature of aristocratic life, in which families moved from one house to another and children sent away from home went to and fro on visits, necessitated the learning of riding by boys and girls alike. Hunting, hawking and shooting with bows were also common to both sexes in adulthood, and there are occasional references to the involvement of children in these pastimes. Prince Arthur had a bow bought for his use in 1492 when he was five and a half,[107] and his fourteen year-old sister Margaret, on her way to be married to

100. *Canterbury Tales*, General Prologue, lines 91–100; Squire's Tale, line 277; *Troilus and Criseyde*, book II, lines 876–82.
101. BL, Additional MS 35295, fol. 262.
102. Wylie, *England under Henry the Fourth*, IV, 159.
103. Edward Hall, *Chronicle Containing the History of England* (London, 1809), 515.
104. BL, MS Cotton Vespasian C. xii, fol. 283v; Leland, *Collectanea*, ed. Hearne, V, 361; N. H. Nicolas, *Privy Purse Expenses of Elizabeth of York* (London, 1830), 29; S. Bentley, *Excerpta Historica* (London, 1831), 125, 133.
105. For references to the practice of these arts by aristocratic women see Giles of Rome, *De Regimine Principum*, book II, part II, chapter 20; William Langland, *Piers Plowman*, B. Text, passus VI, lines 7–16; Chaucer, *The Legend of Good Women*, lines 2350–8.
106. Above, note 20.
107. S. Bentley, *Excerpta Historica*, 88.

James IV of Scotland in 1503, succeeded in shooting a buck while hunting in Alnwick deerpark.[108] It is fair to say that the physical training of girls, however, remained circumscribed compared with that of boys. Aristocratic women required exercise, but their menfolk were a military estate. Even if they did not aspire to knighthood and service in war, they were bound by law to possess arms,[109] and prudence directed that they should know how to use them to guard their property and keep order in their districts. The basic textbook of military training in medieval England was the fourth-century work of Vegetius, the *Epitoma Rei Militaris*, originally intended as a training manual for the whole Roman army but interpreted in medieval times as a guide for the aristocracy in particular.[110] The work was translated into French in 1284, into English prose in 1408, and paraphrased into English verse during the 1450s.[111] It was also drawn upon extensively by Giles of Rome and many writers on chivalry. Vegetius, like Aristotle, indicated *adolescencia*, the years from fourteen to twenty-one, as the period for military training. The activities he recommended included running, throwing weights, casting spears, jousting on foot at the quintain, riding, jousting on horseback, and swimming. Most of these feats can be paralleled in later medieval practice. Edward the Black Prince was only sixteen when he took part in the real battle of Crécy in 1346. John Hastings, earl of Pembroke, was mortally wounded in 1389 at the age of seventeen, as he tilted with an older knight under his master's supervision.[112] An equally ill-fated boy, Edward son of Henry VI, is described by Fortescue in the late 1460s, when he was in his mid teens, giving himself almost entirely to martial exercises: riding, fighting with swords and other weapons, and learning the rules of military discipline.[113] He too experienced battle and death soon afterwards, at Tewkesbury in 1471.

It will now be apparent that the shortage of specialised treatises on aristocratic education in medieval England did not reflect a want of education itself. There might have been little theory but there was much practice. What separated the fourteenth- and fifteenth-century aristocracy from their Tudor and Stuart successors was not a lack of

108. Leland, *Collectanea*, ed. Hearne, IV, 278.

109. On this subject see M. Powicke, *Military Obligation in Medieval England* (Oxford, 1962).

110. For a survey of the history and influence of the work see J.-A. Wisman, 'L'Epitoma rei militaris de Végèce et sa fortune au Moyen Age', *Le Moyen Age*, LXXXV, fourth series, XXXIV (1979), 13–31.

111. The English prose translation has not yet been printed. It is discussed in John Trevisa, *Dialogus inter Militem et Clericum*, ed. Perry, xciv–viii. The English verse paraphrase is *Knyghthode and Bataile*, ed. R. Dyboski & Z. M. Arend, *EETS* OS 201 (1936).

112. *Polychronicon Ranulphi Higden*, ed. Babington & Lumby, IX, 219–20.

113. Fortescue, *De Laudibus Legum Anglie*, ed. Chrimes, 2–3.

education but a lack of consciousness about it. This arose from the nature of medieval education, which was less distinct from life in general than it has since become. In the great household, the chief location of aristocratic upbringing, education was only one of many activities. Most of those who provided it – parents, nurses, clergy and even some tutors – were not specially trained to do so, and often had other duties and interests. Specialised schools and universities existed from the twelfth century onwards, and so did professional masters and mistresses, but their influence, as far as the aristocracy was concerned, only gradually developed during the later middle ages and the sixteenth century. The evolution of a specialised literature of education was complementary to this process; education had to become a distinct process before it could stimulate a distinct genre of writing. It would be difficult to establish that the informal and unspecialised system of education in medieval times was inferior by nature, or served society less well, than the more formal and specialised systems that have succeeded it. As we have seen, the aristocratic curriculum was a wide one. Much of it was common to both sexes. Girls and boys alike were schooled in religion, literacy, deportment, music, dancing, and outdoor exercises. If men were privileged to learn grammar and military techniques, this merely reflected the greater role in government and business which they played in adult life. Ladies were denied this role, but they had something equally distinctive of their own in the cult of the decorative arts. Well-educated noblemen and women came to the court with an experience which encompassed people and places, as well as pursuits. How they fared when they got there, of course, depended on many other factors besides education: personality, family connections, and the circumstances they encountered. But that is another story.

5

The *Familia Regis* and the *Familia Cupidinis*

Richard Firth Green

'Il y a eu des cours d'amour en France de l'an 1150 à l'an 1200. Voilà ce qui est prouvé'; thus wrote Stendhal in 1822, confident that he could count on the support of Andreas Capellanus.[1] Though it might provide a chastening reminder of the vulnerability of all such scholarly certainties, this is not the place to trace in detail the fluctuating fortunes of Andreas' reputation for veracity over the next century and a half: by the 1930s Amy Kelly was already having to paper over the cracks that had appeared in his account, and nowadays most scholars would agree with John Benton that 'with good reason a number of modern historians have been unwilling to believe in the existence of actual "courts of love" as described by Andreas'.[2] Even Benton, however, has no difficulty in accepting that Andreas' flights of fancy might have found more concrete expression in a later century: 'of course there were changes, and to see how literature and behaviour acted on each other between 1100 and 1400 is a fascinating subject . . . There is, for instance, no doubt that in 1400 Charles VI founded a court of love, a serious courtly and literary assembly'.[3] It is with some of the implications of such a view that I wish to deal here.

Over half a century has passed since Huizinga taught us 'to see how literature and behaviour acted on each other' as the middle ages waned, and we need have no difficulty in understanding how the poetic extravagances of the twelfth century could have become the social commonplaces of courtly society in the fifteenth. Not only polite manners but elaborate and costly public spectacles were founded upon the

1. *De l'Amour*, ed. V. Del Litto (Paris, 1969), 314.
2. Kelly, 'Eleanor of Aquitaine and her courts of love', *Spec.*, xii (1937), 3–19; Benton, 'The courts of Champagne as a literary center', *Spec.*, xxxvi (1961), 581.
3. 'Clio and Venus: an historical view of medieval love', in *The Meaning of Courtly Love*, ed. F. X. Newman (Albany, N.Y., 1968), 36.

literary stereotypes of an earlier age, and if the mimic ostentation of a tournament held by René d'Anjou near Saumur in 1446 could re-create the Joyeuse Garde of the *Mort Artu*,[4] why should his contem-poraries not have been led to flesh out the courts of love of Andreas Capellanus in much the same style? In at least one case, the so-called *cour amoureuse* of Charles VI, the evidence that they did so seems overwhelming; yet if Benton's faith in the authenticity of this insti-tution is unlikely ever to appear quite so naive as Stendhal's in its predecessor, even here not everything is quite what at first it might seem.

The founding charter of the *cour amoureuse* tells us that 'à ce jour d'uy fest de tifainne' [the feast of the Epiphany], Charles VI, at the request of Philip of Burgundy and Louis of Bourbon, and in order to pass the time graciously 'en ceste desplaisant et contraire épidemie de pestilence présentement courant en ce très crestien royaume', has appointed 'en son royal hostel I prince de la court d'amours, seigneu-rissant sur les subgès de retenue d'icelle amoureuse court'.[5] The charter then goes on to name three 'grans conservateurs' of this court (the king and the two dukes) and fourteen other 'conservateurs', in-cluding the queen's brother, Louis of Bavaria, and his cousin William (page 206); these five are later mentioned as having endowed a weekly mass in honour of the court (pages 214–15), and their names also appear in a list of witnesses given at the end – a list which includes most, though not all, of the lesser 'conservateurs' and twenty-five other names, that of Marshal Boucicault among them (pages 219–20). The dating clause of the charter reads, 'octroyé humblement en salle royalle, à Mante, le sixième jour de jenvier, l'an de grace nostre seigneur mil quatre cens, et de nostre lie créacion le premier'.[6]

Now, Theodor Straub has shown that on 6 January, 1400, Charles VI was in Paris, Philip of Burgundy was in Neaufle (together with his son John, named as one of the 'conservateurs'), Louis of Bavaria was in Heidelberg, and his cousin William in Quesnoy; the whereabouts of the duke of Bourbon are unknown, but Marshal Boucicault was on crusade. In other words, there is no evidence that any of the important men named in the charter were in Mantes on the day in question. We do know, however, that the queen, Isabel of Bavaria, accompanied by

4. R. S. Loomis, 'Arthurian influence on sport and spectacle', in *Arthurian Literature in the Middle Ages*, ed. R. S. Loomis (Oxford, 1959), 556.

5. In this wretched and malevolent outbreak of plague now running through this most Christian realm . . . in his royal household a prince of the court of love having rule over the retainers of this court of love; C. Potvin, 'La Charte de la cour d'amour', *Bull. de l'acad. royale des sciences, des lettres et de beaux-arts de Belgique*, Third Series, xii (1886), 202–23 (I have silently corrected a number of errors in Potvin's edition).

6. Respectfully granted in the royal hall at Mantes, the sixth day of January, in the year of our lord 1400, and of our happy creation the first (p. 219).

only her ladies-in-waiting and part of her household, left Paris for Mantes to escape the plague on 18 December 1399, and stayed there for a whole month, leaving on 19 January; on the feast of the Epiphany she is known to have made an offering at the High Mass celebrated in Mantes. One final piece in the puzzle is that on 15 January a copy of the *Cents Ballades* was bought for her from a bookseller in Paris.[7] It appears, then, that the whole elaborate superstructure of Charles VI's *cour amoureuse* was erected upon quite modest foundations: a cultivated queen (and Isabel was after all a patron of Christine de Pisan) spending the festive season in enforced exile in a minor royal palace, attended by only a skeleton household, seeks to allay the boredom of waiting for the plague to abate by organizing some kind of literary entertainment (much as the young Florentine courtiers in the *Decameron* had done); upon what was perhaps originally little more than a spontaneous parlour game there later arises a pompous courtly edifice in which the elements of fact and fiction have become inextricably mixed. That Charles VI's *cour amoureuse* must have achieved some measure of actualisation seems undeniable: two membership lists (one dating from 1416 and the other from sometime after 1426) read like a *Who's Who* of French, or rather Burgundian, chivalry;[8] between 1408 and 1413 a verse epistle was addressed to the 'prince d'amours', Pierre de Hauteville, by Amé Malingre;[9] and Hauteville's own position is confirmed by his mention in a *Description of Paris*, written by Gilbert of Metz, librarian to John the Fearless, around 1407, and by mention of his title in the inscription on his tomb;[10] furthermore, in 1410 a herald received eighteen *sols* for bringing news of a 'certaine feste et assemblee' to be held in Paris on April 15 from the 'Prinche d'Amours' to the mayor and aldermen of Amiens.[11] Nevertheless, that this *cour* was ever held on anything like the scale, with the frequency, and in all the ceremonious ritual that its founding charter lays down seems far less likely.

We are left to wonder in what way this later court and its literary remains really differ from those of the courts of twelfth-century Champagne, of which Paul Remy has written, 'à la base ne se trouve qu'un jeu de société, un amusement littéraire centré sur les dilemmes courtois ... André le Chapelain codifie et systématise ces données'.[12]

7. 'Die Gründung des Pariser Minnehofs von 1400', *Zeitscrift für Romanische Philologie*, lxxvii (1961), 8–11.

8. A. Piaget, 'La Cour amoureuse, dite de Charles VI', *Romania*, xx (1891), 423–46, and 'Un Manuscrit de la cour amoureuse de Charles VI', *Romania*, xxxi (1902), 597–8.

9. Piaget, 'La Cour', 449–54.

10. Piaget, 'La Cour', 448–9, and 'La *Belle Dame sans mercy* et ses imitations, II', *Romania*, xxx (1901), 323.

11. Piaget, 'Un Manuscrit', 603.

12. 'Les "cours d'amour": légende et réalité', *Revue de l'Univ. de Bruxelles*, vii (1954–5), 196.

In fact, the differences that exist seem to turn less on the vexed question of the degree to which life imitated art in one case or the other than on questions of emphasis and perspective that have some-times been ignored. Thus, whether fact or fiction, the courts of love of Eleanor and Marie were based on the concept of a court of law, a *curia*, whereas Charles VI's *cour amoureuse* was primarily a court in the domestic sense, a *familia*; again, the courts of Champagne sat in judgment on the finer points of amatory etiquette, the actual behav-iour of lovers, that of Paris, on the other hand, discussed love poetry and the niceties of literary decorum; finally, the earlier courts were presided over by women, whereas the later one was nominally founded by a king and was administered by a 'prince' of love. Each of these statements involves, of course, a degree of over-simplification, but as I hope to show they may help to shed light on some of the distinctive qualities of the court culture of the late middle ages.

It is rarely a simple matter to separate the judicial and the domestic elements that made up any medieval court, real or imaginary, for if the men of the middle ages, in Tout's words, 'did not clearly distinguish between the king in his public and private capacities',[13] neither did they do so with his retinue. Nevertheless, there can be little doubt that the dominant metaphor underlying the chapter in the *De Amore* entitled 'de variis iudiciis amoris' is a legal one;[14] the founding charter of Charles VI's *cour amoureuse*, on the other hand, with its talk of 'noz amoureux subgès de retenue' (page 203) and its inclusion of such officers as 'escuiers d'onneur', 'concierges des vergiers et jardins', and 'huissierz' (page 207) suggests something far closer to a domestic es-tablishment than a court of law – this despite the fact that the *cour* is to sit in judgment on love poems. In Straub's words, 'der Minnehof ist ganz nach dem Vorbild der fürstlichen Höfe gegliedert'.[15] What this shift of emphasis clearly indicates is that the code of love, as a standard of polite behaviour, had achieved a central and unshakeable position in the courtly imagination; no longer need its individual tenets be weighed and tested in some kind of mock-legal process, for they had become enshrined in an established corpus whose essential authority was unquestioned. Thus, in Martial d'Auverne's *Arrêts d'A-mour*, one of the comparatively few late medieval works in which the court of love is exclusively a legal assembly, we are concerned largely with particular torts – should a lady have thrown a bucket of water over her lover? was a man whose mistress had put grass down the back of his shirt justified in knocking her to the ground and pulling

13. T. F. Tout, *Chapters in the Administrative History of Mediaeval England* (Manch-ester, 1920–33), i, 19.
14. Andreas Capellanus, *De Amore*, ed. E. Trojel (2nd ed. Munich, 1964), 271–95.
15. Straub, 'Gründung', 4.

her hair? – not with the statute law which Eleanor and Marie so ably expound in a series of test cases.

By the late middle ages familiarity with this law had become so important a part of the courtier's social equipment that it could be thought of as the foundation of a genteel education. When the court pedagogue, Antoine de La Sale, sought to describe the upbringing of the ideal courtier, he did so in the form of a love story: little Jean de Saintré must first learn to be a lover before he can become a courtier for, as his preceptress tells him, it is the 'vray amoreux gentil homme' who 'quant il est a la messe c'est le plus devot, a table le plus honneste, en compaignie des seigneurs et des dames le plus avenant'.[16] This is why, as John Stevens has pointed out, the first part of the *Roman de la Rose*, the greatest and most influential of all the medieval handbooks of love, 'is also the source and pattern of "curtesy" books',[17] not only a sentimental education, but a courtly one as well. The precepts of Guillaume de Lorris' God of Love,

> Thyn hondis wassh, thy teeth make white,
> And let no filthe upon thee bee.
> Thy nailes blak if thou maist see,
> Voide it awey delyverly,
> And kembe thyn heed right jolily, (2280–4)[18]

must have been echoed by untold masters of henchmen and court tutors throughout the late middle ages. From the notion of the ideal courtier as the perfect lover, it is but a short step to seeing the ideal court as a court of love, and here too the *Roman de la Rose* is a *locus classicus* for the 'medieval conception of the ideal society as one made up of lovers – a "court" of love'.[19] The retinue which surrounds Sir Mirth in his garden is the forerunner of all those later *familiae Cupidinis* in whose flattering glass the courtier looked to find his own reflection.

The appeal of this particular metaphor to the courtly imagination can be sensed in numerous late medieval works. Love's retinue, in which the narrator has long served without reward, is constantly referred to throughout Gower's *Confessio Amantis*, for example, and when this court finally makes its appearance in Book VIII we hardly need the reference to the 'newe guise of Beawme' (2470) to confirm our impression that what is really being discussed is the court of King

---

16. When he is at the Mass is the most devout, at table the best mannered, and in the company of lords and ladies the most gracious; *Jehan de Saintré*, ed. J. Misrahi and C. A. Knudson (Geneva, 1967), 29–30.
17. *Medieval Romance* (London, 1973), 52.
18. Translation in Geoffrey Chaucer, *Works*, ed. Robinson, 586.
19. Stevens, *Romance*, 55.

Richard himself.[20] (Gower's view is far from uncritical, of course, and to appreciate the full irony of Venus' rejection of Amans at the end we should recall that it was the accepted duty of the head of a real household to look after old servants.) 'The glade empire/ Of blisfull Venus' (530–1) in the *Kingis Quair* is likewise seen as *familia* rather than a law court:

> Stude at the dure Fair-Calling, hir vshere,
> That coude his office doon in connyng wise,
> And Secretee, hir thrifty chamberere,
> That besy was in tyme to do seruise (673–6).[21]

A fuller expression of the same motif is to be found in the *Assembly of Ladies*, of which Pearsall has written, 'the poet seems more interested in real households than in allegorical ones, and his language, too, betrays a touch of the busy bureaucrat';[22] but it is perhaps most completely expressed in the poem the *Court of Love* itself:

> 'Goth on,' she said to Philobone, 'and take
> This man with you, and lede him all abowt
> Within the court, and shew him, for my sake,
> What lovers dwell withinne, and all the rowte
> Of officers'. (1023–7)[23]

One passage in the *Confessio Amantis* is particularly interesting in this context; it describes the lover's envy of others who catch his lady's attention:

> Whan I the Court se of Cupide
> Aproche unto my ladi side
> Of hem that lusti ben and freisshe, –
> Thogh it availe hem noght a reishe,
> Bot only that thei ben in speche, –
> My sorwe is thanne noght to seche:
> But whan thei rounen in hire Ere,
> Than groweth al my moste fere,
> And namly whan thei talen longe;
> My sorwes thanne be so stronge
> Of that I se hem wel at ese,
> I can noght telle my desese (ii, 39–50).

The court of Cupid here is clearly neither an allegorical abstraction nor some kind of formally constituted assembly; it refers merely to a

20. *The English Works of John Gower*, ed. Macaulay, ii, 453.
21. Ed. J. Norton-Smith (Oxford, 1971), 97.
22. D. Pearsall, 'The English Chaucerians', in *Chaucer and Chaucerians*, ed. D. S. Brewer (London, 1966), 229.
23. *Chaucerian and Other Pieces*, ed. W. W. Skeat (Oxford, 1897), 436.

group of young courtiers, lovers and lusty bachelors, whom the jealous narrator suspects of being his rivals. No doubt it is in some such sense that we should understand Shirley's reference to 'a squyer that serued in loves court', for whom, he says, Lydgate's 'Ballade, Of Her That Hath All Virtues' was written.[24] It is not difficult to imagine how the 'God of Loves servantz' who listened to Chaucer reading *Troilus and Criseyde* (i, 15) might have seen themselves as constituting such a court, and it is certainly unnecessary to regard every literary allusion to the *familia Cupidinis* as reflecting an actual formal assembly founded along the lines of Charles VI's *cour amoureuse*.

The second point of comparison between the courts of Champagne and the *cour amoureuse* turns on the degree to which each institution discussed literary matters. Though no doubt literary works furnished the original subject matter for many of the cases which come before Eleanor of Aquitaine and the other noblewomen in the *De Amore*, not one of the twenty-one questions discussed involves a poet or a matter of poetic decorum. The main participants in Charles VI's court of love, on the other hand, are twenty-four 'chevaliers, escuiers et autres, ayans experte congnoissance en la science de réthorique, approvez factistes par apparence et renommé, lesquelz aront nom de ministre de la court d'amours et principale auctorité après les grans conservateurs d'icelle',[25] and the main business of this court is to sponsor a literary competition between these ministers on the first Sunday of each month (page 204), with particularly elaborate contests on Saint Valentine's day, in May, and on one of the five feasts of the Virgin (pages 209–11). The charter refers to these meetings as 'puys d'amours' (the extraordinary meetings are called 'puys royaux'), and in many respects (the crowning of the winners, the endowment of the masses, the holding of annual dinners, and the association with the cult of the Virgin) the *cour amoureuse* bears a suspicious resemblance to the minstrel *puys* of the late middle ages, whose ancestry reaches back to the *confréries* of the twelfth and thirteenth centuries.[26] It is more than a little curious that the main external corroboration for the existence of Charles VI's *cour amoureuse* should involve a messenger sent to the mayor and aldermen of Amiens, a city second only to Arras in the fame of its *puy*; that this messenger should have been a herald, and thus a member of a profession still closely associated with that of the minstrel, is also worth noticing. The new code of polite manners

---

24. John Lydgate, *Minor Poems II*, ed. H. N. MacCracken, *EETS* OS 192 (1934), 379.

25. Knights, squires and others, having an expert knowledge of the art of rhetoric, acknowledged poets in their work and by reputation, who shall have the name of 'minister of the court of love' and the main authority under its 'grans conservateurs' (p. 203).

26. E. Faral, *Les Jongleurs en France au Moyen Age* (2nd ed. Paris, 1964), 128–42; see also D. Poirion, *Le Poète et le Prince* (Paris, 1965), 38–40.

ushered in by the *Roman de la Rose* demanded of the courtier-lover that he should be able to turn his hand to verse, and long before the year 1400 court minstrels had been forced to concede the literary side of their vocation to amateurs within the household.[27] Yet when Charles VI's courtiers, hoping perhaps to find in the *cour amoureuse* a vehicle for displaying their poetic skills and to claim for themselves some of the prestige which had once accrued to their professional predecessors, sought a model for their literary assembly, they turned, it would seem, to those very *jongleurs* whom they had exiled from court. This alone might give us grounds for regarding the details of the founding charter with some scepticism.

The *confréries* and *puys* of the minstrels existed in part to maintain standards, and their literary competitions were no doubt regarded as a means of encouraging technical facility; this aspect seems to have been intended to be carried over to the *puys d'amours*, for which each of the twenty-four ministers was required to compose a ballade with a set refrain, chosen by the member whose turn it was to act as host (page 204). A later reflection of such a practice might perhaps be seen in the so-called 'concours de Blois', sponsored by Charles d'Orléans, to which a number of poets (including Villon) contributed ballades, each with the first line 'Je meurs de soif auprés de la fontaine'.[28] This was not the only way in which competition between the ministers might arise, however, for the charter also makes provision 'se aucunes questions, pour plaisant passetempz, sourdoient entre noz subgès en fourme d'amoureux procès pour differentes oppinions soustenir';[29] where these questions are to be debated in writing each side must use a different-coloured ink (black is forbidden, but 'vermeil, vert, bleu, sanguine, violet et pourpre' are all available), the defendant to have first choice of colour (page 213). It seems unlikely that such debates should have been concerned with technical matters, and though *questions d'amour* of the kind raised at the courts of Champagne may have been discussed, the most probable source of controversy at the *cour amoureuse* would have been the merits and propriety of literary works. The celebrated debate over Jean de Meun's portion of the *Roman de la Rose* (a debate which it has been suggested may have been linked in some way with the *cour amoureuse* itself) was after all in progress by this time.[30] One particular passage in the founding charter sets the scene for such a literary controversy:

27. R. F. Green, *Poets and Princepleasers* (Toronto, 1980), 101–10.

28. I die of thirst beside the fountain; Charles d'Orléans, *Poésies*, ed. P. Champion (Paris, 1923–7), i, 191–203, and ii, 560–3.

29. If any questions, as a pleasant pastime, should arise amongst our retainers in the form of an amorous lawsuit, in order to debate opposing positions (p. 212).

30. *Le débat sur le Roman de la Rose*, ed. E. Hicks (Paris, 1977), xliv.

Nous, par meure et très grande déliberacion, avons ordonné et par ces
présentes ordonnons à tous noz amoureux subgès, . . . qu'ilz ne facent
ou par autre facent faire dittierz, complaintes, rondeaux, virelays, balades, lays ou autres quelconques façon et taille de réthorique, rimée
ou en proze, au deshonneur, reproche, amenrissement ou blame de dame
ou dames, damoiselle ou damoiselles, ensemble quelconques femmes,
religieuses ou autres, trespassées ou vivans, pour quelconques cause
que se soit, tant soit griève dolereuse ou desplaisant.[31]

Anyone who disobeys this statute is to have his arms effaced and his
shield painted black, 'comme homme infâme, ennemy d'onneur et
mort au monde' (page 214). The atmosphere which gave rise to such
a provision was clearly the same as the one in which the controversy
over Chartier's *Belle Dame sans Mercy* flourished, and this may have
been just the kind of debate envisaged by the author of the founding
charter (perhaps Pierre de Hauteville himself) when he drew up his
rules for the battle of the coloured inks.

By the late fourteenth century the older style of *débat d'amour*
which is to be found in the *De Amore* seems to have been losing some
of its appeal, to be replaced by the more self-consciously literary con-
troversies, of which the debates over the *Roman de la Rose* and the
Belle Dame sans Mercy are the most conspicuous examples. The two
Judgment poems of Guillaume de Machaut might be seen as marking
a turning point in this respect.[32] The *Jugement dou Roy de Behaingne*,
written around 1340, discusses the question of whether a lady whose
lover has died or a knight whose mistress has deserted him suffers
the more; this is a question which would certainly not have been out
of place at the courts of Champagne. The *Jugement dou Roy de Navarre* (1349), however, describes the trial of the poet himself for having
slandered women in his earlier poem, and thus anticipates Chaucer's
Legend of Good Women and a number of fifteenth-century palinodes
in the same tradition. The taste for more abstract *questions d'amour*
certainly did not die out however:

> Yow loveres axe I now this questioun:
> Who hath the worse, Arcite or Palamoun?[33]

and it appears, though sometimes in a rather burlesque form, in
Martial d'Auverne's *Arrêts d'Amour* (although a number of these

---

31. We, after mature and great deliberation, have decreed and hereby decree to all
our amorous retainers . . . that they write, or cause by others to be written, no ditties,
complaints, rondeaux, virelais, ballades, lays nor any other literary form, in rhyme or
prose, to the dishonour, blame, disparagement or detraction of any lady or ladies, damsel
or damsels, or of women as a whole, whether nuns or otherwise, whether living or dead,
for any cause whatsoever, such as may give serious and unpleasant offence (pp. 213–
14).

32. *Oeuvres*, ed. E. Hoepffner, *SATF* (Paris, 1908), i, 57–282.

33. Chaucer, *Knight's Tale*, 1347–8.

turn out to be themselves based on literary debates such as the one over the *Belle Dame sans Mercy*).[34]

One question, none the less, seems to have dominated all others: it is implicit in the two halves of the *Roman de la Rose* and in the celebrated debate inspired by that work; it is clearly articulated in the *Livre des Cents Ballades* (a copy of which, we might recall, Isabel of Bavaria bought a week or so after the founding of the *cour amoureuse*), and it informed Christine de Pisan's *Epître au Dieu d'Amours*; it appears to have provided the grounds for the contest between the orders of the Flower and the Leaf, and to have inspired the founding of Charles VI's *cour amoureuse* itself, dedicated as it was to upholding 'la glorieuse vertu d'umilité et la constante vertu de léauté' (pages 201–2). This was the question of the conflict between painful service and sensual self-indulgence in love, between the defenders and the exploiters of female virtue. Put like this, of course, the debate was a dead letter, for few were prepared to follow the example set by Regnault de Trie and the lord of Chambrillac in the postscript to the *Cents Ballades* by publicly espousing the latter position; used as a measure of orthodoxy, however, as a way of identifying heretics against Cupid's law, it underlay much of the literary controversy of the later middle ages – yet one more illustration of a shift in focus from the nature of love itself to the role of the poet in the service of love.

In view of what has just been said, the third distinction which I have drawn between the courts of Champagne and Charles VI's *cour amoureuse* – that the first were presided over by women whereas the later one was founded by a man – seems particularly ironic. 'Here was a woman's assize to draw men from the excitements of the tilt and the hunt, from dice and games, to feminine society,' writes Amy Kelly of the twelfth-century courts, 'an assize to outlaw boorishness and compel the tribute of adulation to female majesty'.[35] Yet two hundred years later a *cour amoureuse* which seems to have been first thought up in the household of a French queen is established in the name of her husband and administered by one of his butlers; Isabel of Bavaria is not once mentioned in the founding charter, and every one of the six hundred names on the membership list of 1416 is male. Though the *cour* is said to be founded 'à l'onneur, loenge et recommendacion de toutes dames et damoiselles',[36] women play remarkably little part in its activities: the monthly *puys* are judged by the ministers themselves, the two winners from one meeting acting as judges at the next (pages 204–5), and only at the 'puy royal' on Saint Valentine's day are

---

34. Martial d'Auverne, *Les Arrêts d'Amour*, ed. J. Rychner, *SATF* (Paris, 1951), xxxii–xxxvi.

35. Kelly, 'Eleanor of Aquitaine', 15.

36. To the honour, praise and commendation of all ladies and damsels (p. 213).

the ballades to be submitted to 'les dames telles que on avizera pour les jugier à leur noble avis et bonne discrécion'.[37] Even here, however, their role is limited, for a very revealing provision specifies:

> se en icelles balades y avoit vice de fausse rime, reditte, trop longue ou trop courte ligne en la balade couronnée ou chapelée, on les reporteroit de rechief à icelles dames qui les rejugeroient de nouvel.[38]

From an assize to 'compel the tribute of adulation to female majesty' the courts of love have degenerated into an institution in which women are not even to be trusted to tell a good poem from a bad one. In Martial d'Auverne's *Arrêts d'Amour* the male president of the court and the lords spiritual and temporal are assisted by a panel of ladies, 'deesses' he calls them,

> Toutes legistes et clargesses
> Qui savoient le Decret par cueur (31–2),[39]

but in one case where a lover appeals a decision of these ladies in favour of a woman who had accepted presents from him and then given her love to another, the court upholds the appeal saying that 'il fust mal jugé par les dites dames du Conseil' (page 57).

Nevertheless, the impression that the standards of literary decorum in the courts of the late middle ages were set by women still remains. We may question the authenticity of Pierre de Brantôme's story of Jean de Meun and yet still feel that it expresses a truth about the role of women at court: the poet, he says, for implying in the *Roman de la Rose* that all women are harlots at heart,

> encourut une telle inimitié des dames de la cour pour lors, qu'elles, par une arrestée conjuration et advis de la reine, entreprindrent un jour de le fouetter, et le despouillerent tout nud; et, estans prestes à donner le coup, il les pria qu'au moins celle qui estoit la plus grande putain de toutes commençast la premiere: chacune, de honte, n'osa commencer; et par ainsi il évita le fouet. J'en ay veu l'histoire representée dans une vieille tapisserie des vieux meubles du Louvre.[40]

37. Such ladies as shall be appointed to judge them according to their noble opinion and good taste (p. 210).
38. If there should be in these ballades, either the winner or the runner-up, errors of false rhyme, repetition, or too long or too short a line, they are to be sent back to the said ladies who shall judge them once more (p. 210).
39. All lady lawyers and clerks who knew the law by heart (p. 4).
40. Incurred such an enmity amongst the court ladies of the day that, by a preconceived plan arranged by the queen, they set a day to beat him and stripped him naked; and when they were on the point of beating him, he asked that at least she who was the greatest harlot of all should strike the first blow: none, for shame, dared begin, and thus he escaped a beating. I have seen the story portrayed on an old tapestry amongst the old furnishings of the Louvre; *Les Dames Galantes*, ed. M. Rat (Paris, 1960), 129.

Christine de Pisan, after all, if she could not whip the living Jean de Meun did at least castigate his memory, and she seems to have had the support of Isabel of Bavaria in this. Nor is Brantôme alone; other sixteenth-century writers give a similar impression that the ladies of earlier courts had constituted some kind of board of censors always ready to reprimand the erring poet: 'for that som Ladies in the Court tooke offence at Chaucers large speeches against the vntruth of women,' writes Speght of the *Legend of Good Women*, 'the Queene enioyned him to compile this booke in the commendation of sundry maydens and wiues, who shewed themselues faithfull to faithlesse men';[41] and Stow reports that Hoccleve's *Littera Cupidinis* 'gate him such hatred among the gentlewomen of the Court that he was inforced to recant'.[42] Finally, we have the case of Alain Chartier, compelled to defend himself for his *Belle Dame sans Mercy* in an *Excusacion* which he submits to the judgement of ladies ('Pour ce me rens a vostre court,/ Mes dames' [235–6]).[43]

We might stop for a moment to ask ourselves who these ladies were of whom the court poet went in such fear. The king's household, with the exception of a few menial officers like laundresses, was all male, and the queen's establishment was largely so. A list of members of the English royal household in 1368, for instance, includes 375 names, of which only thirty-one are women,[44] and fully confirms Mark Girouard's suggestion that 'women made up a minute proportion of the total household'. As he says, 'it is hard to believe that the majority of the household was totally celibate, but the whereabouts of its women, licit or illicit, remains mysterious'.[45] Women authors have left little mark on the courtly literature of the late middle ages, and though both the *Flower and the Leaf* and the *Assembly of Ladies* purport to be by women, and a handful of lyrics almost certainly are so,[46] Christine de Pisan is unique among writers of any stature. No doubt feminine society was all the more valued because of its comparative rarity, and perhaps this fact might be taken to explain the almost morbid fascination it held for the courtly imagination; but there are, nevertheless, some curious inconsistencies in the masculine facade of deference to female authority. How is it, for example, that all three of Christine de Pisan's opponents in the debate over the *Roman de la*

41. E. P. Hammond, *Chaucer: A Bibliographical Manual* (London, 1908), 380.

42. Thomas Hoccleve, *Minor Poems*, ed. F. J. Furnivall and I. Gollancz, rev. J. Mitchell and A. I. Doyle, *EETS* ES 61 and 73 (1970), 92.

43. Alain Chartier, *La Belle Dame sans Mercy et les Poésies Lyriques*, ed. A. Piaget (2nd ed. Geneva, 1949), 44.

44. *Chaucer Life-Records*, ed. M. M. Crow and C. C. Olson (Oxford, 1966), 94–7.

45. *Life in the English Country House* (New Haven, 1978), 27.

46. See *The Floure and the Leafe and the Assembly of Ladies*, ed. D. A. Pearsall (London, 1962), 15, and *Secular Lyrics of the XIVth and XVth Centuries*, ed. R. H. Robbins (2nd ed. Oxford, 1955), 218–20.

Rose are to be found in Charles VI's *cour amoureuse* (two of them, Jean de Montreuil and Gontier Col, as ministers)?[47] And what precisely are the implications of Alain Chartier's condemnation for having written the *Belle Dame sans Mercy*?

The *Belle Dame* is neither allegory nor dream. In the realistic setting of courtly diversion (in an interval between dances following a formal banquet) the poet hears a debate between a lady and her unwelcome suitor. The lady, described as a 'garnison de tous biens' (147),[48] is, like Criseyde, her 'owene womman, wel at ese' ('Je suy franche et franche vueil estre' [286]); knowing of no way to distinguish true protestations of love from hypocritical ones,

> Vous et autres qui ainsi jurent
> Et se condempnent et maudirent,
> Ne cuidez que leurs sermens durent
> Fors tant comme les mots se dient (345–8),[49]

she refuses to take his chronic love-sickness seriously:

> Si gracieuse maladie
> Ne met gaires de gens a mort (265–6).[50]

Her suitor, calling her marble-hearted (689), and complaining that true lovers are made to suffer for the sins of cynical seducers (743–4), wanders off disconsolate to his death, but we are certainly not encouraged to lay the blame for this at the lady's door. As she says herself:

> Qui me dit que je suis amee,
> Se bien croire je l'en vouloye,
> Me doit il tenir pour blasmee
> S'a son vouloir je ne foloye? (681–4)[51]

Through the poem there runs a thread of legal imagery: the ladies in the banquet scene at the beginning are described as 'juges' (79); yet when the lover protests that men who betray their ladies' love deserve a double death, the lady replies pointedly:

47. Piaget, 'La Cour', 429–30, 443.
48. 'A garnison she was of al goodnesse' (175); this and the following translations are taken from Sir Richard Roos's version, in Skeat, *Chaucerian and Other Pieces*, 299–326.
49. 'Ye and other, that swere suche othes faste,/ And so condempne and cursen to and fro,/ Ful sikerly, ye wene your othes laste/ No lenger than the wordes ben ago!' (373–6).
50. 'This sicknesse is right esy to endure,/ But fewe people it causeth for to dy' (293–4).
51. 'What-ever he be that sayth he loveth me,/ And peraventure, I leve that it be so,/ Ought he be wroth, or shulde I blamed be,/ Though I did noght as he wolde have me do?' (709–12).

Sur telz meffais n'a court ne juge
A qui on puisse recourir.
L'un les maldit, l'autre les juge,
Mais je n'en ay veu nul mourir (585–8).[52]

Most striking of all is her very last speech to him:

Riens ne vous nuit fors vous meismes.
De vous mesmes juge soyez (763–4).[53]

The lady apparently regards the court of Cupid in its legal guise in much the same way as Gower had thought of the *familia Cupidinis*: not, that is, as a formal assembly however playfully realised, but as the metaphorical expression of an aspect of courtly society – in this case, its jurisdiction over all forms of polite behaviour. The lady's implication that deference to women as the ultimate social arbiters is nothing but a hypocritical fiction, the product of masculine self-interest, is supported by the curious reception which the *Belle Dame* itself received.

The debate over Chartier's poem, which was still alive in the sixteenth century, was evidently initiated by a rival poet, Pierre de Nesson; and if we did not have Nesson's own testimony that a sentence of public banishment from Issoudun ('present son roy et trestout le commun') was in reality nothing more than a practical joke which he had worked up 'par moquerie' with the aid of a drunken town-crier, we might believe that Chartier had actually been condemned by a formal session of the *cour amoureuse*.[54] A letter addressed to the ladies of the court by a group of unnamed 'loyaulz serviteurs' asking for judgment against the *Belle Dame* specifically mentions this court (33) and attacks the poem in terms which seem deliberately to recall the wording of its founding charter: 'et en adviendra dommage et esloingnement aux humbles servans et amendrissement de vostre povoir, se par vous n'y est pourveu' (35–8).[55] That anyone could have expected a poem which defends the right of women to reject unwelcome suitors to have been proscribed by a female tribunal might seem the most egregious piece of masculine effrontery; that a letter exists, sent 'par les dames a Alain', demanding that he answer the charges against him would be quite as astonishing, were it not signed by a woman, Catherine de l'Isle-Bouchard, whose love-life was scandalous even by

52. 'There is no juge y-set of such trespace/ By which of right oon may recovered be;/ Oon curseth fast, another doth menace,/ Yet dyeth non, as ferre as I can see' (613–16).
53. 'There hurteth you nothing but your conceyt;/ Be juge your-self; for so ye shal it fynde' (791–92).
54. A. Piaget and E. Droz, *Pierre de Nesson et ses Oeuvres* (Paris, 1925), 17–18.
55. There shall come of it the misery and rejection of your humble servants, and a diminution of your authority, if it is not attended to by you; Chartier, *Belle Dame*, 35–6.

the standards of the corrupt and cynical court of the king of Bourges.[56] It is little wonder that Chartier in his *Excusacion* is unrepentant (nor perhaps that this response did not satisfy Catherine). To be fair, he was not without defenders, René d'Anjou among them, but the whole incident seems to confirm our impression of the *cour amoureuse* as, not only an elaborate fiction, but also the embodiment of male hypocrisy. If Catherine was prepared to go along with the game, most court ladies, one feels, would have sided with the cultivated Margaret of Scotland, who is said to have kissed the sleeping Chartier on the lips, with the words, 'je n'ay pas baisé l'homme, mais la precieuse bouche de laquelle sont yssuz et sortis tant de bons motz et vertueuses parolles',[57] or with Parlamente in Margaret of Navarre's *Heptameron*, who says of the *Belle Dame*, 'si est sa doctrine autant proffitable aux jeunes dames que nulle que je sache'.[58]

It is of course easy to be cynical about any failure to live up to an ideal. When we find Froissart's chivalrous heroes behaving with the predictable brutality of professional soldiers we must guard against the temptation to dismiss the code they professed as so much empty rhetoric; so too, we should be ready to recognise that the presence among the ranks of the *cour amoureuse* of a man guilty of attempted rape, or of another who abandoned his wife for one of the duchess of Burgundy's ladies-in-waiting,[59] need not render altogether meaningless the ideals of that institution. Nevertheless, it is difficult not to feel that men in the late middle ages put less store by living up to the code of the chamber than they did that of the battlefield; as Huizinga, not a historian to underestimate the power of an ideal, points out, 'medieval literature shows little true pity for woman, little compassion for her weakness and the dangers and pains which love has in store for her'.[60] The *cour amoureuse* was very far from being Amy Kelly's 'woman's assize'; it grew out of a tradition which, in Poirion's words, 'a enfermé la littérature dans un univers essentiellement masculin: la dame que l'on consulte est imaginée par ou pour l'amant. Objet d'un culte ou jouet des désirs, l'idole féminine ne pouvait réellement parler: son oracle n'était qu'un écho déguisé'.[61]

---

56. Catherine de l'Isle-Bouchard, having seduced Pierre de Giac away from his wife, subsequently eloped with his murderer, the influential Georges de la Trémoille, and married him, 'Dont tout le monde fut esmerveillé'. One of the other two names signed to this letter may be that of Jeanne de Bouthéon, who was reputed to be the king's mistress. Poirion, *Le Poète*, 47.

57. I have not kissed the man, but the precious lips from which have come such good words and virtuous speeches; J. C. Laidlaw, *Poetical Works of Alain Chartier* (Cambridge, 1974), 13 (the story is probably apocryphal).

58. Its teaching is as useful to young ladies as any that I know of; quoted in A. Piaget, '*La Belle Dame sans Mercy* et ses imitations, VI', *Romania*, xxxiv (1905), 596.

59. Piaget, 'La Cour', 447.

60. J. Huizinga, *The Waning of the Middle Ages*, tr. F. Hopman (London, 1924), 114.

61. Poirion, *Le Poète*, 131.

If I have spent rather a long time on Charles VI's *cour amoureuse* it is because its founding charter remains the most important witness to the court-of-love tradition in the late middle ages. I have suggested that this charter represents a largely fictional elaboration of a quite modest original, and that the direction taken by this fiction tells us a good deal about the cultural aspirations of the closed, familial society which nurtured it. I should like now to turn to the English court to see if what we have already learnt can help us to understand a handful of literary reflections of the tradition preserved there. No English document survives which might be taken with any confidence to support the view that actual courts of love were ever held; such references as Lydgate's 'squyer that serued in loves court' are at best ambiguous, and what objective historical evidence there is is negative, suggesting, as we should expect, that if the courts of love achieved any degree of realisation at all it must have been on a very modest scale.[62] Several allegorical poems attest to the popularity of the tradition in England,[63] but it is not with these that I am primarily concerned; I wish rather to look at four works which seem to me to reflect the kind of social transposition of the allegorical impulse already discussed in relation to the French court. I shall begin with the simplest.

The nineteenth and twentieth poems in the series in Bodley MS Fairfax 16, attributed by MacCracken to the duke of Suffolk, are an attack on John Lydgate.[64] The first, 'How the louer ys sett to serue the floure', begins by establishing the poet's credentials as a loyal lover whose faithful service to one flower commits him to honouring 'flours all' (8–10); after a brief encomium on Chaucer, he comes to his real subject:

And to the monke of bury now speke I, –
For thy connyng ys syche, and eke thy grace,
After Chaucer to occupye his place. (26–8)

The immediate object of his scorn is Lydgate's poem 'Beware the blind',[65] a crude piece of anti-feminist satire, which nevertheless invites the attack by addressing itself to lovers:

Loke well about, ye that louers be;
Lat nat youre lustes leede yow to dotage (1–2).[66]

62. Green, *Poets and Princepleasers*, 122.
63. See W. A. Neilson, *The Origins and Sources of the Court of Love* (Cambridge, Mass., 1899), 135–68 and 228–40.
64. H. N. MacCracken, 'An English friend of Charles of Orléans', *PMLA*, xxvi (1911), 168–74.
65. A. G. Rigg, 'Some notes on Trinity College, Cambridge, MS. 0.9.38', *N & Q*, ccxi (1966), 327–8.
66. Robbins, *Secular Lyrics*, 224–5.

At least one other reader, probably John Shirley, was also struck by its indecorousness, for a note in one of the manuscripts urges: 'Do not Reade thys but hyde your eye'.[67] The target would be difficult to miss, but the poet's marksmanship is none the less creditable: he not only castigates Lydgate for his discourtesy but also parodies the pomposity of his style, so that when he writes 'thy corupt speche enfectyth alle the air' (68) one is tempted to see a double-meaning. What is most interesting about the poem, however, is its introduction of legal machinery:

> O thou vnhappy man, go hyde thy face;
> The court ys set, thy falshed is [out] tryed;
> Wyth-draw, I rede, for now thou art aspyed. (75–7)

The poet concludes by advising Lydgate to find himself a lawyer and to be prepared to make recompense for his offences (82–3). There follows a poem, entitled simply 'Parlement', of no great originality, in which various lovers present their 'byllys' to Cupid and discuss aspects of love; it seems, however, to be linked to the poem which precedes it by its mention of,

> how that of tymes past
> Myche peple vsyd loue to countirplete
> Whiche lyeth not in thair powers for to trete, (45–7)

an apparent reference to Lydgate and his clerical status.

These two poems, I feel, bring us close to the reality of the court of love tradition. If in their place we had only a recantation of the kind which Lydgate is clearly being expected to make, we may be fairly sure that the monk would have cast himself as defendant in a law suit brought before Cupid, and some later commentator like Stow or Speght might well have concluded that he had drawn upon himself the wrath of the gentlewomen of the court. Yet we can readily appreciate that the quarrel is purely a literary one and that the question of discourtesy to women is little more than a stalking horse. As with Pierre de Nesson and Alain Chartier, we are concerned with the attack of one poet upon another, and the tribunal before which the offender is to be tried is simply the familial coterie within which their poems circulated; judgment need imply nothing more than the general censure or approval of this group, and punishment exclusion from the fashionable amusements of its inner circle. The elaborate machinery of Cupid's court, in other words, can be seen as merely the metaphorical embellishment of a literary feud; there is no compulsion to regard it as reflecting a formalised social ritual.

---

67. Robbins, *Secular Lyrics*, 290, n.

In my second example the boot is on the other foot: we find a courtly writer anticipating censure and cleverly circumventing it. When earl Rivers set about translating the *Dicts and Sayings of the Philosophers* for his young charge, Edward Prince of Wales, thinking 'ful necessary to my said lord the vnderstandyng therof',[68] he came across a passage which must have put him in something of a quandary. As moral tutor he no doubt felt it his duty to bring to the prince's attention the opinion, attributed to Socrates, that 'who someuer wyll acquere and gete scyence, late hym neuer put hym in the gouernaunce of a woman',[69] but as the queen's brother and a man with a reputation for chivalry to protect he can hardly have relished being held responsible for such a statement. He did in fact omit it, and several like it ('and the said Socrates had many seyinges ayenst women whiche is not translated'),[70] but whether it was he who then saved 'the trouble of an index' by relegating it to an appendix (and compounded the hypocrisy by putting the blame on his printer), or whether it was Caxton himself, we shall probably never know. Even in the second event, I find it difficult to believe that the earl was not a conspirator; Caxton's dedication to textual accuracy was not so great that he would have been prepared to risk both his patron's anger and his readers' disapproval on that ground alone, particularly in what, as one of the first books to be printed in England, must have been a somewhat speculative undertaking. There is an air of disingenuousness about the excuses he makes on the earl's behalf: 'I am not in certayn wheder it was in my lordis copye or not or ellis perauenture that the wynde had blowe ouer the leef' (he knew that that was untrue);[71] he gives out the reason that Rivers himself must have wished to be publicised: 'but I suppose that som fayr lady hath desired hym to leue it out of his booke Or ellys he was amerous on somme noble lady. for whos loue he wold not sette yt in hys book. or ellys for the very affectyon. loue and good wylle that he hath vnto alle ladyes and Gentylwomen. he thought that Socrates spared the sothe' (pages 20–2). Caxton, however, does his best to protect his own interests as well: Socrates, he says, was clearly writing about Greek women not 'of them of this Royaume' (page 24), and in any case his views are not as extreme as one might have feared (pages 28–30). One has the strong impression that 'in satisfyeng of all parties' the printer has got himself into a very awkward situation.

As this incident suggests, the polite fiction of female sovereignty

68. R. Hittmair, 'Earl Rivers' Einleitung zu seiner Übertragung der *Weisheitsprüche der Philosophen*', *Anglia*, lix (1935), 335.

69. *The Prologues and Epilogues of William Caxton*, ed. W. J. B. Crotch, EETS OS 176 (1928), 26.

70. *The Dicts and Sayings of the Philosophers*, ed. C. F. Bühler, EETS OS 211 (1941), 345.

71. *Prologues and Epilogues*, 24.

could not be lightly disregarded by those who wanted to cultivate a reputation for chivalry. Rivers, who seems to have wished to cast himself in the same mould as Marshal Boucicault and Jacques de Lalaing (he had already risked his life in a joust with the Bastard of Burgundy after his sister's ladies-in-waiting had tied an 'emprise' to his right thigh – 'and whan I had it, it was nerer my hert then my knee'),[72] was obviously not insensitive to such considerations. It is perhaps churlish to recall that the earl shared his family's taste for lucrative marriages (at one time he even aspired as high as Mary of Burgundy),[73] and that, despite his hair shirt, he is known to have fathered at least one illegitimate child, but nevertheless the impression remains that his chivalrous attitude to women owed as much to its publicity value as to genuine sentiment. The sceptical remarks of the Knight of the Tower's wife seem worth quoting in this context: 'for they that saye that alle the honour and worshyppe whiche they gete and haue is comynge to them by theyre peramours ... but how be hit that they saye that for them and for theyr loue they done hit/ In good feyth/ they done it only for to enhaunce them self/ and for to drawe vnto them the grace and vayne glory of the world.'[74]

While we may easily appreciate how a man in Rivers' position might wish to maintain his good standing in the court of love, the implications of its censure for someone lower down the social scale are more difficult to determine. Chaucer's prologue to the *Legend of Good Women* is both the best known and the most elusive of the works reflecting the court-of-love tradition in England. Does the poet's apparent intention to send his palinode to Queen Anne 'at Eltham or at Sheene' (F. 497) imply that it was written, as Lydgate says, at her request, and because, in Speght's words, 'some Ladies in the Court tooke offence at Chaucers large speeches against the vntruth of women',[75] or is it all an elaborate fiction? I have already suggested that we should beware of taking protestations of subservience to female authority too literally, and we have already seen how Isabel of Bavaria's patronage of Christine de Pisan did not prevent some members of the French court defending the *Roman de la Rose*, 'that is an heresye ayeins my lawe' (F. 330). If Chaucer's alleged offences in translating the *Roman* and writing in *Troilus and Criseyde* of a woman notorious for her 'untrouth' are not as easily defended as Chartier's in the case of the *Belle Dame sans Mercy*, they are hardly very grave; he does, after all, everything he can to exonerate Criseyde: 'iwis, I wolde excuse hire yet for routhe' (V. 1099). One passage in the *Troilus* seems to

72. *Excerpta Historica*, ed. S. Bentley (London, 1831), 178.
73. C. Ross, *Edward IV* (London, 1974), 251.
74. *The Book of the Knight of the Tower*, ed. M. Y. Offord, *EETS* SS 2 (1971), 164.
75. Hammond, *Bibliographical Manual*, 59 and 380.

point clearly to the *Legend's* being part of a contrived literary amusement:

> Bysechyng every lady bright of hewe,
> And every gentil womman, what she be,
> That al be that Criseyde was untrewe,
> That for that gilt she be nat wroth with me.
> Ye may hire giltes in other bokes se;
> And gladlier I wol write, yif yow leste,
> Penelopëes trouthe and good Alceste (V. 1772–8).

This, it seems to me, is less an attempt to forestall possible criticism than a conscious effort to provoke it; Chaucer is offering up his poem as the subject of fashionable debate much as the author of the *Cents Ballades*, which deals with a similar theme, was to do.[76] At all events he seems to have had in mind something like the *Legend of Good Women* even before he had finished the *Troilus* and given Queen Anne a chance to criticise it.

If there is little reason to ascribe the genesis of the *Legend of Good Women* to formal courts of love, or even to companies of the Flower and the Leaf, the poem nevertheless belongs to the world of Cupid's courtiers. It was clearly written for that informal *cour amoureuse* which sprang into being wherever members of the *familia regis* fell to discussing love poetry and, as with the *Lenvoy a Scogan*, where Chaucer appears for the prosecution rather than the defence (a further hint that the game might be set afoot without the help of the ladies), we can sense the presence of a tight-knit group of initiates playing with literary and social conventions at which we can now but guess. My final example concerns a poet who was only on the outer edge of such a group.

Though Thomas Hoccleve might have wished to be taken for a 'verray gentil man',[77] his social position was far humbler than that of Chaucer. As a clerk of the Privy Seal he was not truly a member of the *familia regis* at all, and when he fell foul of Cupid's court we can sense the genuine puzzlement of an outsider made the butt of a joke which he cannot fully understand. Hoccleve had good reason to be puzzled, for the poem which caused all the trouble was his translation of Christine de Pisan's *Epître au Dieu d'Amours*, that first call to arms in the feminist campaign against Jean de Meun. Hoccleve completed his translation in 1402 when the debate over the *Roman de la Rose* was at its height, but it was not until twenty years later that he found himself having to answer for it.[78] The question is raised at the

---

76. Chaucer may have known the *Cents Ballades*; see Robinson's note on 'Merciles Beaute' (1. 26), in *Works*, 866.

77. 'La Male Regle', 184, in *Minor Poems*, 31.

78. J. H. Kern, 'Die Datierung von Hoccleve's Dialog', *Anglia*, xl (1916), 370–3.

end of his *Dialogus cum Amico* where he is discussing the possibility of writing something for Humphrey of Gloucester, whose

> lust and his desir
> Is / as it wel sit / to his hy degree,
> ffor his desport / & mirthe in honestee,
> With ladyes / to haue daliance (703–6),

and it is tempting to link it in some way with the duke's politically embarrassing liaison with Jacqueline of Hainault. Whether or not Jacqueline anticipated Catherine de l'Isle-Bouchard's role in the controversy over the *Belle Dame sans Mercy*, Hoccleve's alleged ruffling of feminine sensibilities is even more extraordinary than Chartier's. Christine de Pisan's *Epître au Dieu d'Amours* is an out-and-out attack on male hypocrisy and a defence of female virtue, and it seems almost inconceivable that any lady should be 'swart wrooth' (line 756) with Hoccleve for having translated it. No wonder he protests,

> Who so lookith aright / ther-in may see
> That they me oghten haue in greet cheertee,
> And elles / woot I neuere what is what; (776–8)

and a little later,

> My ladyes all / as wisly god me blesse,
> Why that yee meeued been / can I nat knowe:
> ....
> But I your freend be / byte me the crowe!
> I am al othir to yow / than yee weene. (806–11)

It is of course possible that the whole business is a somewhat contrived fiction designed to introduce the tale of Jeruselaus' wife, which is Hoccleve's own legend of a good woman, written 'in honur & plesance/ Or yow, my ladyes' (*Dialogus*, 821–2), but his stubborn return to the theme of the *Littera Cupidinis* during the course of it suggests otherwise:

> Shee change nolde hir vertuous maneere;
> The lessons that they in Ouyde had red,
> Halp hem right noght / they wenten thens vnsped. (481–3)

Unlike the subtle ironies of Chaucer's Ovidian saints' lives, which seem to presuppose the knowing connivance of a sophisticated audience, the unambiguous morality of this tale of wifely constancy from the *Gesta Romanorum* implies the work of a man out of touch with the inner circle of the court. What Gloucester, who was the twenty-one year old Jacqueline's third husband, must have made of it one hesitates to think.

The four examples from late middle English literature that I have chosen provide far from unambiguous evidence about the reality of the court of love tradition, but then, as I have tried to show, the apparently unshakeable testimony of the founding charter of Charles VI's *cour amoureuse* is hardly much more dependable. If the courts of love in the late middle ages were indeed little more than a literary embellishment of one side of life in the real court (their plaintiffs court poets, their lawsuits literary debates, their 'billes' actual poems) then it is in the literature itself that we might hope to come closest to the reality. In the mockery of 'How the louer', in Rivers' exaggerated delicacy, Chaucer's self-irony, and Hoccleve's bafflement we may get some sense of that closed, predominantly masculine, and self-consciously literary society which preened itself before the flattering looking-glass of the *familia Cupidinis*.

6

Middle Scots Poets and Patrons

Denton Fox

When one contemplates the landscape of Middle Scots verse, it seems hardly a fair field full of folk – unless, of course, one includes the modern scholars. Robert Henryson, William Dunbar, and Gavin Douglas loom up solidly enough, respectable and even imposing figures, though not gigantic. James I is a rather misty figure on the edge of the field: we are not altogether sure that he wrote the *Kingis Quair*, and in any case this is often thought to be an English poem, not a Scots one. Sir David Lindsay is in the background, solid enough, to be sure, but it is a little doubtful whether a poet born in 1490, about the time that Caxton died, can be called a Middle Scots poet – though one might wish to adopt the plausible hypothesis that the middle ages lingered on in Scotland for a very long time. Apart from that, the figures seem either small (though not always short-winded), or, often, exceedingly wraith-like: Blind Harry, Clerk of Tranent, Huchoun of the Auld Ryall, and other descendants of Ossian. One might even think that, if it were not for Henryson, Dunbar, and Douglas, the term 'Middle Scots literature' would seem as superfluous (in England if not in Scotland) as 'Middle Kentish literature'. Certainly much of the other Scots verse would blend in remarkably well with Middle English literature. To correspond to the English *Legendaries* there is the Scots *Legends of the Saints*; there are similarly Scots versions of the *Secreta Secretorum*, the *Seven Sages*, the *Troy Book*, the Alexander legend, not to mention various imposing metrical chronicles.

All these works are Scottish enough in language, and some of them, such as the chronicles, are Scottish in subject, but they can be accounted for without any need to hypothesise a specifically Scots literary tradition. I would like here to cast an eye, briefly, erratically, but roughly chronologically, over Middle Scots verse and its relationship to the court, in order to see whether Henryson, Dunbar, and

Douglas are solitary and inexplicable figures, or whether there are any specifically Scots traditions behind them. While I am wary about making any easy distinctions between courtly and popular verse, I will restrict myself mostly to poems which have some degree of rhetorical sophistication, poems in which the manner is at least as important as the matter. This is a distinction that would be familiar to Henryson, Dunbar, and Douglas: they all, in different ways, distinguish between the 'polite termes of sweit rhetore' and 'hamelie language and . . . termes rude'.[1]

I would like particularly to keep an eye on the poet's audience, both the immediate audience for which he composed, and the later audience which read his works. I would make two initial assumptions, both of them, perhaps, both obvious and questionable. The first would be that a poet, at least a pre-romantic poet, is not likely to write poems unless he has an audience which will in some ways reward him – the reward of course need not be financial. The second is that a poem is more likely to survive if it continues to find readers, or, to put it another way, if it fits into an enduring literary tradition – the poet himself may, of course, like Chaucer or Langland, sharply modify this tradition.

Turning now to the Scots poets themselves, it seems hardly polite to overlook completely Barbour's *Bruce*, even though this work is outside our province in that it is, or purports to be, factual, and in that the matter is more important than the manner. But it is a work which has no precise Middle English counterpart, while it does have Scots successors: the *Wallace*, written about 1470, and, if you like, David Lindsay's *Squire Meldrum*.

The reasons why the *Bruce* was written are not far to seek. Barbour was an important official under Robert II, the grandson of the hero of the *Bruce*. Robert II came to the throne in 1371; his claim to the throne was through his grandfather, but the claim was debated by the first earl of Douglas, who, however, was not the grandson of the Bruce.[2] Barbour's poem, which was finished in 1376,[3] seems clearly to have a political motivation – as did, presumably, the lost genealogy he wrote tracing the Stewarts back to their Trojan ancestors. It is pleasing to note that Robert II rewarded Barbour handsomely for his services.[4]

One might go further, though this is very speculative, and suggest that there may be some connection between the *Bruce* and Froissart, the French chronicler. Froissart, who apparently wrote his first chronicle in verse,[5] and was court-poet to Philippa of Hainault, came to

1. Henryson, *Fables*, 3, 36: *Poems*, ed. D. Fox (Oxford, 1981). *polite* 'polished'.
2. Ranald Nicholson, *Scotland: The Later Middle Ages* (Edinburgh, 1974), 185.
3. See *The Bruce*, ed. W. M. Mackenzie (London, 1909), 448.
4. See the memoir in *The Bruce*, ed. W. W. Skeat, Scottish Text Society, 1st Series, 31–3 (Edinburgh and London, 1894).
5. See Normand R. Cartier, 'The Lost Chronicle', *Spec.*, xxxvi (1961), 424–34.

Scotland in 1365, in the course of his research for a chronicle glorifying Philippa's family, and spent fifteen weeks with King David, the uncle of Robert II.[6] Even if the idea for the *Bruce* had nothing to do with Froissart, there is clearly a similarity between the aims of the two authors.

The much later *Wallace*, incidentally, seems also to be a work which must have been produced for family or political reasons. The origins of it are too obscure to allow one to speak with confidence, but it seems very likely that this extremely unhistorical glorification of William Wallace, whom earlier chronicles had styled as 'chief of brigands', had some connection with the Wallace family; it is also possible that this very anti-English poem had some connection with the anti-English party in late fifteenth-century Scotland.[7]

While the *Bruce* had a royal patron, and the *Wallace* presumably at least a noble patron, their eventual audience was far from courtly: these poems were perhaps more widely read in the seventeenth and eighteenth centuries, at least, than any other Middle Scots poems. But they seem important more for social or cultural history than for literary history. Their popularity in the fifteenth and sixteenth centuries would seem to be connected with the peculiar importance of the central government, which, however weak, was the great force giving Scotland an identity, since the Lowlanders were much closer to the English, geographically, in blood, and in culture, than they were to the Highlanders, whom they despised. And of course these poems have the pleasing features that they purport to be historical, they are filled with bloody action, have impressive heroes, and convey the impression that the English are evil but feeble.

The *Kingis Quair*, for all its merits, should be passed over in silence here: whether its language be regarded as Scots or English, it is presumably a product of the English court, not the Scots court. It is a poem which survives in only one manuscript, and which seems to have had little, if any, influence on the main course of Scots verse, though there are interesting linguistic similarities between it and the *Quare of Jelusy* and *Lancelot of the Laik*.[8]

But Richard Holland's *Buke of the Howlat* (the owl), written about

6. See A. H. Diverres, 'Jean Froissart's journey to Scotland', *Forum for Modern Language Studies*, i (1965), 54–63.

7. These matters are discussed by Matthew P. McDiarmid, in the introduction to his edition: *Hary's Wallace*, Scottish Text Society, 4th series, 4–5 (Edinburgh and London, 1968–9). It should be noted, however, that McDiarmid's dating of the poem, his theory that its author also wrote *Rauf Coilyear* and *Golagros and Gawane*, and his high estimation of the *Wallace's* worth, have not been universally accepted. See the reviews by, for instance, Priscilla Bawcutt (*Medium Aevum*, xxix [1970], 224–8) and Florence Ridley (*Studies in Scottish Literature*, vii [1970], 195–9).

8. See the introductions to *Lancelot of the Laik*, ed. M. M. Gray, Scottish Text Society, 2nd series, 2 (Edinburgh and London, 1912), and *The Kingis Quair and The Quare of Jelusy*, ed. Alexander Lawson (London, 1910).

1450, should certainly be considered.[9] In this poem, the owl, ashamed of his appearance, appeals against Nature to the pope, that is, to 'the plesant Pacok, preciouss and pure' (line 81). The pope agrees to call a council to consider the matter, and summons the members: 'Swannis ... In quhyte rocatis ... war bischopis blist' (171–3); the cock, as chanter; the raven, as rural dean, and a vast quantity of other birds – the poem is an immense aviary. But they cannot decide, and so they call in the emperor, the eagle, and the whole secular state – another great array of birds. So they have a grand banquet, entertained by, among others, the nightingale as minstrel, the jay as juggler, and the rook as a disruptive Irish bard who speaks gibberish. Finally the council agrees to ask Nature to help the owl; she does, and each bird lends him a feather; the owl then becomes, in his beauty, so over-bearing that the birds all complain, and Nature strips him again. The most peculiar thing about this peculiar poem is that the green wood-pecker, who, as pursuivant, rides before the eagle-emperor, bears coat-armour with devices. Three stanzas are spent describing the papal and various royal arms; then twenty stanzas, or more than a quarter of the poem, are devoted to a description of the arms of various Doug-lases, and, in particular, to a long and unhistorical account of how Sir James Douglas took the Bruce's heart to Jerusalem and then died fighting against the Saracens. The poem is plainly a beast fable, a genre which seems to have flourished greatly in Scotland, but beyond that it becomes somewhat baffling. Various attempts have been made to make it into a historical allegory, but none of them seems very satisfactory. The council must be a reference to the church councils that were so important in the first half of the century: one might suppose Holland to be a conciliarist, since it is not flattering to show the pope as a peacock; but then one might suppose him to be a papalist, since it is hardly flattering to represent a council as a flock of twitter-ing birds.

A possible solution would be to suppose that the very discontinuity between the Douglases and the birds is the major point of the poem. The birds are only simulacra of humans: they flock gaudily, banquet ridiculously, discuss absurd question, and the owl, in particular, is envious, proud, and changeable. The Douglases, especially Sir James, act meaningfully, and are shown as surpassingly human and constant: 'O Dowglass, O Dowglass,/ Tender and trewe!' (402–3). This would seem, then, to be an extremely partisan poem, where the Douglases are set apart from the rest of the world, and to be a poem written for a patron. This seems to be confirmed by the records, which show that Holland was always closely associated with the Douglases, and that

9. In *Scottish Alliterative Poems*, ed. F. J. Amours, Scottish Text Society, 1st series, 27, 38 (Edinburgh and London, 1892–7).

in 1482, when James III outlawed James, the ninth earl of Douglas, Holland was one of the three followers of Douglas who were specifically excluded from any pardon.[10]

Before considering the metrical forms of these poems, perhaps we should turn to Henryson, the major poet of the century. His dates are a bit shadowy: one might guess that his *floruit* was about 1475, but all one can safely say is that he wrote in the last half of the century.

To a literary taxonomist, the most obvious thing about Henryson is how Chaucerian his verse forms are, at least in his three long poems, the *Fables*, the *Testament of Cresseid*, and *Orpheus*. These poems are written mostly in rhyme royal, with occasional changes to the Monk's Tale stanza in the *moralitates* of the *Fables*. The formal complaint of Cresseid is in a complicated nine-line stanza with two rhymes which goes back to Chaucer's *Compleynt of Anelida*; Orpheus's lament is in a ten-line variant of this stanza. The *moralitas* to *Orpheus* is in decasyllabic couplets.

It would be useless to deny, in view of Henryson's obvious other debts to Chaucer, that he is likely to have been influenced by him in the metrical patterns of his lines, as well as of his stanzas. The real question, I suppose, is why Henryson was able to write ten-syllable lines which are, to our taste, excellently metrical, while many English poets in this century were not. No certain answer is possible, though one can make conjectures. It is possible that Chaucer's influence was less strong on the Scots poets, because of dialectal differences, among other things, and so the Scots were content to follow Chaucer's example in adding two syllables to the traditional octosyllabic line, and did not follow the more hazardous course of trying to imitate Chaucer's rhythms. The *Bruce*, for instance, like Andrew of Wyntoun's chronicle and many other works, was written in competent enough octosyllabic couplets. The author of the *Wallace* shows occasionally and not always happily, in his rhetorical touches, that he has read at least a little Chaucer, but by and large he contents himself with straightforwardly following his predecessors, and simply adding a couple more syllables to their line.

Another possibility is that we misinterpret fifteenth-century English poetry: our ears are now so attuned to the regular pentameter line that we assume all fifteenth-century poets were groping, however unskilfully, towards this line. But in fact some of them write lines which, by our standards, are perfectly regular; others follow principles which are quite different but sometimes no less fixed. It may have happened that in the comparatively small area of lowland Scotland the more-or-less iambic pentameter line was, by chance, the option chosen, much to the historical advantage of these poets. Certainly

10. *Scottish Alliterative Poems*, xxv.

there are a number of Scots poems in such iambic pentameter lines in the last half of the fifteenth century: besides Henryson and the *Wallace*, for instance, there are *The Thre Prestis of Peblis*, perhaps written in the 1480s; *The Contemplacioun of Synnaris*, written before 1499; *The Talis of the Fyve Bestis*, probably a late fifteenth-century work. Henryson is the only poet who shows himself to be metrically skilful, but the poems all seem fairly regular – it is hard to be sure how regular, because there is often textual corruption, or uncertainties about pronunciation and accentuation, or because modern editors emend silently for metrical reasons. The dates of these works are too uncertain to allow any tracing of influences; all we can say is that a tradition of more or less regular pentameter lines became established in Scotland, where it did not in contemporary England.

But Henryson also knew alliterative poems, such as the *Buke of the Howlat*, and it is interesting to contemplate whether this is of any importance. The alliterative tradition, of course, flourished much more in Scotland than in England during the late fifteenth and the sixteenth centuries. *Scotish Ffeilde*, an account of the battle of Flodden, must have been written after 1513, and is usually thought to be the last English alliterative poem; alliterative poetry was copied and, in the case of *Piers Plowman* and *Pierce the Ploughman's Crede*, printed in England in the sixteenth century, but it is thought that probably little English alliterative poetry of much importance was written after the first few years of the fifteenth century;[11] even the fifteenth-century interest in it seems to be largely regional. But in Scotland the last alliterative poem is apparently Polwart and Montgomerie's *Flyting* of 1582, and this does not seem to be a freak, since James VI and I, in his 'Reulis and Cautelis to be Obseruit and Eschewit in Scottis Poesie' of 1584, recommends alliterative verse, which he calls 'tumbling' (that is, not syllabically regular), for flyting or invectives. Henryson, Dunbar, Douglas, and even Lindsay (for a single stanza) all wrote alliterative verse – they use it for special purposes, to be sure, but they show themselves proficient at it. This seems unusual: it is hard to be sure, since so much English alliterative poetry is anonymous, but it must have been rare for an English poet to write both alliterative and syllabic verse, since not only different techniques but different vocabularies are involved. When Chaucer's Parson says 'I am a Southren man, / I kan nat gesste "rum, ram, ruf," by lettre', he may be expressing not only Chaucer's disdain for alliterative verse, but also a simple fact about 'Southren' men. So one of the distinguishing marks of Middle Scots verse, perhaps, is the way in which poets have access to both the alliterative and the syllabic traditions.

But the question remains: in what ways was the alliterative trad-

<hr/>

11. Thorlac Turville-Petre, *The Alliterative Revival* (Cambridge, 1977), 122.

ition important for Henryson's verse? It supplied him, obviously, with a quantity of traditional alliterative phrases, which he used freely, especially in mock-heroic contexts: the dogs chasing Chantecleir and the fox 'but baid, thay braidet ouer the bent; / As fyre off flint thay ouer the feildis flaw'. But this trick is not unknown among Southern poets. Most obviously, of course, the alliterative tradition accounts, presumably, for the very high degree of alliteration in Henryson's syllabic verse. The effectiveness of alliteration in the seasonal, particularly the winterly, descriptions by Henryson and other Scots poets has often been commented on. But heavy alliteration can also be used powerfully in a high style, as in Orpheus's lament:

Fair weill, my place; fair weile, plesance and play;
And welcome, woddis wyld and wilsome way,
My wikit werd in wildernes to wair!
My rob ryall and all my riche array
Changit sall be in rude russat of gray . . .

In a more impalpable way, it seems likely that many of Henryson's best lines owe much of their strength to alliteration. For instance, 'O fair Cresseid . . . how was thow fortunait / To change in filth all thy feminitie'. It seems true that alliteration is an important and constant part of the texture of the verse of Henryson, as also of Dunbar and Douglas.

I would guess, too, that there were other and less obvious ways in which the alliterative tradition influenced Henryson. Most Scots alliterative verse is, like the *Howlat*, written in a thirteen-line rhymed stanza which consists, usually, of nine four-stress lines and a wheel of four two-stress lines. This is a fairly intricate stanza, not a stanza that one can drone on in, and, because of the pounding wheel at the end, it is a powerfully end-stopped stanza. In its better examples the stanzas are carefully planned and highly wrought. It is tempting to suppose that Henryson's concise and careful stanzas owe something to this tradition: he clearly paid a great deal of attention to the construction of each stanza and consistently treats them as self-contained units. In the first thousand lines of the *Fables*, for instance, I have noticed only one instance of a run-on stanza (620–1), though there are rather more in the *Testament*, where he is imitating Chaucer. At the very least, it is certain that the alliterative tradition gave Henryson, and the other Scots poets, an extremely useful source of 'fine language'. Although people think, not altogether accurately, that polysyllabic Latinisms, the so-called 'aureate terms', are a conspicuous feature of Middle Scots poetry, in Henryson, at least, lines like 'Now is my breist with stormie stoundis stad, / Wrappit in wo, ane wretch full will of wane!' (*Testament* 542–3), with the ornamental terms drawn from the alliterative

tradition, are vastly more common than such Latinisms as 'In mor-
alitie exemplatiue prudent' (*Fables* 2591).

There remain, however, the questions of why Henryson wrote at all,
and who his audience were. The *Bruce* and the *Howlat* were works
written for patrons; although external evidence is lacking for the
Wallace, everything points to patronage for that work as well. But
Henryson's works do not seem to be written for a patron. It is true
that he does say, in the prologue to his *Fables*, that he was writing 'be
requeist and precept of ane lord, / Of quhome the name it neidis not
record', but I am not inclined to put very much weight on this: poets
sometimes alluded to such pretended 'requests' merely as a way of
emphasising their own modesty.

At the risk of being frivolous, one might suggest that among the
reasons for Henryson's poetry was that he had the good luck, or good
sense, to settle in Dunfermline, in Fife. Although Dunfermline is only,
in an air-line, about twelve miles from Edinburgh, it is on the north
side of the Firth of Forth, which, though only a little over a mile wide
at that point, and passable enough by ferry, is a very effective obstacle
to an invading army. Wallace, at the end of the thirteenth century,
had begun the strategy which was to continue for many years: to
invade England, and then to retreat, burning the Scots towns south
of the Forth and turning the country into a desert, so that the invading
army could find no sustenance. One can see that this would be an
effective strategy, but it is possible that it might have caused a certain
amount of inconvenience and disruption of social intercourse for the
natives, even apart from the ravages of the invading English. Dunfermline must have been altogether more apt for poetic tranquillity.
Perhaps because of its protected situation, it was comparatively a
place of much more importance in the fifteenth century than it is now.
It had been created a royal burgh in the twelfth century; many of the
Scots kings either resided or were buried there; its Benedictine abbey,
founded in 1124, became one of the most important monastic establishments in Scotland, and owned most of the lands in western Fife,
as well as much land elsewhere. As master of the grammar school in
the abbey, Henryson is likely to have held a position of some importance. One can only conjecture about his relations with the abbey, the
burgesses, the aristocracy, and the court. But it seems clear from the
internal evidence of his poetry that he could count on a reasonably
learned and sophisticated audience. The *Fables* contain Latin quota-
tions and a good many legal details: they are presumably intended for
an audience which had been pushed through Gualterus Anglicus's
fables at school. The *Testament* would hardly make sense to an audience unacquainted with Chaucer's *Troilus*; *Orpheus* is a very bookish
poem.

In any case it seems likely that in the second half of the fifteenth century, or considerably later than in England, something like a reading public, albeit a very small one, was slowly beginning to arise in Scotland. The public of any sort was of course not all that large. While any estimate of the population of medieval Scotland must be even more speculative (and that is saying a great deal) than estimates of the population of England, Russell guesses that the population of Scotland in the middle of the fourteenth century, before the plague, was 550,000, and that it was about 350,000 in 1377; the decline is likely to have continued until some time in the early or middle sixteenth century.[12] But these figures are too large, for several reasons. First, we are concerned only with the English-speaking lowlands, not with the highlands, and the highlands, whose population has grown comparatively little over the centuries, contained a far greater percentage of the population in medieval Scotland than they do now.[13] Secondly, in Scotland, the civil wars and the wars against the English seem to have caused much greater destruction among the ordinary people than the Wars of the Roses did in England. Thirdly, even by medieval standards, an unusually large percentage of the population appears to have lived on the land, rather than in villages and cities, and our concern is with the literate townspeople and courtiers, not with the peasants. Froissart describes Edinburgh, at the end of the fourteenth century, as a town with less than four hundred houses: this would be a population of about 1,500.[14] By the middle of the sixteenth century the population is said to be 9,000. Glasgow, about 1450, had perhaps less than 2,000 inhabitants; by the middle of the sixteenth century its population was perhaps under 4,500. By way of comparison, London is thought to have had a population of about 80,000 in the middle of the sixteenth century. However, learning did make some headway in Scotland during the fifteenth century – the university of St. Andrews was founded in 1411, Glasgow in 1451, and Aberdeen in 1495; burgesses did, at least intermittently, prosper; and the very existence of works like *The Thre Prestis of Peblis* and *The Talis of the Fyve Bestis* presupposes a reading public.

But we should move on to William Dunbar and Gavin Douglas. These poets were both demonstrably influenced by Henryson, so we

12. Josiah Cox Russell, *British Medieval Population* (Albuquerque, 1948), 362; for the decline after 1377 see T. H. Hollingsworth, *Historical Demography* (Ithaca, N.Y., 1969), Appendix 3. If one accepts the argument advanced by T. M. Cooper, 'The numbers and the distribution of the population of medieval Scotland', *Scottish Historical Review*, xxvi (1947), 2–9, that the population of medieval Scotland was about a fifth that of England, and uses Hollingsworth's figures for the population of England (p. 386), one arrives at these figures for Scotland: in 1348, 730,000; in 1377, 450,000; in 1444, 234,000.

13. See Cooper, 6–9.

14. This and the following figures, all of which must be regarded as extremely speculative, are taken from Russell, 359–60, 298.

do now have something like a definite tradition. Although Dunbar
was born around 1456, and so was some twenty years younger than
Douglas, it is striking that all of the poems by Dunbar which we can
date, and also Douglas's two important poems, the *Palice of Honour*
and his translation of the *Aeneid*, all fall in the period 1500–13.
Douglas lived on until 1522; though we know nothing of Dunbar's
death, there is no reason to suppose that he did not also live on past
1513. The obvious explanation for the coincidence is that 1500–13
were the gaudy years of James IV's reign. James IV came to the
throne in 1488 as a boy of 15, having rebelled against his father, and
having been implicated in his death. There was a time of many
troubles, domestic and foreign, but from 1499 on negotiations were
under way for the marriage of James to Princess Margaret, Henry
VII's daughter. The marriage took place in 1503, and from then until
1511 there was peace in England, and indeed about as large a measure
of internal peace as medieval Scotland ever knew. The records show
James, during this period, as being deeply religious, strenuously un-
faithful, and altogether active. He travelled steadily, while adminis-
tering justice, playing chess, hunting, making pilgrimages, visiting
mistresses, hawking, making surgical experiments on his subjects,
paying them damages for the aforesaid, experimenting on deafmutes,
playing the lute, jousting, playing backgammon, golf, cards, tennis,
and dice, striking anvils, casting artillery, building ships and palaces.[15] Especially, he liked giving money to people: minstrels, alche-
mists, physicians and other quacks, would-be aviators, pipers,
buffoons, jugglers, musicians, beggars, guisers, tightrope-dancers, fal-
coners, goldsmiths, French dog-fanciers, and even poets. He lived, to
be sure, far above his means, or the means of Scotland, a poor country:
Froissart records the French soldiers in Scotland as saying, 'We never
knewe what povertie ment tyll nowe'.[16] And James seems also to have
had ideas above his station in life, with his plans to lead a grand
crusade against the Turks. It was not prudent of him to lead his people
to the point where, as a foreign observer commented, 'they think
themselves the most powerful kingdom that exists',[17] and certainly
James seems to have shared in the inclination toward self-destruction
that was common to so many of the Stewarts: James II, who managed
to blow himself up with one of his own cannon, seems emblematic of
them all. But while it lasted, it was a good party.

There is no question, then, about the causes for Dunbar's poetry. He
was a court poet; James rewarded him very handsomely, as the records
show, but never gave him the benefice which he begged for so often:

15. See R. L. Mackie, *King James IV of Scotland* (Edinburgh and London, 1958).
16. Diverres, 61.
17. Nicholson, 575.

James, very sensibly, had no desire to let Dunbar grow fat in silence. But when the music stopped in 1513, at Flodden, Dunbar stopped singing. It is worth considering whether Douglas, too, was not in some sense a court poet. He was of course of a very much higher social rank than Dunbar, but he was at least as much a courtier as a churchman, and was dependant on the king. In 1497 James decided a complaint in favour of Douglas; in 1498 the reversion of the parsonage of Glenholm, which was in the king's gift, was given to Douglas; in or about 1501 Douglas dedicated the *Palice of Honour* to James; in 1503 Douglas was given the provostry of St. Giles', Edinburgh, an important benefice, and again one in the king's gift.[18] There is ample evidence to show that Douglas was a very ambitious and self-interested man; it seems very probable that at least one of his motives in translating the *Aeneid* was to increase his reputation for learning and so put him in the way of higher offices. In 1514, after Flodden, Douglas was angling for the archbishopric of St. Andrews, and Henry VIII, prodded by his sister, James's queen, who in turn had doubtless been prodded by Douglas, wrote to the pope in support of Douglas (whom he did not know), praising him for his 'extraordinary learning'.[19]

But though it is easy enough to guess what Dunbar's and Douglas's social and economic motives might have been, it is less easy to see what their literary environment was – what sort of poetry was flourishing when they started writing. However, I think some useful light can be thrown on this by the Chepman and Myllar prints, and by the Asloan MS. In 1507, at James IV's request, Chepman and Myllar set up a press in Edinburgh. Except for a breviary, all of their surviving productions are in the vernacular: there are nine tracts, now bound together, and fragments of the *Wallace* and the *Buke of the Howlat*.[20] All of these survive only in single copies, and presumably there were other publications which have been lost. These prints need to be considered in conjunction with the Asloan MS, with which they have a curious connection. The Asloan MS, an anthology of prose and verse, was compiled some time between 1513 and 1530 by John Asloan, whom we know from other sources as a scribe and a notary.[21] Unfortunately, though the original table of contents has survived, much of the MS has been lost: thirty-five items, all or almost all poems, are missing completely, while some of the remaining poems are partly missing. The MS must originally have been very large: it now contains seventeen poems and over ten thousand lines of verse; if one adds to

18. Priscilla Bawcutt, *Gavin Douglas* (Edinburgh, 1976), 7–8, 47–9.
19. Bawcutt, 12.
20. A facsimile has been edited by William Beattie: *The Chepman and Myllar Prints*, Edinburgh Bibliographical Society (Oxford, 1950).
21. *The Asloan Manuscript*, ed. W. A. Craigie, Scottish Text Society, 2nd Series, 14, 16 (Edinburgh and London, 1923–5).

this the missing parts of these poems and the fourteen poems listed in the table of contents, missing in the MS, but which we know from other sources, the total rises to eighteen thousand. How many lines were in the twenty poems that were listed in the table of contents but are otherwise unknown is anyone's guess, but the MS presumably had originally over twenty-five thousand lines of verse, and so would have been roughly comparable to the Bannatyne MS, which has about thirty thousand.[22]

The Asloan MS and the Chepman and Myllar prints have a very considerable overlap. Eleven Chepman and Myllar publications exist, in whole or in fragments; all or the major part of seven or eight of these publications occur, or occurred, also in the Asloan MS (and it is clear why some of the others, the very long *Wallace*, for instance, do not appear in the MS).[23] In all cases where there is enough evidence, it can be established that the versions in the print and in the MS are very close textually, so that it seems fairly certain that the MS version was copied from a Chepman and Myllar print or another closely related print. And it seems very likely that other pieces in the MS, perhaps many others, were copied from prints. This is worth stressing, since it helps to establish that the Chepman and Myllar prints and the Asloan MS both furnish something like a standard collection or at least sampling of the corpus of verse known in Scotland in the early sixteenth century. The Chepman and Myllar prints were commercial ventures, and the printers must have chosen poems for which they thought there would be a demand.[24] John Asloan appears, from the prose which he chose to put in his anthology, to be a man of no very advanced tastes or ideas, and he seems, in his selections of verse, to be copying out what other people read, and printed, not to be following any recherché interests of his own.

The surprising thing about both the prints and the MS is the extreme heterogeneity of the verse. One of the prints has in it both an

22. If one assumes that the twenty missing poems had the same average length as the others, the figure would be 29,600 lines. But this is not a safe assumption, since twelve of the twenty unknown poems have 'ballat' in their titles, but only six of the extant poems. These six poems average less than one hundred lines. However, some of the unknown poems have titles which suggest considerable length.

23. The words 'major part' are added because some of the prints consist of a long poem and one or two short poems. Some of the missing 'ballats' in the MS may be identical with these short poems: the titles in the table of contents of the MS are too vague to be of much help. Chepman and Myllar Tract V, *De Regimine Principum Bonum Consilium*, might correspond to 'þe Regiment of King*is* with þe buke of phisnomy', a missing item in the MS (though this sounds more like a version of the *Secreta Secretorum*), or, perhaps more likely, to 'þe buke of curtasy and nortur', another missing item, or to neither.

24. A possible exception is the shortest print, Tract IX, Dunbar's 'Welcome to Lord Bernard Stewart', an official poem, and perhaps printed at the king's command. It is not in the MS.

alliterative romance and a short poem by Lydgate; another has both Dunbar's *Flyting* and Henryson's serious 'Praise of Age'. In the MS, Dunbar's aureate poem on the Virgin, 'Hale sterne superne, hale in eterne', is followed by two alliterative romances; Lydgate's *Complaint of the Black Knight* is sandwiched in between two other hymns to the Virgin. The poems are in all metres, genres, and stylistic levels.

The obvious point here is that extreme heterogeneity of metres, genres, and stylistic levels is precisely the hallmark of Dunbar, a poet who skates easily from the obscene to the sublime, and to all points in between. But this great range seems to be, at least to some degree, a quality of other Scots poets, too. Henryson's short poems are a very mixed lot: 'The Annunciation', 'Sum Practysis of Medecyne', 'The Praise of Age', 'Robene and Makyne', for instance, while there is a very considerable stylistic range within the *Fables*. Douglas uses some nine different metrical forms in his prologues; Lindsay writes in a great variety of metrical forms, stylistic levels, and genres.

If one looks at Dunbar's poetry in the light of the Asloan MS and the Chepman and Myllar prints, one can see the number of poetic traditions that were available to him. To name some of them, for instance, there is the Chaucerian-Lydgatian high style, the Middle English and Lydgatian moral lyric; the Latinate religious lyric; alliterative verse; the Chaucerian-Henrysonian narrative mode; the comic dramatic mode, as in 'The Manner of the Crying of ane Playe'. It would take too long to trace all these strands, but I might comment briefly on one poem, as an example. The Asloan MS contains, or did contain, a fifteenth-century poem named *Colkelbie Sow*. The first part of this poem, a burlesque account of a peasant festivity and ensuing brawl, consists largely of comic catalogues: the guests include

An ald monk, a lechour
A drunkin drechour . . .
And a fanyeit flatterar . . .

And so on for fifty lines. It would seem very possible that some of Dunbar's more sophisticated catalogues are in this same tradition, as for instance his

Fenyeouris, fleichouris, and flatteraris;
Cryaris, craikaris, and clatteraris; . . .
Monsouris of France, gud clarat-cunnaris . . .
('Remonstrance to the King')

Certainly Dunbar had *Colkelbie Sow* in mind, since he mentions it in this same poem. One might also speculate that Douglas, in constructing the *Palice of Honour* largely out of catalogues, may have been influenced by poems like *Colkelbie Sow* – which, again, he mentions explicitly.

The genre of the first part of *Colkelbie Sow* is, I suppose, that of exuberant and burlesque accounts of the activities of peasants, or at least of the lower orders. Some of Dunbar's poems would seem to belong to this tradition, 'The Tournament' of the Soutars and Tailors, for instance, or the peasants' wooing poem, 'In Secreit Place this Hyndir Nycht', while Henryson's 'Sum Practysis of Medecine' and 'Robene and Makyne' may not be unrelated. Indeed, there is a very strong tradition of Scots poetry which is intensely energetic and about peasants – *Peblis to the Play* and *Christis Kirk on the Grene* are perhaps the two most notable examples.[25] It is probably here, if anywhere, that continuity between Middle Scots and eighteenth-century Scots poetry should be looked for.

There is, however, the large question, which I have been avoiding, of the French influence on Dunbar and the other Scots poets. The Scots critics, whom one sometimes suspects of being anti-English, stress Dunbar's French sources: so Janet Smith, following Aeneas J. G. Mackay, says that 'he owed more of a debt to the French than to the English poets'.[26] The trouble is that it is not easy to see precisely what his French sources were. Pierrepont Nichols wrote a long dissertation at Harvard in the twenties in which he worked laboriously through the French verse that Dunbar might have known. The fruits of this dissertation were two articles in *PMLA*, one titled 'Lydgate's Influence on the Aureate Terms of the Scottish Chaucerians', and the other, 'William Dunbar as a Scottish Lydgatian'.[27] As far as I know, no one has ever established any specific French source for any of Dunbar's poems. This is not to deny that some of his poems look as if they might have a little French blood in them: his 'Dregy', for instance, contains two perfect triolets, a form which the handbooks say is not recorded in English before the seventeenth century.

There seem to be two possible explanations. On the one hand, it is possible that Dunbar had a wide knowledge of French poetry, and was generally influenced by it, but, with his lofty spirit, disdained to do any direct borrowing. I cannot deny that this may be the case, but there are three possible difficulties. One is that there is no evidence that Dunbar knew any French. The second is that he did not, as far as I can see, have a particularly lofty spirit: I think that if he found anything worth stealing, and if no one was watching, he would steal

25. See A. H. MacLaine, 'The *Christis Kirk* tradition: its evolution in Scots poetry to Burns', *Studies in Scottish Literature*, ii (1964–5), 3–18, 111–24, 163–82, 234–50. It should be noted that the *Christis Kirk* stanza, with its bob and wheel, and its frequently heavy alliteration, must be related to the alliterative stanza discussed above.

26. *The French Background of Middle Scots Literature* (Edinburgh and London, 1934), 60.

27. 'Sources and influences traceable in the poetry of William Dunbar', Diss. Harvard 1923; *PMLA*, xlvii (1932), 516–22; *PMLA*, xlvi (1931), 214–24.

it. The third is that poets from Chaucer to T. S. Eliot, when they are genuinely influenced by poetry in a foreign language, have usually made some direct imitations or even translations.

The other explanation is that whatever French influence there is on Dunbar's poetry – and perhaps there is not, in fact, all that much of it – comes not directly but secondhand, and that, in particular, there must have been a fairly large body of Scots poetry, written in the late fifteenth and early sixteenth century, that is now lost. Here again, the Asloan MS gives some evidence. A few of the twenty untraceable items in its table of contents may be untraceable because the title is not helpful – an item listed as 'a ballat of our lady' may or may not survive elsewhere. But some of the items are undoubtedly lost: one would give a lot to recover 'the buke of the otter and the ele', and more to recover Master Robert Henryson's 'Dreme On fut by forth', a poem which appears in a later list as the single work by Henryson worth mentioning.[28] Other evidence is provided by Dunbar, who in his 'Lament for the Makers', lists twenty-four poets. Three of these are English: Chaucer, Lydgate, and Gower. Seven are Scots poets whom we know something about: Andrew of Wyntoun, Holland, Barbour, Gilbert Hay, Henryson, Walter Kennedy, and (if he should be included here) Blind Harry. The other fourteen are poets whom we know nothing, or next to nothing, about. For three of them, single poems may survive, though the attributions are not certain; a fourth, Mersar, has three short poems attributed to him in the Bannatyne MS. Some of the others have names which occur also in the records, though the identification is usually not secure. There is other evidence to show that these poets are not simply figments of Dunbar's imagination. Lindsay, in 'The Testament of the Papyngo', lists nine dead Scots poets: of the three we do not know, Mersar and Rowle also appear in Dunbar's list, and the third, 'Quintyng', may or may not be the same man as Dunbar's 'Quintyne Schaw', but is probably to be identified with 'Quintine with ane Huttok on his heid', one of the three Scots poets named by Douglas in the *Palice of Honour*. Also, we do not, of course, have the complete works of even the poets we do know something about. Walter Kennedy is an interesting case: besides his share in the *Flyting* of Dunbar and Kennedy, five poems survive with his name attached. They are remarkable more for piety, or, in one case, for obscenity, than for great merit, and yet his contemporaries thought highly of him. Dunbar gives him a whole stanza in his 'Lament for the Makers'; Douglas makes him at least equal to Dunbar, when he speaks of 'Greit Kennedie and Dunbar yit vndeid' (*Palice of Honour*, 923), as does Lindsay, who writes, 'Or quho can now the workis cuntrafait / Off Kennedie, with

28. *The Complaynt of Scotland*, ed. A. M. Stewart, Scottish Text Society, 4th Series, 11 (Edinburgh, 1979), 50.

termes aureait?' ('Papyngo', 15–16). While it is possible that these poets were all incompetent critics, it seems much more likely that Kennedy's best work has not survived.

There is a curious list of forty-eight tales and stories, in verse and in prose, in *The Complaynt of Scotland*, though this work was not written until *c.* 1550, and so needs to be treated with some care. The first is 'the taylis of cantirberrye', and some of the others are presumably English. Authors are not given, but one finds such recognisable items as the *Wallace*, the *Bruce*, *Rauf Coilyear*, *Golagrus and Gawene*, Dunbar's *Golden Targe*, Douglas's *Palice of Honour*, and a variety of further works, some of which can be identified with some degree of plausibility, and some of which can not, such as 'Opheus kyng of portingal'.[29] Many of these works were doubtless popular, but some of them are more learned: 'the tail of the amours of leander and hero', for instance.

It seems likely that a far smaller proportion of Middle Scots verse has survived than of Middle English verse, perhaps because of the violence of the Scottish Reformation. Dunbar's poems, or some of them, were probably gathered into collections, and the compilers of the Bannatyne and Maitland Folio manuscripts must have had access to the collections. Other lyric poets were not so lucky: a poem or two might survive, copied by chance on the flyleaf of a manuscript which escaped the attention of the reformers, but otherwise all would be lost. There were, almost certainly, a number of good and bad poets writing short poems around Dunbar's time: presumably they had to some extent different styles; presumably some of them had some acquaintance with French verse; and presumably there was some mutual influence. Which is about all we can say, I think, about the French influence on Dunbar.

There remains the question of how the court influenced the verse of Dunbar and Douglas. On the one hand, it is true that it was all-important, in that it provided the poets with the necessary incentives. It is also important, at least in Dunbar's case, because the court must have dictated the genres, and often even the subjects, of his poems. His petitionary poems are an obvious example, as is his epithalamion for James and Margaret, 'The Thrissill and the Rois', and his poems on Bernard Steward, Lord of Aubigny. But even beyond this, it seems likely that he wrote mostly to command: one imagines the king calling now for an obscene ditty, and now for a pious exhortation. On the other hand, they did not write coterie verse, except in the very limited sense that some of Dunbar's occasional poems would be more intelligible if one knew precisely what court occasion was behind them. There is no special court style: both Dunbar and Douglas are distin-

---

29. *The Complaynt of Scotland*, 50.

guished by the fact that they use so many styles. And, as far as one can judge from the surviving early prints and from the manuscript anthologies, there seem to have been no perceptible differences between the tastes of the court and the tastes of the reading public.

To sum up, then, I would guess that in the first decade of the sixteenth century Scots poetry could be described as a fair, if smallish field, and reasonably full of folk: if all of the verse had survived, we might still think that Dunbar and Douglas overtopped the others, but they would not seem such isolated figures. The court provided the impetus for these poets, but the poetry reached an audience far wider than the court. The most distinguishing common feature of these very different poets, I think, is that they were open to more different kinds of influence, had more various literary traditions behind them, and were less swamped by Chaucer and Lydgate, than the English poets. No English poet between Chaucer and Spenser, perhaps, was able to write in so many different ways. The only possible exception is Skelton, and I would like to think that one of his assets was that he was a Northerner. He is sometimes said to have been born in Yorkshire: as far as I know, there is no solid evidence for this, but his family, as the name indicates (Skelton vs. Shilton or Shelton), was presumably from Yorkshire or Cumberland. And poems like *Colkelbie Sow* would seem a very good source for Skeltonics. I might also venture a couple of generalisations: one, that he was perhaps the best English poet between Chaucer and Wyatt partly because he did have such a stylistic range; the other, that the instability and only partial success of many of his poems, as it seems to me, is because he was such an isolated figure, and had such difficulty in finding useful traditions to work in.

The importance of the court to Scots poetry can be seen by looking at what happened after 1513. When James IV died at Flodden in that year, the crown was next to bankrupt, James V was seventeen months old, and the country was in confusion. Nor can James V's reign be counted a success: the kindest thing a recent Scottish historian can say about him is that he 'is not to be judged by Scottish standards. He was, after all, half a Tudor by birth'.[30] It is hardly surprising if some of the poems from this period belong to that least attractive of medieval genres, the poem which is intended to be a complaint but which sounds more like a whine.

James V did, however, have court poets, two of whom provide an instructive contrast. Sir David Lindsay is famous; the other, William Stewart, is chiefly remembered, if at all, and cursed, for his sixty-thousand line metrical translation of Hector Boece's history of Scotland, which was commissioned by James V's mother, for the benefit of

---

30. Gordon Donaldson, *Scotland: James V to James VII* (Edinburgh and London, 1965), 62.

her son.[31] It has not been noticed, apparently, that Stewart is in some sense Dunbar's heir. Twelve poems in the Bannatyne MS and the Maitland Folio MS are ascribed to William Stewart, or simply to Stewart; some of them are addressed to James V. These poems are very similar to Dunbar's in their metrical forms, in their range of styles, and sometimes even in their subjects. They are also far from contemptible: if the other short poems which he presumably wrote had survived, he might now be a poet of some reputation. But he belonged, one suspects, to a poetic tradition which was dying.

Though Sir David Lindsay cannot be done justice to here, one might suggest that, though he is recognisably the heir of Henryson, Dunbar, and Douglas, his poetry seems distinctly more diffuse, or, to put it a different way, some of his poems are extremely agreeable, but light, and in general his passion was directed less towards poetic form than towards social or political goals. Lindsay's own career spans two worlds: he was, first, a court poet, writing ceremonial and occasional verse for James V; he was also a social and religious reformer, writing for a more general audience. And it was the more general audience which was going to control the day: if Lindsay's poetry was much printed and read, not only in the sixteenth century but also in the seventeenth and eighteenth centuries, while the verse of Henryson, Dunbar, and Douglas was largely forgotten, this was more because people liked Lindsay's excellent ideas than because they admired the beauties of his verse.

Some indication of how effectively the reformation put the lid on not only court poetry but on any poetry of a non-utilitarian sort can be seen by going through Aldis's *List of Books Printed in Scotland Before 1700*.[32] Of the first nineteen items – these are works printed up to 1540 – twelve are in vernacular verse, and only one of these is openly didactic. Of the fifty items published between 1550 and 1569, most are religious, and only eight are in vernacular verse: of these five are abusive political broadsides by Robert Sempill; the other three are by Lindsay. Two of these three are *The Monarche*: how this work was read can be seen by an entry in Mr James Melvill's *Diary*. Speaking of the year 1568, when he was twelve, he says: 'I remember therin twa benefites; ane the reiding of the Storie of the Scripture that wintar . . . and of Dauid Lindsayes book, quhilk my eldest sistar, Isbell, wald reid and sing, namelie, concerning the letter iudgment, the peanes of Hell, and the ioyes of Heavin, wherbe sche wald caus me bathe to greit and be glad'.[33]

31. *The Buik of the Croniclis of Scotland or, A Metrical Version of the History of Hector Boece*, ed. William B. Turnbull, Rolls Series (London, 1858).

32. Harry G. Aldis, *A List of Books Printed in Scotland Before 1700* (Edinburgh, 1904; reprinted with additions, 1970).

33. *The Diary of Mr James Melvill 1556–1601*, Bannatyne Club, No. 34 (Edinburgh, 1829), 15.

Later in the century, of course, there would come a time when James VI and I could again afford ingenious lovely things. But such poet-musicians as Alexander Montgomerie and Alexander Scott are outside the scope of this book.

7

The 'Court Style' in Medieval English Architecture: a review

H. M. Colvin

In recent writings on English medieval architecture the concept of a 'court style' has assumed an important place. The expression was, I believe, first used by the late Maurice Hastings in an article published in the *Architectural Review* in 1949,[1] and subsequently in his book on *St. Stephen's Chapel* (1955). Geoffrey Webb took it up in his Pelican volume on British Architecture in the Middle Ages (1956) and it is frequently met with both in Jean Bony's brilliant book on *The English Decorated Style* (1979) and in John Harvey's complementary volume on *The Perpendicular Style* (1978).

Hastings sought to find a 'court style' exemplified in St. Stephen's Chapel (begun in 1292, but not completed until the reign of Edward III), a building in which he also saw the origins of the Perpendicular style, which could thus be connected at its birth with the court. With St. Stephen's Chapel he associated other buildings in London and Westminster, including Old St. Paul's, the Guildhall, and the Grey-friars' and Blackfriars' churches. What these had in common, he said, was the fact that 'they were the work of, or supervised by, the King's masons'. Geoffrey Webb and Jean Bony both use the term freely in connection with such buildings as the Eleanor Crosses, the bishop of Ely's chapel in Holborn and Merton College Chapel, which share common stylistic characteristics. For them, as for John Harvey, the 'court style' is simply the prevailing architectural style favoured by the court, which sets the pace for the rest of the country. 'The royal taste', Harvey says, 'set a fashion which was soon universal and which had a natural growth under a succession of chief architects, the master masons to the Crown, and their pupils'. The fashion which he, like Hastings, is particularly concerned to trace is the one known to us as

1. 'The court style', *Architectural Review*, cv (1949).

'Perpendicular', whose dissemination he attributes to 'the highest levels of the Court', though his account of its genesis differs from (and is to be preferred to) that of Hastings.[2]

As the medieval English kings were, almost without exception, great builders, it is not unreasonable to suppose that, at any given time, there was a recognisable architectural style associated with the royal court. If, however, the idea of a 'court style' is to have any real meaning, it must be demonstrated either that the architectural taste of the court was in advance (or perhaps, since courts are sometimes conservative places, in arrear) of the taste of the country as a whole, or at least that it was marked by some characteristic idiosyncrasy: in short that it had some aesthetic identity that can be singled out by the architectural historian. And it must be shown that that identity was either consciously fostered by the personal interest of the king or his leading courtiers, or else maintained (perhaps less consciously) by a body of architectural designers – master masons and master carpenters – forming part of the royal establishment. There may be some periods when this is self-evidently true: Henry III's leadership in taste, his leaning towards French architectural forms, is well-known: so is the leadership in Tudor domestic architecture given by the palace-building activity of Henry VII and Henry VIII. But in the two intervening centuries the architectural patronage of the court is less easy to define, much less easy to distinguish from that of the secular lords and the great ecclesiastical corporations. The personal initiative of the king is often difficult to discern, partly because the loss of the Privy Seal records has deprived us of much of the documentary evidence upon which to assess it, partly because building, unlike literature or painting, is to some extent a necessity rather than a luxury, and does not necessarily imply any conscious patronage of architecture as an art. Moreover, at a time when every great lord, whether secular or ecclesiastical, was in some sense a courtier, how are we to distinguish between the court and the courtiers?

The stock of houses used by the court was, moreover, being constantly renewed, and as constantly depleted, by confiscation on the one hand and by grant on the other. Of the eighty-odd houses owned by the Crown between 1066 and 1485, almost half had been acquired from a former baronial or ecclesiastical owner by forfeiture, purchase or inheritance, and very few indeed remained continuously in royal occupation from the twelfth century to the fifteenth: effectively only Westminster, Woodstock and Clarendon.[3] So most royal houses must

2. *The Perpendicular Style* (London, 1978), 14, 44.
3. For the relevant details see *The History of the King's Works*, ed. H. M. Colvin, ii (London, 1963), chap. xiv ('The King's Houses 1066–1485', by R. A. Brown and H. M. Colvin).

have been indistinguishable (except, perhaps, by heraldic insignia) from private ones, and only Westminster was normally referred to as a 'palace'.[4] It is above all at Westminster that we must look for signs of a 'court style'. For not only was Westminster the heart of the court, it was the headquarters of the royal works.

Now, as we have seen, the idea of a 'court style' in architecture implies a body of expertise to maintain it, and previous writers have seen the officers of the royal works in this role. It has indeed been natural to suppose that an organisation that in the seventeenth and eighteenth centuries formed the core of the architectural profession in England fulfilled something of the same function in the fourteenth and fifteenth. Such a supposition is explicit in John Harvey's paper 'The medieval office of works', published in 1941,[5] and it has been implicit in much that has been written since. Harvey started with the assumption that there was a central office of works at Westminster from 1256 onwards and that this office was served by a regular succession of master craftsmen holding established posts giving them authority over all the king's works south of Trent. 1256 was the year in which Henry III, dissatisfied with the conduct of his works in the traditional way by sheriffs and other local officials, entrusted them to two experienced craftsmen directly responsible to himself: Master John of Gloucester as master mason and Master Alexander the carpenter for his trade. This was seen by Knoop and Jones as 'marking the beginning of the Office of Works',[6] and Harvey concurred. In a sense this is true, but it must be emphasised that the appointments made in 1256 were personal and perhaps experimental, and did not in fact outlast the lives of the two individuals concerned. Master John died in 1260, Master Alexander probably in 1269, but it is doubtful whether he executed his functions effectively after the débacle of Lewes. Thereafter there were no permanent offices held by chief craftsmen with general authority over the king's works in their respective trades until 1336 – nor were there clerks of the works with similar authority. Master James of St. George's position as 'master of the king's works in Wales' from 1278 to 1307 was unique and personal to himself. When works were ordered at one of the king's houses or castles the appropriate craftsmen were of course engaged, but even at Westminster there was no regular succession of master masons and master carpenters throughout the reigns of Edward I, Edward II and Edward III.[7]

In 1336, however, another set of appointments was made which in

4. Op. cit., i, 120, n. 4.
5. *Journal of the British Archaeological Association*, 3rd. ser. vi (1941).
6. *An Introduction to Freemasonry* (Manchester, 1937), 62.
7. See *History of the King's Works* i, 105–8, 175–8.

the case of the carpenter (but not that of the mason) did prove to be permanent. But the authority of the craftsmen concerned was formally limited to the Tower of London and to the king's castles south of Trent. For some reason no mention was made of Westminster or of the royal manor-houses. It is difficult to follow Harvey in his assertion that these appointments 'mark the definite assumption of control by Edward III over the architectural establishment'.[8] We know too little of the circumstances in which they were made to justify so large a claim. They may just as well be interpreted as an attempt to make better provision for routine maintenance. But for the Black Death, in which both the mason, William of Ramsey, and his successor, John atte Green, perished, it is possible that they would have *created* an architectural establishment, but as it was there was to be no Master Mason of all the king's works for over a quarter of a century, and it was not until 1378 that a properly constituted office of works was established, with a Clerk of the King's Works at its head, in a form that was to last, with modifications, right up to the era of economical reform in the eighteenth century. This, it may be noted, was undoubtedly an administrative measure attributable rather (to adopt modern terminology) to the civil service than to the court, for it was effected during the king's minority, and at a time when no works of any importance were either in progress or in contemplation. In fact there is good reason to attribute it to the initiative of the Treasurer, Thomas Brantingham.[9] It is, therefore, only from the reign of Richard II onwards that there was at Westminster an established corps of craftsmen who may, by the continuity of their offices, and the prestige of their official appointments, have formed the personnel of a 'court school'. In the twelfth and thirteenth centuries, and for much of the fourteenth, craftsmen were recruited as and when they were required, moving from private to royal service and back again as the king's needs and their own ambitions might dictate. Some, like James of St. George and probably Henry 'de Reyns', might be fetched from abroad to serve the king in his works. Others, like John of Gloucester, Robert of Beverley, Michael of Canterbury or William of Ramsey, bore the names of places with famous churches of their own, and are at least as likely to have learned their skill in local ecclesiastical workshops as in the royal yard at Westminster. Once engaged, it is true, some of these men spent most or all of their careers in the king's service. But for others the royal employment was only an incident, however important, in their lives, and the Crown was only one of many possible patrons. The fact that the Crown is also (with one or two exceptions) the only medieval patron of architecture to have preserved the bulk of its administrative records intact means that the careers of many

8. *The Perpendicular Style* (1978), 50.
9. *History of the King's Works* i, 189–90, 210.

medieval masons and carpenters are known only because at some time
or other they served the king. The extent of their work for private
patrons can never be known. In these circumstances it is easy to
exaggerate the role of the Crown as a patron of medieval craftsmen
and to assume that because a man is referred to as 'the king's mason'
or 'the king's carpenter', he was a permanent employee of the court.
Generally the term has no such significance, and only the granting of
a title of office, or the payment of a regular fee, can prove that a
craftsman was permanently retained. Even then, the king might have
no monopoly of his services. In the reign of Edward III the mason
William of Wynford was retained simultaneously by the king and the
dean and chapter of Wells.[10] Henry Yevele had a large and flourishing
architectural practice that was in no way inhibited by his promotion,
in 1378, to be the king's master mason.[11] Yevele, like many other
prominent craftsmen employed by the king, was a citizen of London,
and the proximity of the city must never be forgotten in any attempt
to assess the importance of Westminster as an artistic centre. London
was the home of many of the craftsmen employed by the king at his
palace, and in the later middle ages at least, its gilds and companies
would have formed a framework for their lives which must have been
at least as important as the royal service.[12] Indeed, when Hastings,
and after him Professor Bony, speak of 'the Court Style of London', or
of 'the Court Style based in London', they seem to be recognising that
the court was only the most prestigious of London's customers, and
that what they really mean is 'the metropolitan style', or 'the style in
fashion at London and Westminster'. St. Stephen's Chapel and the
Eleanor Crosses may mark important innovations in Gothic design,
but (as Harvey has shown) it was in the City, at St. Paul's Cathedral,
in the new Chapter House begun in 1332, that William of Ramsey
inaugurated the Perpendicular style four years before he entered the
royal service as master mason at the Tower of London.[13]

Even in Westminster itself the king was not the only patron of
building craftsmen. For the abbey maintained its own works organisation and provided almost continuous employment for masons, some
of whom passed from the service of the monks to that of the crown.[14]

10. J. H. Harvey, *English Mediaeval Architects* (London, 1954), 308.
11. Op. cit., 312–19. Harvey's work on Yevele has been the subject of a critical review
by A. D. McLees in which the limitations of the documentary evidence are stressed in
a salutary manner, though little attention is paid to architectural evidence: *Jnl. of the
British Archaeological Association* 3rd. ser. xxxvi (1973).
12. For the London Masons' Company and its antecedents, see D. Knoop and G. P.
Jones, *The Medieval Mason* (Manchester 1933, reprinted with corrections 1967).
13. J. H. Harvey, 'The origins of the Perpendicular style', in *Studies in Building
History*, ed. E. M. Jope (London, 1961), and *The Perpendicular Style* (1978).
14. Notably William Colchester and William Redman. Redman's father was master
mason to the abbey before him, and William had had twenty years' experience in the
abbey works before he became the king's Master Mason in 1519.

Westminster Abbey was exceptional because the completion of its nave was a major task that went on intermittently from 1376 almost until the dissolution.[15] But other great abbeys were also nurseries of building craftsmen. When Henry VI began to build King's College Chapel it was Reginald Ely, an East Anglian, not a Westminster mason, who received the commission, and Simon Clerk and John Wastell, who continued his work, were both connected with Bury St. Edmund's.[16] At Eton, Henry at first entrusted the works to his Master Mason, Robert Westerley, but by the time the design was completely revised in 1448 Westerley's place at Eton had been taken by John Smyth, a Canterbury mason who had been his second-in-command; and when Smyth became master mason of Westminster Abbey in 1453 the Bury mason Simon Clerk took his place at Eton.[17] Thus the two great royal chapels were effectively designed by masons from outside the office of the king's works, and although in the early sixteenth century there was to be some consultation between the masons employed by the king at Westminster and those at work on the chapel at Cambridge, the building that, as Horace Walpole put it, is 'alone sufficient to ennoble any age', cannot be regarded in any real sense as a product of a 'court school'. If we were to look for a Lancastrian 'court style' the place to find it would have been in Henry V's new house at Sheen, with its satellite religious houses at Sheen and Syon, of which we know little as works of architecture, possibly also in Humphrey, duke of Gloucester's manor-house at Greenwich, of which we know even less. In King's College Chapel only in the portion built by Henry VII does the elaborate heraldic display directly reflect the taste of a later court and remind us that if anyone deserves to be 'taxed with vain expense' in connection with the building of King's College Chapel it is Henry VII rather than the 'royal saint' his kinsman.

It is by no means my purpose to belittle the importance of the king's works in the history of medieval English architecture. That the Crown sought the services of the most eminent architectural designers is unquestionable, and that it provided many of them with exceptional opportunities to display their skill is obvious. Moreover, by the use, from Edward III's time onwards, of its powers of impressment, it sucked workmen from all over the country into its works, giving them involuntary experience of working under its chosen masters, experience which (however unwelcome) must sometimes have transformed the ideas of a provincial mason confronted for the first time with the

15. R. B. Rackham, 'The nave of Westminster', *Proceedings of the British Academy*, iv (1909–10).

16. See their biographies by the late Arthur Oswald in J. H. Harvey's *English Mediaeval Architects* (1954).

17. *History of the King's Works* i, 280, 284.

innovations of a Michael of Canterbury or a William of Ramsey.[18] The importance of impressment as a vehicle of architectural influence may indeed have been considerable. But the concept of a 'court style' remains ill-defined and requires careful handling if it is not to degenerate into a mere cliché devoid of any real historical validity.

How far, then, can the idea of a 'court style' in medieval English architecture be regarded as acceptable? Must we reject it as too imprecise to be worth retaining, or can it be redefined in such a way as to serve a useful historical function? Some examples may help to suggest contexts in which the term can be legitimately employed, others where it can not.

As an example of the former I have already mentioned the building activities of Henry III. By his personal enthusiasm and his employment of a master mason with French experience, he was able to build in Westminster a major exemplar of the French rayonnant style which had its architectural progeny at Hereford, Hailes, Salisbury and elsewhere.[19] Here the aesthetic initiative undoubtedly lay with the court, indeed with the king himself, and as Hailes Abbey was founded by his brother Richard, earl of Cornwall, and as Hereford Cathedral was rebuilt under the auspices of Henry's protégé the Savoyard bishop Peter of Aigueblanche, we can legitimately associate a specific style with Henry III's court. Moreover it was, as we have seen, in Henry's reign that a first attempt was made to establish some degree of central control over all the king's works: an attempt that failed to survive the collapse of Henry's government, but one that may nevertheless serve to underline the connection between a court style and a central works organisation.

Edward I again imported a foreign master to design the castles which were his great architectural achievement, and as the court was for much of his reign on a war footing, the distinctive type of 'concentric' castle associated with Master James of St. George might well be regarded as exemplifying the 'court style' of a warrior king. However it is to the exquisitely elegant Eleanor Crosses, with their complex geometrical forms, including ogee arches (the earliest known) that the term has been more generally applied. They were indeed built by masons who, with one exception, all had previous connections of one kind or another with the royal works,[20] and although none of these masons held any specific office at court, and probably met one another quite as often in the London Guildhall as in the Great Hall at Westminster, their workmanship must have received the approval of the

18. On the exercise of the right of impressment see *History of the King's Works* i, 180–4.
  19. Op. cit., i, 154–5.
  20. Op. cit., i, 483.

queen's executors, one of whom was the chancellor, the discriminating Robert Burnell, bishop of Bath and Wells. To that extent the Eleanor Crosses may be said to represent the taste of Edward I's court in the 1290s, though they may equally well be said to represent the decorative style favoured by the leading London masons of the day.

Edward II is, perhaps, more likely than his father to have consciously fostered a court style, for we have evidence of alterations to a ship (the *Margaret* of Westminster that was to fetch Queen Isabella from France) and the building of a new chamber in the palace being done *per proprium divisamentum Regis*, and his critics' complaints of his addiction to base and mechanical arts take on a new significance when we find that he retained a group of twelve to twenty carpenters who travelled round with him everywhere and were responsible both for the maintenance of the household carts and boats and for repairs and minor alterations to the castles and manor-houses visited by the king. They were paid by the Chamber, and much of their work was done at the group of manors directly administered by that household department, notably Burstwick, Byfleet, Cowick, Easthampstead, Hadleigh and King's Langley. As virtually nothing now remains of any of these buildings we are not in a position to judge to what extent Edward II's houses exemplified a recognisable 'court style'. But the employment, in 1325, of eleven of these *carpentarii de familia regis* on the woodwork of St. Stephen's Chapel does provide a tenuous link between the most important royal work of the 1320s and the inner circle of Edward II's court.[21]

As for St. Stephen's Chapel itself, it was begun by a mason whose background was in Canterbury, and completed by another who had strong connections with Norwich.[22] Though both of them had become established in London before they were engaged on the chapel, they brought with them styles already developed in Kent and East Anglia, a circumstance which serves to demonstrate how far the court was from being the seat of an established 'school' in the reigns of the first two Edwards. Indeed, when Master Michael of Canterbury began work on the chapel in 1292 there was evidently neither workshop nor masons' lodge at Westminster, since one of the first tasks was the erection of these necessary buildings.[23] Moreover from 1297 to 1320 and again from 1325 to 1331 work had to be suspended as a result of national crises, so (although continuity was maintained by the re-employment of Master Michael of Canterbury in 1320, and of Master Thomas of Canterbury – perhaps his son, certainly a relation – in 1331) West-

21. Op. cit., i, 179–80, 506.
22. For Master Michael of Canterbury see Harvey, *English Mediaeval Architects* (1954), 52, and for Master William of Ramsey ibid., 215–28 and also Harvey, *The Perpendicular Style*, 47–8.
23. *History of the King's Works* i, 510.

minster was hardly the home of a continuously active masons' shop throughout the period when it is particularly supposed to have been the centre of diffusion of a 'court style'. It would be nearer the truth to represent St. Stephen's Chapel (as at last structurally completed – though not yet glazed or furnished – in 1348) as the showpiece of the London masons of the early fourteenth century.

Edward III's enormously expensive works at Windsor probably deserve more attention in this context than they have received, but so little has survived the successive remodellings of the seventeenth, eighteenth and nineteenth centuries that it is difficult to characterise the architectural style of his new buildings in the Upper Ward. However the surviving portions of the college of St. George which he built in the Lower Ward show that this was an early – though not the earliest – example of Perpendicular design,[24] and had they survived intact Edward III's works in the Upper Ward might well figure more prominently than they do in the history of English medieval architecture. They do at least illustrate the way in which membership of the court could serve to disseminate new architectural ideas, for it was undoubtedly from Windsor that both New College, Oxford, and Winchester College derived important features of their distinctive planning, and their founder, William of Wykeham, was of course the clerk of Edward III's works at Windsor.[25]

Richard II is well known as the rebuilder of Westminster Hall, whose hammer-beam roof is, of course, one of the supreme achievements of medieval English architecture. So large and ambitious a roof must have had predecessors, and several possible candidates have been put forward. Among them are the roofs (all destroyed) of the great halls of Arundel Castle, Dartington Hall and Kenilworth Castle. As the first was built by Richard's 'governor', the earl of Arundel, the second by his half-brother John Holand, earl of Huntingdon, and the third by his uncle, John of Gaunt, we are perhaps entitled to think of the hammer-beam roof as something particularly favoured by Richard II's court, especially as at Dartington the White Hart badge is prominent in the still surviving porch.[26] Moreover, although we do not know who was employed to build the roofs of the three baronial halls, the master-carpenter at Westminster was Hugh Herland, who had been the king's Master Carpenter since the 1370s. He was the succes-

24. See J. H. Harvey in *Report of the Society of the Friends of St. George's* (Windsor, 1961), 52–5.
25. On the relationship between New College and Winchester College on the one hand and Windsor Castle on the other, see Harvey, *The Perpendicular Style*, 133, and Gervase Jackson-Stops's contribution to *New College, Oxford*, ed. J. Buxton and Penry Williams (Oxford, 1979), 149–64.
26. For the hammer-beam roof see A. Emery, *Dartington Hall* (Oxford, 1970), 237–44.

sor (and almost certainly the son) of William Herland, who had held the same office from 1354 to 1375 in succession to William Hurley, the designer of the octagon at Ely, an earlier tour-de-force of English carpentry. Here in fact we have an authentic case of the cumulative experience of three generations of men closely associated with the royal works and we can legitimately regard the roof of Westminster Hall as a product of the 'court school' of carpenters.

The tradition of expertise in structural and decorative carpentry was, indeed, a marked feature of the royal works in the later middle ages. The timber-framed roof, more or less decorative in character, is as characteristic a feature of English fifteenth-century churches as the stone-vaulted roof is of French ones. It is, therefore, interesting to find that when Henry V decided to build a royal palace at Rouen in 1419, he employed French masons, but English carpenters.[27] Again it is the roof, rather than the masonry, that marks Edward IV's great hall at Eltham as a major architectural achievement. Here pendants have taken the place of angels as the characteristic decoration of the hammer-beams, and, as Geoffrey Webb observed, when the same effect is achieved in stone, as in the Divinity School at Oxford and later in Henry VII's Chapel at Westminster, it is tempting to see it as a case of the masons emulating the carpenters.[28]

This does not exhaust the episodes in the history of the king's works in late medieval England which might deserve consideration in this discussion, but I hope I have said enough to indicate the degree of caution with which a judicious historian, whether of architecture or of culture, should approach the concept of a 'court style'. There are, of course, other, more technical, criteria which also need to be borne in mind. Once it has become institutionalised, a body like the office of the king's works is liable to develop certain tricks of execution that can be recognised as characteristic. Mouldings are a case in point. In recent years a great deal of valuable work has been done on mouldings by John Harvey, Richard Morris and Eileen Roberts, and although much of it has been directed towards the association of specific mouldings with individual masters, rather than with the royal works as such, Morris has identified one moulding whose diffusion can be related to Edward I's works in North Wales.[29] More of this painstaking analysis of mouldings might well help to build up a stylistic identikit of the royal works at particular periods. Meanwhile some characteristic methods of jointing employed by the king's carpenters in the

27. *History of the King's Works* i, 461.

28. *Architecture in Britain: the Middle Ages* (Harmondsworth, 1956), 194, 200.

29. Richard K. Morris, 'The development of later Gothic mouldings in England *c.* 1250–1400', *Architectural History*, xxi (1978), 27.

Tudor period have been observed by Cecil Hewitt.[30] I am not aware that any detailed study has yet been made of the brickwork of the Tudor royal palaces, but (although it was not until 1609 that an office of Master Bricklayer was established) the exact specification of the size of bricks to be used at Woking in 1534[31] might suggest that as early as the reign of Henry VIII the officers of the king's works were moving towards some degree of standardisation. Draughtsmanship is another sphere in which a sense of corporate identity can be expressed. In the eighteenth century, for instance, the Office of Works and the Office of Ordnance each had a characteristic style of draughtsmanship that is quite distinctive. The sum total of medieval or Tudor architectural drawings surviving in English archives is too pitifully small for any such office styles to be distinguished today, but throughout the fifteenth century there was in the office of the Clerk of the King's works at Westminster a 'long oak chest made to keep the patrons [i.e. drawings] and instruments belonging to the chief mason',[32] and if we could inspect its contents it would not be surprising if we could recognise some conventions of presentation, perhaps even some recurrent motifs, as characteristic of the royal works. If we could, we should have gone far towards identifying that 'court style' which it has been the purpose of this paper to confine within somewhat narrower, and, I hope, more intellectually acceptable limits than it has sometimes been allowed to assume in the past.

---

30. In a note appended to Sir W. Addison, *Queen Elizabeth's Hunting Lodge and Epping Forest Museum* (Loughton, 1978).
31. *History of the King's Works* iv, 162.
32. Op. cit., i, 201.

8

Painting and Manuscript Illumination for Royal Patrons in the Later Middle Ages

J. J. G. Alexander

The first part of this paper aims to survey the surviving evidence of royal patronage of painting and manuscript illumination in the fourteenth and fifteenth centuries from Edward III to Henry VII. The paper confines itself, with a few exceptions, to paintings and illuminated manuscripts for which there is good evidence that they were owned or commissioned by English kings or queens or by the heir to the throne. As regards royal patronage of the figural arts in general, I do not propose to discuss sculpture, stained glass, textiles including tapestries, or applied arts including metalwork, though clearly all these were objects of considerable expenditure; and especially the textiles and the precious metalwork were far more important in terms of such expenditure than the painting and manuscript illumination. Probably an even smaller proportion of this material survives than of the painting and illumination, however.

In the second part of the paper some evidence from royal inventories and accounts informing us of objects no longer extant will be examined. I will conclude with some short remarks comparing the position in England with that on the Continent.

The first two manuscripts in this chronological survey were presented to Edward III by Walter de Milmete at some time between the proclamation of Edward as Keeper of the Realm on 26 October 1326 and his father's death in September 1327. These are the Pseudo-Aristotle *Secreta Secretorum* (BL. Add. 47680, formerly at Holkham, pl.1) and Milmete's own compilation *De Nobilitatibus Sapientiis et Prudentiis Regum* (Christ Church, Oxford, E.11).[1] Both manuscripts

1. M. R. James, *The Treatise of Walter de Milmete* (Roxburghe Club, 1913).

are sumptuously decorated with miniatures, borders including very imaginative grotesques, and initials. These were executed by a number of different artists, presumably to speed up the production of the manuscripts. In Milmete's treatise there are a number of pages with drawings which are presumably unfinished and were intended to be painted. Some pages of the Pseudo-Aristotle are also unfinished. Some of these artists' styles relate them to an illuminator named the 'Master of the Queen Mary Psalter after the Psalter (BL. Royal 2 B VII) confiscated by Baldwin Smith, a London customs officer, in 1553 and presented to Queen Mary.[2] It has been suggested often that the Queen Mary Psalter because of the scale and quality of its illumination could have been a royal commission, but there is no positive evidence for this. A third manuscript, a small Psalter (Dr Williams Library, London, Ancient 6) bears the arms of England and of Hainault and was probably therefore made for Philippa of Hainault whom Edward married on 24 January 1328.[3] Its tiny size (10.2 × 7 cm.) relates it to the contemporary French Hours of Jeanne d'Évreux, queen of France, and to the Hours of Queen Catherine, wife of Henry V, mentioned later. The illumination is also by an associate of the Queen Mary Master, and though it is not very lavish, being confined to historiated intials at the liturgical division of the Psalms, it might well have been a wedding gift since the date 1328 would fit perfectly. A more lavishly illuminated larger Psalter (Bodl. MS Douce 131) has a donor portrait on f.110 (pl.2) which, though damaged, may have originally worn the arms of England and France and thus be identifiable with Edward III.[4] The fact that the Virgin holds a sceptre crowned by a bird is possibly confirmatory evidence, as it may be a reference to the English royal sceptre and in particular to the Staff of St. Edward.[5] The same

2. G. F. Warner, *Queen Mary's Psalter* (London, 1912).

3. *English Illuminated Manuscripts 700–1500*, no. 65, Bibliotheque Royale Albert Ier, Brussels, 1973. Exhibition catalogue by C. M. Kauffmann, J. J. G. Alexander.

4. O. Pächt, J. J. G. Alexander, *Illuminated Manuscripts in the Bodleian Library, Oxford* (3 vols), vol. 3, 1973, no. 590, pl. lxii–iii.

5. See H. D. W. Sitwell, M. Holmes, *The English Regalia* (London, 1972), 9–10. Edward I is represented holding such a sceptre in a Memorandum Roll of 1297–8: J. Chancellor, *The Life and Times of Edward I* (London, 1981), pl. p. 137. I am grateful to Dr M. Twycross for drawing my attention to this representation. Various royal sceptres surmounted by a 'merlot', presumably the martlet of Edward the Confessor's mythical arms, are described in the inventories, e.g. three in 1356, Palgrave, 3, 226. It is also no doubt correctly represented by Smith as held by the standing Magus at St. Stephen's, Westminster, as against Topham, see below and pl. 3. Otto III was already represented with a bird-topped sceptre (Munich, Bayr, Staatsbibl., Clm. 4453). In the 12th century a number of English ecclesiastical seals show the Virgin with a bird-topped sceptre. For these see A. Heslop, 'The Virgin Mary's regalia and twelfth-century English seals', in *The Vanishing Past, Studies of Medieval Art, Liturgy and Metrology presented to Christopher Hohler*, eds. A. Borg, A. Martindale, *British Archaeological Reports International Series*, 111 (1981). Clearly the iconography of the English royal sceptres needs more investigation than I have been able to devote to it.

bird-topped staff was carried by the standing Magus in St. Stephen's Chapel according to Smith (pl.3). To these four manuscripts can be added a fifth, another Psalter, also containing the arms of England and of Hainault (BL. Harley 2899).[6] Professor Lucy Freeman Sandler, at present writing a volume on English fourteenth-century illumination, considers this book, which has a Sarum calendar, to be English. Since the royal arms are not quartered with those of France, it seems fairly certain that it dates before January 1340 when Edward assumed the title of king of France.

The major piece of artistic patronage of Edward III was St. Stephen's Chapel, Westminster, whose interior must have been one of the richest decorated interiors of the later middle ages in Europe. The documentation is exceptionally detailed, and we know from it that the painters, of whom Master Hugh of St. Albans was the leader, were able to start work in the completed building in March 1350. It is doubly tragic that the Chapel was destroyed in its upper level in 1834, in that, unlike the Painted Chamber of Henry III in the palace, there are rather few antiquarian drawings of it, and the descriptions of Topham in 1795 and of Smith in 1807 give us little information on the detailed contents of the considerable cycles in the Chapel.[7] It seems these had largely been destroyed already by the late eighteenth century. Some fragments of the wall paintings are preserved in the British Museum.

The Chapel was not very large, measuring 90 × 30 ft., and the paintings were correspondingly small in size. At the east end was shown above and left of the altar the Adoration of the Magi (pl.4) and on the right the Presentation in the Temple and the Adoration of the Shepherds extending round the corner on the south wall. The way Joseph and the Virgin hold up the child's swaddling clothes in the last scene is very unusual. Below, on the left, Edward III kneeling is presented by St. George to the Virgin and Child above. The parallel with the Magi above is obviously intentional. The figures are labelled and behind the king are the Black Prince, the dukes of Clarence, Lancaster and York, and at the end the smaller figure of Thomas of Woodstock, duke of Gloucester, who was born in 1355. All these figures

6. A. G. Watson, *Catalogue of Dated and Datable Manuscripts c. 700–1600 in the Department of Manuscripts, the British Library,* 2 vols (London, 1979), no. 711; Paris, BN, Fr. 571, Brunetto Latini, with English illumination, may perhaps have been made in connection with Edward's marriage to Philippa. I am grateful to Professor Sandler for letting me see the descriptions of these manuscripts from her forthcoming book.

7. J. Topham, *Some account of the Collegiate Chapel of St. Stephen at Westminster* (London, Society of Antiquaries, 1795); J. T. Smith, *Antiquities of Westminster* (London, 1807); E. W. Tristram, *English Wall Painting of the Fourteenth Century* (London, 1955); R. Allen Brown, H. M. Colvin, A. J. Taylor, *The History of the King's Works,* vols 1, 2. *The Middle Ages* (London, 1963), especially 518ff. I am grateful to Mr Nigel Morgan for allowing me to read a paper contributed to a Symposium on St. Stephen's Chapel held in 1976.

were quite small, about a quarter life size, and the standing Magus above measured only two feet (pl.3). To the right Queen Philippa and her daughters were shown, and here the Presentation above is reversed so that Simeon is unusually on the left. The parallelism with the royal figures below is thus again made clear. The standing king (pl.3) carries the bird-topped sceptre which also appears in the Douce Psalter and which may refer to the English royal sceptre. The royal figures kneel in a series of little Gothic arched chambers so that the arrangements resembles the predella of an altarpiece or the figures of mourners on the base of a tomb.

On the long walls of the Chapel below each of the five windows on either side were eight scenes, four above and four below. These are the scenes of which a few from the stories of Job and Tobit originally at the east end to north and south now survive. We do not know the subjects of the stained glass windows, so there seems little chance of reconstructing the whole programme. The Marriage at Cana was also recorded, so we have to think of a cycle of Old and New Testament scenes, probably as extensive as that in the glass of the Ste. Chapelle, Paris. It is interesting to speculate on the origin of the very extensive Old Testament cycles which appear in English fourteenth-century manuscripts such as the Queen Mary Psalter or the Tickhill Psalter. Scenes from Job also appear a little later, in the 1370s, in the Copenhagen and Bodleian Bohun Psalters which I shall mention later. There seem to be resemblances of the scenes of the death of Job's children. Possibly one could make some deductions about other scenes in the Chapel by detailed study of the Bohun manuscripts.

Stylistic sources are also problematic, again because we have so little with which to compare the paintings. In general Italian influence has been detected. This is most obvious in the perspective architectural niches at the east end. On the lower level of the north and south walls were standing angels holding ornate cloths which recall the angels, who, however, do not have cloths, painted by Cimabue in the Upper Church, Assisi, in the 1290s. Perhaps the best parallel to the Chapel as a whole is the almost contemporary work for the Emperor Charles IV at Karlstein, Prague.[8] There is a similar use of gold embossed decoration and also of perspective arcades on a lower level, though without figures. Bohemian painting was strongly influenced by Italian art at this period, but Italian influences reached England by various channels in the early fourteenth century, and another possible source of ideas are the frescoes done for Clement VI in the Papal Palace at

---

8. G. Schmidt, 'Malerei bis 1450', in K. M. Swoboda *ed.*, *Gotik in Böhmen* (Munich, 1969), 194, and *Die Parler und der schöne Stil 1350–1400*, ed. A. Legner (Cologne, 1978), 3, 236ff.

Avignon by Matteo di Giovanetti and assistants from 1343 onwards with striking experiments in illusionistic effects.[9]

The French wars resulted in a number of manuscripts being taken and brought back to England. Thus we know that a *Bible Historiale* (BL Royal 19 D II) was taken at Poitiers in 1356 with King Jean le Bon and bought by the earl of Salisbury for 100 marks.[10] The same note in the manuscript tells us that he gave it to his wife Elizabeth and her executors sold it for £40. Perhaps at the same date a copy of the *Miracles de la Vierge* (Paris, BN, n. acq. fr. 24541) was captured, since a note in the inventory of Charles V says of it 'racheteez des Anglais'.[11] This manuscript was probably made for Jeanne de Bourgogne, wife of Philip VI, and the illumination has been attributed to Jean Pucelle, the leading illuminator working for the French court in the years c. 1320 to his death in 1334.

A copy of Chandos Herald's Life of the Black Prince (University of London Library MS 1) contains the arms of England in the initial at the beginning of the text. D. B. Tyson in her edition of the text does not comment on the arms and she calls the quality of the illumination poor.[12] However, though the illuminator is not particularly gifted, his style clearly relates to that found in English manuscripts of the 1380s–90s, and he may be the same artist who illuminated a manuscript made for Richard II in 1391 to be mentioned shortly. The representation of the Black Prince seems clearly to derive from that we have seen in St. Stephen's Chapel (pl.5). Above him is the Trinity in the iconography known as that of the Throne of Mercy, and this was similarly painted on the tester of the prince's tomb at Canterbury. The prince's devotion to the Trinity is amply documented. Dr Tyson shows that corruptions in the text of this manuscript mean that it derives from the original, written, she argues, in 1385–6, via at least one and probably several intermediaries. The arms and the style would nevertheless seem to me to entitle us to believe this copy was made for Richard II.

The manuscript just referred to, made for Richard II in 1391, is a book of Geomancy (MS Bodley 581).[13] That the king had it made is stated in the text, but there are no royal arms. A second copy (BL

9. E. Castelnuovo, 'Avignone rievocata', *Paragone Arte*, x no. 119 (1959), 41, espec. pl. 7.

10. G. F. Warner, J. P. Wilson, *Catalogue of Western Manuscripts in the Old Royal and King's Collections*, 4 vols (British Museum, 1921), 341–2, pl. 111.

11. Exhibition, *La Librairie de Charles V*, (Bibliothèque Nationale, Paris, 1968), no. 151.

12. D. B. Tyson, 'La vie du Prince Noir by Chandos Herald. Edited from the manuscript in the University of London Library', *Beihefte zur Zeitschrift für Romanische Philologie*, CXLVII (Tübingen, 1975). R. Barber, *Edward, Prince of Wales and Aquitaine* (London, 1978).

13. Pächt, Alexander, op. cit., vol. 3, no. 673. See also above, pp. 41–2.

Royal 12 C V) has a similar set of illustrations, but the quality of illumination is less good and presumably, therefore, the Bodley manuscript is the dedication copy.[14] Also of *c*. 1395 is a copy of Roger Dymmok's *Liber Contra Duodecim Errores*, with the King's portrait crowned and throned and with his arms and badges (Cambridge, Trinity Hall, MS 17).[15]

It is only a presumption that the so-called *Liber Regalis* now at Westminster belonged to Richard. It contains the coronation order with four miniatures of the coronation of a king (f.1v), of a king and queen (f.20), of a queen alone (f.29) and of the funeral of a king (f.33v). A twin manuscript exists at Pamplona in Spain. This omits the miniature of the king and queen crowned, but contains the other three. The Pamplona manuscript unfortunately has no indication of its earlier history. Ullmann has shown that the text in both manuscripts is close to that in the great Missal made for Abbot Nicholas Lytlington of Westminster in 1383–4.[16] It has been suggested that the Westminster manuscript was made for the coronation of Anne of Bohemia in 1382. The Pamplona manuscript derives its pictures from it and is probably of the 1390s.

There can be no reasonable doubt that the copy of Philippe de Mézières' Epistle urging the foundation of a new Crusading Order (BL Royal 20 B VI) is the dedication copy to Richard of 1395–6.[17] The illumination in this is French and shows on folio 2 the presentation scene to the king with, on the preceding verso, the crown of thorns flanked by the crowns of the kings of England and France.

The Wilton Diptych remains still controversial as to purpose, date and origin. J. J. N. Palmer has strongly re-asserted the historical evidence for connecting the making of the Diptych with the projected alliance of Charles VI and Richard II for a crusade and dating it to between May and December 1395, connecting it, as M. V. Clarke already did in 1931, with the Mézières manuscript.[18] On the other

14. Warner, Gilson, op. cit., vol. 2, 23.

15. S. Whittingham, 'The chronology of the portraits of Richard II', *Burlington Mag.*, cxiii (1971), 16, pl. 24.

16. W. Ullmann, *Liber Regie Capelle*, (Henry Bradshaw Society, 92, 1961). For the Pamplona manuscript see F. Idoate, 'Un Ceremonial de coronación de los reyes de Inglaterra', *Hispania Sacra*, vi (1953), 151–80, figs. 1–3. Professor V. J. Scattergood draws my attention to the will of William Kyng, draper, 11 Nov. 1394, who left to the rector and parishioners of St James Garlekhythe his bible in French and another book called *Liber Regalis: Calendar of Wills Proved and Enrolled in the Court of Husting, London, ed.* R. R. Sharpe (London, 1890), ii, 312–3. It was to be chained, and if this was really a Coronation Order it seems a most strange use for it.

17. Warner, Gilson, op. cit., vol. 2, 363, pl. 115. M. V. Clarke, 'The Wilton Diptych', *Burl. Mag.*, lviii (1931), 283–94, pls. IA, B.

18. J. J. N. Palmer, *England, France and Christendom* (London, 1972). J. Harvey, 'The Wilton Diptych, a re-examination', *Archaeologia*, xcviii (1961), 1–28, also argues for a date *c*. 1394–5. G. Henderson, *Gothic* (Harmondsworth, 1967), Appendix I, argues for *c*. 1397.

hand the closest comparisons adduced by Francis Wormald, particularly in Lombard art, but also in French and English art, are of the early fifteenth century.[19] This is a period in which we have a fair number of dated or datable works and which has received a lot of attention from art historians in recent years. Though at other periods it would be foolhardy to assert as it were 'after and not before 1400', Wormald's arguments still command respect, and this is a case where art historical and historical evidence are in conflict. If 1395 is accepted as the date, then certain readjustments in other areas will be necessary. Margaret Rickert also detected differences in style between the two parts of the Diptych. One hypothesis, admittedly far-fetched but nevertheless one that we should perhaps consider, since it would accommodate some of these difficulties, is that the Diptych might be a copy made in the early fifteenth century, perhaps *c.* 1413, the date of the moving of Richard's remains, of a late fourteenth-century picture. It would be accurate in details of fashion and heraldry but updated stylistically.

The painter is likely to be English, on the grounds that the style mixes French and Italian sources and that it does not fit into the much richer surviving context of either French or northern Italian art. The impression is of a less spatial rendering of motifs seen elsewhere and an emphasis on flat highly decorated pattern-making, seen especially in the textiles, which is characteristic of English art of the period. But we have to admit that it is an isolated masterpiece without a context and that unless some unexpected new piece of evidence turns up it is likely to remain a bone of contention.

The damaged wall paintings in the Byward Tower of the Tower of London appear to be of the late fourteenth century and, though undocumented, may be a result of Richard II's patronage.[20] There was also once the polyptych from the Hospice of St. Thomas at Rome with donor portraits of the king and Anne of Bohemia.[21]

As a result of his second marriage to Isabella, daughter of Charles VI, on 12 March 1396 Richard received as a gift from his father-in-law the Belleville Breviary (BN lat 10483–4), a *de luxe* manuscript illuminated, like the *Miracles de la Vierge* discussed earlier, by Jean Pucelle about 1323–6.[22] This would rank as one of the most important surviving fourteenth-century French illuminated manuscripts. As far

19. F. Wormald, 'The Wilton Diptych', *JWCI* xvii (1954), 191–203.
20. Tristram, op. cit., 193–4, pls. 8b, 9a, b, 10.
21. Whittingham, op. cit., 12–13, pl. 17.
22. *Charles V* (op. cit, n. 11), no. 132. The great Bible, BL Royal 1 E IX, Warner, Gilson, op. cit., vol. 1, 21–2, formerly thought to have been made for Richard II, has more recently been dated *c.* 1410 and connected with Herman Scheerre, see Rickert, *Painting in Britain*, 171, 248 n. 83, pls. 170 a, 174. There is no evidence of royal ownership.

as I can see, however, there is no sign of any influence on English art of this remarkable book which only remained a short time in England.

No illuminated manuscript commissioned by Henry IV as king appears to survive. Perhaps the fact that he returned the Belleville Breviary to France as a gift to Jean de Berry means he did not value such things. However both his wives owned important manuscripts. Those belonging to his first wife, Mary Bohun, whom he married in July 1380, presumably passed to Henry on her death in 1394.[23] A Psalter in the Bodleian (MS Auct. D 4 4) seems to have been begun for her father, Humphrey de Bohun, who died in 1373, since he is mentioned in the prayers, and finished for her. There is a portrait of her later in the book. A second Psalter (Copenhagen, Kgl. Bibl. Thott 547) has the arms of Bohun together with those of England and France quarterly and of John of Gaunt, and again there is a portrait of Mary (f.1). A third Psalter owned by Humphrey and again perhaps finished for Mary is in the British Library (Egerton 3277) and a fourth Psalter (Oxford, Exeter College, MS 47) belonging to this group of manuscripts was again made for Humphrey de Bohun, but was later owned by Elizabeth of York, wife of Henry VII. Perhaps it too came into royal possession through Mary Bohun. A fifth Bohun manuscript, now in Cambridge, which belonged to Henry VI will be mentioned later. Henry IV's second wife, Joan, daughter of Charles of Navarre, wrote her name in a fine quality French illuminated Psalter of c.1220–30, which she presumably brought with her from France when she married Henry on 7 February 1403 (John Rylands University Library, Manchester, Latin 22, pl.6).[24]

Henry V is portrayed as still Prince of Wales on f.37 in a copy of Hoccleve's *Regement of Princes* written in 1411–12 (BL Arundel 38, pl.7).[25] The royal arms with label are on f.1 so it seems likely that this is the dedication copy. The illuminator is very close in style to Hermann Scheerre, a German or Netherlandish artist, who signed a Book of Prayers in the British Library and in whose workshop, no doubt in London, a number of important English manuscripts were illuminated, including the Nevill Hours at Berkeley Castle (see frontispiece).[26] Mrs Spriggs in her study of the Hours suggests that the 'Master of the Pentecost' is an associate of Scheerre with a special talent for portraiture, Possibly he rather than Scheerre is the artist

23. M. R. James, E. G. Millar, *The Bohun Manuscripts* (Roxburghe Club, 1936).

24. M. R. James, *A Descriptive Catalogue of the Latin Manuscripts in the John Rylands Library at Manchester* (London, 1921), 64–71, pls. 48–50, reprinted with additional notes by F. Taylor (Munich, 1980).

25. *English Illuminated Manuscripts 700–1500* (op. cit.) no. 78.

26. G. M. Spriggs, 'The Nevill Hours and the school of Herman Scheerre', *JWCI*, xxxvii (1974), 104–30. For Scheerre see also D. H. Turner, 'The Wyndham Payne Crucifixion', *BLJ*, ii (1976), 8–26.

Plate 1. Pseudo-Aristotle, *Secreta Secretorum*. BL MS Additional 47680, folio 17.

Plate 2. Initial 'A' with Edward III (?) kneeling before the Virgin and Child. Oxford, Bodleian Library, MS Douce 131, folio 110.

Plate 3. East end of St. Stephen's Chapel, Westminster. Magus with a bird-topped staff (after Smith).

Plate 4. East end of St. Stephen's Chapel, Westminster. Adoration of the Magi with Edward III and his children kneeling below (after Smith).

Plate 5. The Black Prince kneeling before the Trinity. University of London Library MS 1, folio 3v-4.

Plate 6. Scenes from the life of Christ. John Rylands University
Library, Manchester, MS Latin 22, folio 9.

Plate 7. Hoccleve presenting the book to Henry, Prince of Wales.
BL MS Arundel 38, folio 37.

Plate 8. Annunciation with arms of Queen Catherine. Private Collection, Lancs.

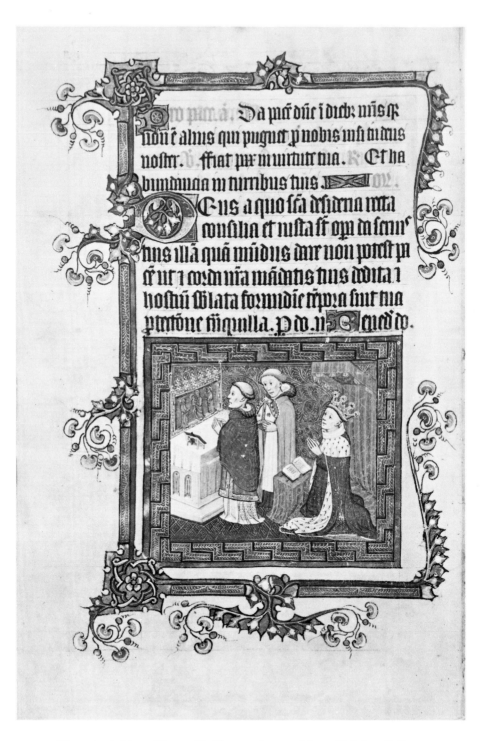

Plate 9. A king, Henry V (?), praying at Mass. Trinity College, Cambridge, MS B 117, folio 31v.

Plate 10. Henry VI adoring Christ as Man of Sorrows. BL MS Cotton Domitian A XVII, folio 98.

Plate 11. Henry VI kneeling at the shrine of St. Edmund. BL MS Harley 2278, folio 4v.

Plate 12. Henry VI and the Knights of the Garter. BL MS Royal 15 E VI, folio 439.

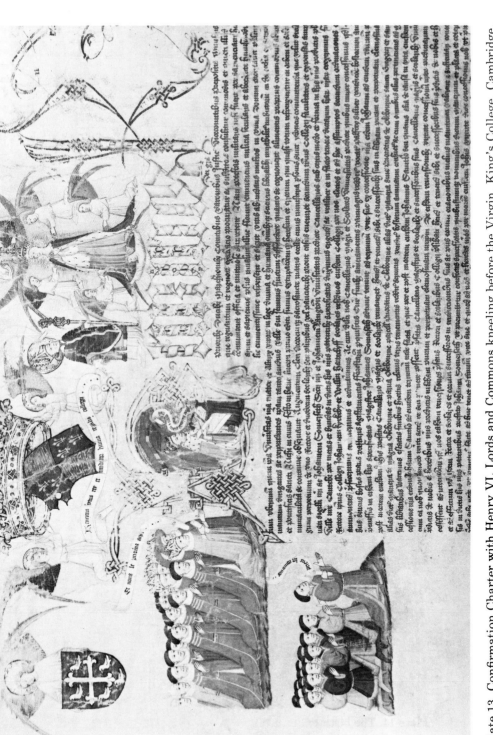

Plate 13. Confirmation Charter with Henry VI, Lords and Commons kneeling before the Virgin. King's College, Cambridge.

Plate 14. The birth of Julius Caesar. BL MS Royal 17 F II, folio 9.

Plate 15. Original illuminated insignia of Henry Bolingbroke? Huntington Library MS EL 26 A 17, folio 1r.

Plate 16. *Above and right:* An anonymous late thirteenth-century song with French text, in conductus style: "Volez oyer le castoy". Corpus Christi College, Cambridge, MS 8, flyleaf.

Volez oyer le castoy,
  Cum Gynot pert sa peyne
D'un' amiette k'il ad
  Ke trop luy est lungtayne?
[Noit] e jour va proyant
  K'ele ne soyt pas vyleine:
    Mes amerousette,
    Douce camousette,
    Kar eez pité
    De voz amourettes!

The principal melody is in the lowest line, and could be sung with two instruments taking the lines above. Otherwise three voices could sing all three lines. The form is that of the Ballade, with a first music section repeated for lines 1 & 2, 3 & 4, and what appears to be a refrain to close, though this is not noted in N. van den Boogard, *Rondeaux et Refrains du XIIe siècle au début du XIVe*, (Paris, 1969). The continental French Motet and Refrain repertory contains many comparable texts, e.g.:

    Ci mi tient maus d'amer!   *Amouretes,*
Haro! je n'i puis durer,   *Amouretes m'ont navré*
  Douce kamusete!   (G. Raynaud, *Recueil de Motets français,*
                      (Paris, 1881), I, 143, 29).

This is not a Motet, however, but is more reminiscent of the polyphonic Rondeau settings of Adam de la Hale (*Lyric Works*, ed. N. Wilkins, CMM 44, American Institute of Musicology, 1967.)

Vo - lez   o - yer   le cas - toy, Cum Gy - not pert sa   pey -
[Would you like to hear the sad story of how Gynot wastes his efforts

- ne D'un' a - mi - et - te k'il ad   Ke trop luy est lung - tay -
for a lady love of his, who keeps herself at too great a distance?

- ne? Noit e   jour va   proy - ant K'e - le   ne soyt pas   vy - lei - ne: *Mes*
Night and day he goes begging her not to be unkind: *My*

a - me - rou - set - te, Dou - ce ca - mou - set - te, Kar
dearest love, with your sweet upturned nose, do

e - ez pi - té De voz a - mou - ret - tes!
have pity on your lover!]

Vpon the mynstraultes / to make chere
And hem / to the feyth / of crist for to bryng
Good chere / for ther in may ye no thyng ere
Els that chere / a meritory cheryng
That is the chese / vn to the conqueryng
Of celestial blisse / that is endlesse
To the whiche your bryng the auctor of pees, Amen.

Explicit liber de principum Regimine.

Verba compilatoris ad librum.

O litel book / whoo zaff the hardynesse
Thi wordes to pronounce / in the presence
Of kynges þmyr / and prynces worthynesse
Seth thow al naked art / of eloquence
And whi approchest thow / his excellence
Vnclothed / saue thi shirtte / bare al soo
I am right sure / his humble pacience
The zeueth hardynesse / for to do soo

But o thyng wot y / welle goo where thow goo
I am so priuee / vn to thi sentence
Thow hast and art / and wilt be euer moo
To his hynesse / of suche reuerolence
That of thow canst nat / to hym bere reuerence
In wordes / thi chierte / nat is the lesse
And if lust be / to his magnificence
So be thi wed / his welwher shal witnesse

Iste liber constat Alueredo Corneburgh De Camera Regis

Plate 17. An inscription in the hand of John Shirley. Huntington Library MS EL 26 A 13, folio 115/120r.

Plate 18. An unidentified *Gloria* in late fourteenth-century French Ars Nova notation. Corpus Christi College, Cambridge, MS 329, binding strips.

of Arundel 38. The workshop was also responsible for the historiated initials, one representing Henry IV, added to the first volume of the Great Cowcher Books of the Duchy of Lancaster, presumably a royal commission, between 1402 and 1407.[27] The Chaucer, *Troilus and Criseyde*, which also has the arms of Henry as Prince of Wales (New York, Morgan Library, M. 817), has a fine historiated initial which, though damaged, appears to be more in the style of the artist Johannes who signed a miniature in the well-known Marco Polo manuscript in the Bodleian Library (MS Bodley 264).[28]

Henry V married Catherine de Valois, daughter of Charles VI of France, on 2 June 1420 and a small Book of Hours bears the arms of England and France modern dimidiated (Private Collection, Lancashire, pl.8).[29] It is of the use of Paris, so must have been made for the queen's personal use. The illumination, comprising fifteen miniatures, is of high quality and certainly English. A larger and more ornate Hours illuminated by the same artist might also have been a royal commission, for though it has no royal arms a miniature on f. 31v shows a king praying at Mass (Cambridge, Trinity College, MS B.117, pl.9).[30] A Bible with important illumination of the early fourteenth-century (Paris, Bibliothèque Mazarine, MS 34) has a fifteenth-century inscription 'Henricus quintus rex Anglie Fundator S.', referring, that is, to the Charterhouse at Sheen which Henry founded in 1414.[31] Two copies of Jean Galopez' French translation of the Pseudo-Bonaventura *Meditationes Vitae Christi* dedicated to Henry V survive, and both have royal arms and presentation miniatures in French style (BL Royal 20 B IV and Cambridge, Corpus Christi College, MS 213).[32]

27. As recognised by A. I. Doyle, M. B. Parkes, 'The production of copies of the *Canterbury Tales* and the *Confessio Amantis* in the early fifteenth century', *Medieval Scribes, Manuscripts and Libraries*, ed. M. B. Parkes, A. G. Watson (London, 1978), 196 n. 82. The initials are reproduced by R. Somerville, *History of the Duchy of Lancaster*, i (London, 1953), pls. ii, vii.

28. C. F. Bühler, 'Notes on the Campsall manuscript of Chaucer's *Troilus and Criseyde*', *Speculum*, xx (1945), 457–60. For the Marco Polo see Pächt, Alexander, op. cit., vol. 3, no. 792, pl. lxxv.

29. Exhibition, *Medieval and Renaissance Treasures in the North West*, Whitworth Art Gallery, 1976, no. 47. A manuscript with private prayers possibly made for Queen Catherine is Bodl. MS Lat. liturg. f. 9, Pächt, Alexander, op.cit., vol. 1, no. 659, 3, no. 870.

30. J. J. G. Alexander, 'William Abell 'Lymour' and 15th-century English illumination', in A. Rosenauer, G. Weber (Eds), *Kunsthistorische Forschungen Otto Pächt zu ehren* (Salzburg, 1972), 169, pl. 6.

31. A. Molinier, *Catalogue des Manuscrits de la Bibliothèque Mazarine I* (Paris, 1885), 12. Prof Lucy Freeman Sandler will include this MS in her volume and I am again grateful to her for letting me see her description.

32. Warner, Gilson, op. cit., vol. 2, 360–1. M. R. James, *A Descriptive Catalogue of the Manuscripts in the Library of Corpus Christi College, Cambridge* (Cambridge, 1910), 510–11. The Cambridge manuscript is reproduced in R. Strong, *Tudor and Jacobean Portraits*, National Portrait Gallery, 2 vols (London, 1969), pl. 280.

Henry's two brothers, John, duke of Bedford and Humphrey, duke of Gloucester, cannot be entirely omitted from this paper. Bedford owned three exceptional illuminated manuscripts, the Hours and Psalter illuminated by the Scheerre atelier after 1415 and perhaps as late as c. 1420–2 (BL Add. 42131), and two manuscripts illuminated by the leading Parisian illuminator of the period who receives his name, the Bedford Master, from this commission, an Hours, use of Sarum, (BL Add. 18850), and a Breviary, also use of Sarum (Paris BN, latin 17294).[33] The Hours was probably executed on the occasion of the duke's marriage to Anne of Burgundy in 1423.

The particular interest of duke Humphrey's library is, of course, in the evidence it provides for his connection with the humanists in Italy.[34] He does not seem to have commissioned any illuminated manuscripts to equal those of his brother, and his Psalter of c. 1440 is by a fairly ordinary English illuminator (BL Royal 2 B I).[35] He did, however, own some splendid earlier books, especially the East Anglian early-fourteenth century Psalter of the St. Omer family, to which he had certain again fairly mediocre additions made (BL Add. 39810).[36] Bedford sent home to his brother a Livy of c. 1370 from the French Royal Library in 1427 (Paris, Bibliothèque Ste. Geneviève, MS 777)[37] and it has been conjectured that a *Songe du Vergier* which had belonged to Charles V reached him in the same way (BL Royal 19 C IV).[38] Bedford bought the French Royal Library in 1425 and its later fate seems somewhat obscure, though it seems to have been brought to Rouen after 1429 and at least part of it came to England later.[39]

The French Bedford Hours was presented by the duchess Anne to Henry VI on Christmas Day 1431, and it was probably then, or slightly

---

33. For Bedford's books see M. J. Barber, 'The books and patronage of learning of a fifteenth-century prince', *The Book Collector*, xii (1963), 308–15. For the Bedford Master see most recently M. Meiss, *The De Levis Hours and the Bedford Workshop* (New Haven, 1972), E. P. Spencer, *The Sobieski Hours* (Roxburge Club, 1977) and J. Backhouse 'A reappraisal of the Bedford hours', *B.L.J.*, vii (1981), 47–69. For Scheerre see above note 26, and for the Bedford Hours especially D. H. Turner, 'The Bedford Hours and Psalter', *Apollo* (June, 1962), 265ff.

34. R. Weiss, *Humanism in England during the fifteenth century* (3rd edn. Oxford, 1967). Exhibition, *Duke Humphrey and English Humanism in the fifteenth century*, (Bodleian Library Oxford, 1970).

35. Warner, Gilson, op. cit., vol. 1, 38. *Duke Humphrey*, (op. cit.) no. 8A. Alexander, 'Abell', op. cit., note 30 above, 169. It is interesting that the miniature of the Duke kneeling before Christ as man of Sorrows is based on the miniature on f.98 of BL Cotton Domitian A XVII, Henry VI's Psalter to be discussed below.

36. M. Rickert, *Painting in Britain. The Middle Ages* (2nd ed., Harmondsworth, 1965), 130–2, 134, 181–3, pls. 133, 182a.

37. *Charles V* (op. cit.) no. 189.

38. *Charles V* (op. cit.), no. 187. F. Avril, *Manuscript Painting at the Court of France. The Fourteenth Century* (New York, 1978), pl. 31.

39. L. Delisle, *Le Cabinet des Manuscrits de la Bibliothèque Nationale* 4 vols. (Paris, 1868–81), 1, 52–3, 3, 313–4, 389.

earlier, that it was further enriched by five full-page miniatures including the well-known portraits of the duke and duchess. Henry VI also owned another fine quality French manuscript, a Psalter (BL Cotton Domitian A XVII, pl.10).[40] A kneeling figure is shown in seven of its miniatures wearing a robe with the royal arms of England. D. H. Turner has pointed out, however, that these are painted over another coat-of-arms and has conjectured that the original owner might have been Louis of France, eldest son of Charles VI, who died in 1415, aged 18. Henry VI is also represented in the copy of John Lydgate's *Life of St. Edmund* (BL Harley 2278, pl.11), made for him to commemorate his visit to Bury St. Edmunds at Christmas 1433.[41] On the occasion of his marriage to Margaret of Anjou in 1445 John Talbot, first earl of Shrewsbury, who had escorted the queen from France, presented her with a very grand large volume of poems and romances (BL Royal 15 E VI, pl.12).[42] A prefatory miniature shows the presentation of the book by Talbot to the queen, who is enthroned holding the king's hand, and on the opposite page is an ornate genealogical tree showing the union of the crowns of England and France in Henry. Below are shown Humphrey, duke of Gloucester and Richard, duke of York. The various artists, employed, no doubt as for the Milmete manuscripts, for the sake of speed, are all French, followers of the Bedford Master, one miniature perhaps even being by the Master himself, but they were working probably in Rouen. At the end of the volume is an interesting miniature of the Chapter of the Order of the Garter. From the royal accounts and inventories it is clear that there were a number of representations of St. George in precious metal. This may represent a cult image, perhaps at Windsor, and it would be interesting to study the iconography of the patron saint of the Order of the Garter.[43]

Henry VI gave manuscripts to various religious houses, for example a Bible (MS Bodley 277)[44] and a *Lives of the Fathers* (Cambridge, King's College, MS 4)[45] donated to the London Charterhouse. His major preoccupation, however, was with his two foundations at Eton

40. D. H. Turner, *Illuminated manuscripts exhibited in the Grenville Library* (British Museum, London, 1967), 44. M. Meiss, *French Painting in the time of Jean de Berry. The Limbourgs and their Contemporaries* (London, 1974), 207f., 375, 405, 467 n. 532, figs. 526, 600.

41. Rickert, op. cit., 183, pl. 183a. BL Cotton Cleopatra A XIII once contained a portrait of Henry VI. See *Schools of illumination. Reproductions from Manuscripts in the British Museum. Part IV* (London, 1922), pl. 15.

42. Warner, Gilson, op. cit., vol. 2, 177–9, pl. 96.

43. W. A. Rees-Jones, *Saint George, the Order of St. George and the Church of St. George at Stamford* (Stamford, 1937), has some valuable material, but does not attempt a full investigation.

44. Pächt, Alexander, op. cit., vol. 3, no. 880.

45. M. R. James, *A Descriptive Catalogue of the Manuscripts other than Oriental in the Library of King's College, Cambridge* (Cambridge, 1895), 8–11.

and Cambridge, and for these the foundation charters of March 1446 survive showing the king, lords and commons kneeling before the Virgin. They have almost identical illumination and the Eton accounts give us the name of the illuminator, William Abell (pl.13).[46] The illuminations in a Bible Concordance (Cambridge, King's College, MS 40) are also attributable to Abell and this manuscript, therefore, is probably a donation from the king.[47] Abell is also the artist of the illuminated prayer roll in which Margaret of Anjou is depicted kneeling (Oxford, Jesus College, MS 124).[48] As was mentioned earlier one of the group of Bohun manuscripts, the Riches Psalter (Cambridge, Fitzwilliam Museum, MS 38 1950), has the royal arms and those of Anjou added as well as those of John Stafford, Chancellor 1432–50, archbishop of Canterbury 1443–52.[49]

Edward IV is the only English king to have had a major collection of illuminated manuscripts which survive. These are now amongst the Royal manuscripts given to the nation by George III and now in the British Library. Surprisingly only one manuscript, so far as I know, has gone astray, a Josephus now in the Soane Museum, London (MS 1), though others may have been destroyed.[50] Warner and Gilson list over fifty volumes, some of them like the king's Froissart being a single work in several volumes, others containing a number of different texts. There are a few earlier manuscripts, but the bulk are large vellum copies of historical or literary works produced in Flanders and presumably commissioned specially for Edward. Some have dates or place of production, for example a *Faits des Romains* (Royal 17 F II), made at Bruges in 1479 with a large miniature showing the Birth of Julius Caesar (pl.14) and thirty-nine smaller miniatures. Many have the royal arms, the arms of Edward's two eldest sons and the Yorkist badges. Not all the manuscripts in Warner and Gilson's list contain royal arms, however, so there may be some manuscripts which were not Edward's, and conversely others may have to be added to the list. There is no early catalogue of the manuscripts (though they are mostly identifiable in the catalogue of books at Richmond Palace in 1535) and apparently no records of payments for them. A detailed palaeographical, codicological and art-historical examination might well establish

46. Alexander, 'Abell' op. cit., note 30 above, 167, fig. 2.

47. Ibid., 167.

48. Ibid., 167.

49. James, Millar, op.cit. Exhibition, *Illuminated Manuscripts in the Fitzwilliam Museum, Cambridge* (Cambridge, 1966), no. 56.

50. E. G. Millar, 'Les Manuscrits à peintures du Sir John Soane's Museum et du Royal College of Physicians de Londres', *Société française de reproductions de manuscrits à peintures*, iv (1914–20), 89–94, pl. xxviii. For this and Edward's other manuscripts see M. Kekewich, 'Edward IV, William Caxton and literary patronage in Yorkist England', *MLR*, lxvi (1971), 481–7. Warner and Gilson give a list of manuscripts which they consider were made for Edward in Flanders in volume 1, pp. xi–xii.

dates, place of production and workshops responsible for many of these manuscripts. This has been done recently, for instance, by M. A. Derolez for the library of Raphael de Marcatellis, Abbot of St. Bavon, Ghent, who died in 1536 and who owned a rather similar collection of *de luxe* manuscripts.[51] It has been suggested that Edward's friendship with Louis de Gruythuyse, with whom he stayed in exile in 1470–1 and whom he created earl of Winchester, was partly responsible for his acquisition of these manuscripts, since Gruythuyse himself had a splendid library. The Soane Museum Josephus originally belonged to Gruythuyse and his arms are overpainted with those of the king, so it may have been a gift. However, such dates as there are in the books themselves, mostly 1479 and 1480, perhaps suggest that Edward acquired the majority of them over a short period and together. A wardrobe account of 1480 lists payments for the binding of a number of them by Pierre Baudwyn.[52] Art historians have in the past been rather dismissive of the illuminators responsible, though Winkler baptized one of them the 'Master of Edward IV'.[53] Recently Professor Otto Pächt has shown the importance of Flemish illuminators of this group for the history of landscape painting, however.[54]

One English manuscript surviving, made for Edward IV, is copied from Caxton's edition of November 1477 of earl Rivers' translation of the *Dicts and Sayings of the Philosophers* (London, Lambeth Palace, MS 265).[55] The prefatory miniature shows the earl presenting the manuscript to the king. Two illuminated manuscripts owned by Richard III are known, a Book of Hours of *c.* 1420–40 of rather mediocre quality which may have come to him from his wife, Anne Neville,[56] and a Vegetius in English (BL Royal 18 A XII).[57] It is also possible that he owned a late fourteenth-century *Chronique de S. Denis* with two hundred and nine miniatures by a French artist, since it has an apparently autograph inscription 'Richard Gloucestre' (BL Royal 20 C VII).[58]

With Henry VII we come to the first recorded officer of the library, Quentin Poulet, a Fleming from Lille to whom the king granted as keeper of the king's library an annuity of ten marks out of the customs

51. A. Derolez, *The Library of Raphael de Marcatellis* (Ghent, 1979).

52. BL Harley 4780. See A. R. Myers, *The Household of Edward IV* (Manchester, 1959).

53. F. Winckler, *Die Flämische Buchmalerei* (Leipzig, 1925, repr. Amsterdam, 1978), 137.

54. O. Pächt, 'La Terre de Flandre', *Pantheon*, xxxvi (1978), 3–16.

55. M. R. James, *A Descriptive Catalogue of the Manuscripts in the Library of Lambeth Palace. The medieval manuscripts* (Cambridge, 1932), 412–14. Strong, op. cit., pl. 162.

56. James, op. cit, note 55 above, 650–4. *Richard III*, National Portrait Gallery (London, 1973), exhibition catalogue by P. Tudor-Craig, no. 51, pls. 12–13.

57. Warner, Gilson, op. cit., vol. 2, 267. *Richard III* (op. cit.), no. 131, pls. 10–11.

58. Warner, Gilson, op. cit., vol. 2, 372–3.

of the port of Bristol in 1492.[59] Warner and Gilson consider that a number of manuscripts containing a monogram 'HR' are likely to have been Henry VII's rather than Henry VIII's. Henry VII may have owned the fine French Book of Hours by the Master of Sir John Fastolf (Bodleian Library, MS Auct. D. inf. 2.11) traditionally known as the Breviary of Henry VII, though it has no conclusive evidence of his ownership.[60] An important English Book of Hours of *c.* 1420 belonged to Queen Elizabeth of York (BL Additional 50001),[61] and a Flemish late fifteenth-century Book of Hours of Sarum Use (Chatsworth, Devonshire Collection) has a touching inscription from the king to his daughter Margaret: 'Remember your kind and loving father in your good prayers Henry'.[62]

Independent portrait panels of the English kings should also be included in this survey as evidence of their patronage. These usually survive in a number of versions, which have been recorded and their iconography studied by Dr Strong. The earliest is the large portrait of Richard II in Westminster Abbey.[63] No authentic portrait type appears to survive for Henry IV, but for Henry V a number of copies survive of a profile portrait. Strong considers the best to be that in the Royal Collection which he dates to the late fifteenth century.[64] He accounts for the profile position and the hands in prayer by deriving them from a lost votive picture. However, the portraits of Jean le Bon of France (died 1364) and of Louis of Anjou (*c.* 1415) provide good parallels for independent profile portraits, and it would be perfectly reasonable to posit a lost original done in Paris *c.* 1420 to which the hands might have been added in later versions.[65] Strong also considers the Henry VI portraits, of which there are again many versions, one at Windsor being the best, to be based on an *ad vivum* likeness made in the 1450s.[66] The earliest and best portrait of Edward IV is that in the Royal Collection which Strong considers to be an *ad vivum* original, and this type was engraved as early as 1472.[67] The earliest version of the Richard III portrait is that in the Royal Collection of the late fifteenth century, possible contemporary or else a copy of an *ad vivum* likeness.[68] The painting of Henry VI made by the German painter Michael Sittow in 1505 in connection with marriage negotiations with

59. Ibid., vol. 1, xiii.
60. Pächt, Alexander, op. cit., vol. 1, no. 670, pl. liii.
61. Rickert, op. cit., 174–6, pl. 177.
62. *Medieval Treasures*, (op. cit.), no. 55.
63. Rickert, op. cit., 160–1, pl. 162. Strong, op.cit. 261, pl. 508.
64. Strong, op. cit., 144–5, pl. 282.
65. M. Meiss, *French Painting in the Time of Jean de Berry. The late XIV century and the patronage of the Duke* (London, 1967), pls. 490, 505–8.
66. Strong, op. cit., 145–8, pl. 283. *Richard III*, (op. cit.), p. 4, pl. 43.
67. Strong, 87, pl. 161. *Richard III*, p. 8, pl. 40.
68. Strong, 262–4, pl. 515. *Richard III*, p. 44, pl. 26.

the Emperor Maximilian is in the National Portrait Gallery, and another portrait type is known through copies.[69]

Turning now from what survives to what is described in accounts and inventories, we may gain some impression of how much has been lost. No doubt much unpublished material survives to be discovered in the Public Record Office and elsewhere, and moreover the incompleteness of the records also requires us to be cautious in interpreting the evidence.

It seems that Richard II is the first to employ someone with the title of 'king's painter'.[70] This was Gilbert Prince, who is paid £44 in 1377, the first year of the reign, for ornamenting Edward III's bed curtains and for making four small banners of minstrels trumpets. Much of the work done was in connection with tournaments, devices on banners, etc., but some of the sums paid are very considerable, for instance £650 13s 7½d in 1392–3, 'for the performance of divers works of his art'. Gilbert appears frequently in the accounts according to Tout and was succeeded at the end of the reign by Thomas Lytlington, alias Prince, painter and citizen of London, who accompanied the king to Ireland in 1399.[71] In 1394 Thomas was paid £289 16s 6d for painting five chambers, two small chapels and one great chapel with stags with gilded antlers at the manor at Windsor.[72] Thomas did not provide the covering for the tomb of Queen Anne, however. This was done in 1395 by John Haxey, who also painted an image to correspond with another of the king placed opposite in the choir of the Abbey.[73] The 'image' seems to me likely to have been a statue representing the queen rather than a portrait painting. Richard II also had his own embroiderer in 1382, John of Cologne, who may either have been his own designer or had designs made for him by the king's painter.[74]

Under Henry IV, Thomas Gloucester petitioned for the office of king's painter which he held until some time after 1413.[75] John Stratford is recorded between 1453 and 1473[76] and John Serle from 1474 to 1505.[77] So far as I know nothing has ever been attributed to any of these painters.

69. Strong, 149–52, pls. 290, 293.

70. Colvin *et al.*, op. cit., 227, 1052. F. Devon, *Issues of the Exchequer*, (London, 1837), 207, 252, 258. T. F. Tout, *Chapters in Administrative History of Medieval England: the Wardrobe, the Chamber and the small seals* (6 vols) (Manchester, 1920–30), vol. 4, 391, n. 8.

71. Colvin *et al.*, op. cit., 227. Tout, op. cit., vol. 4, 391, n. 8.

72. Colvin *et al.*, op. cit., 1007–8.

73. Devon, op. cit., 262.

74. Tout, op. cit., vol. 4, 390. The king's tailor was responsible for binding books. Thus Walter Ralphs used gold cloth for binding five books of devotion. Ibid. 388, n. 6.

75. Colvin *et al.*, op. cit., 1052.

76. Ibid., 1052.

77. Ibid., 1052.

A number of panels are referred to in the king's chapels in the time of Henry III, the word being 'tabulae'. Some of these may have been altar frontals, but others were altarpieces proper which are only just beginning to appear in Italy at this date.[78] In 1412 Henry IV was given a picture in a travelling case by Jean sans Peur, duke of Burgundy, but unfortunately neither the artist's name nor the subject are recorded.[79] In 1424–5 a Flemish wooden gilded panel of Ss. Mary and John was bought for the chapel of Carmarthen Castle.[80] As regards the decorations of the kings' palaces and castles, a remarkably large proportion of the wall paintings recorded were executed for Henry III and thus fall outside the period of this survey. Clearly no succeeding king was anything like as active, Edward III's work on St. Stephen's Chapel being the only exception and standing out the more because of this. Remarking on this, H. M. Colvin says that the lack of reference to wall paintings in the fifteenth century is probably caused by the fact that by this time tapestries were commonly used as wall coverings.

In considering evidence for manuscripts owned by the kings of England, my concern is primarily with texts likely to have been illuminated. However, in such references as I have found there is rarely any mention of illumination. Service books we know by experience of surviving books are those most likely to be illuminated. A number of romances which are referred to are also likely to have been illustrated. The values attached to books are some indication, but a high value may reflect the value of the binding rather than of the book itself.

There appears to have been no regular library or office of librarian as such until Henry VII, as we have seen. Under Henry III Ralph Dunion, the keeper of the king's wardrobe, is referred to as 'custos librorum'.[81] In 1251–2 he was also responsible for giving colours to Master William for wall paintings. Presumably the books owned by succeeding kings continued to be the responsibility of the wardrobe, but I have come across no later references to a 'custos librorum'. In 1323/4 Bishop Stapleton's calendar lists the books kept in a green chest (*in coffro viridi*).[82] The list includes a book *de regimine principum*.

In 1358 a detailed inventory of the possessions of Edward II's queen, Isabella, lists a number of service books from her chapel (*de capella*).[83]

78. Particularly interesting in connection with the Wilton Diptych is a reference to a Diptych for St. Stephen's Chapel in the King's Palace at Guildford, Surrey, showing the Crucifixion and Christ in Majesty 'eisdem tabulis conjungendis ita quod claudi et apiriri possint'. Colvin *et al.*, op. cit., 951–2.

79. L. E. S. de Laborde, *Les ducs de Bourgogne* (Paris, 1849), 1, 45.

80. Colvin *et al.*, op. cit., 601.

81. Tout, op. cit., vol. 1, 256 n. 1. Smith, op. cit. (note 7 above), 57. Tristram, op. cit., 575.

82. F. Palgrave, *The Ancient Kalendars and Inventories of the Treasury of His Majesty's Exchequer* (3 vols) (London, 1836), vol. 1, 106.

83. Ibid., vol. 3, 239, 244.

There were three missals, a portiforium (now more commonly referred to as a breviary), two antiphonals, two graduals, and a martyrology. The prices attached to these books are listed. There were some other books, including some romances, one of which, 'Perceval and Gawain', later belonged to Richard II. The king would obviously always have had his own *capella* service books,[84] and there would also have been service books for the royal chapels, usually one for the queen as well as one for the king, in the royal castles. Thus the service books bought for the chapel at Nottingham Castle in 1251 were listed.[85]

In 1359 Edward III gave the abbot of the Cistercian house of St Mary Graces, London £6 13s 4d for a bible which the Abbot had bought for his house.[86] In 1335 he bought a book of romance from Isabella de Lancaster, a nun at Amesbury, Wiltshire, for one hundred marks.[87] In 1365 he paid the two sheriffs of London for a bible and a breviary, a Juvenal and three books of Romances which had belonged to Henry of Tatton.[88] In 1367–8 he bought certain missals and breviaries for £74.[89] Tout also records that Isabella of Hainault had her own illuminator who was paid along with her fiddler and her midwife.[90]

The Black Prince bequeathed a missal and breviary for use in his chantry at Canterbury.[91] A list of fourteen manuscripts entered on a memorandum roll of 1384/5 has recently been shown to refer in all probability to books inherited by Richard II from his grandfather, of which he probably only retained a bible in French, a *Romance of the Rose* and the 'Perceval and Gawain' which had belonged probably to Queen Isabella.[92] Expenses in connection with the binding of nineteen books are recorded from 1385–8.[93] In 1395 Richard II sent Pope Urban VI a book of the Miracles of Edward II, but whether this was illustrated or not is not recorded.[94] Philip the Bold of Burgundy is said to have made a gift of books to Richard and his uncles in 1389.[95] The

---

84. For capella books see R. Branner, 'The Ste-Chapelle and the *Capella Regis* in the Thirteenth Century', *Gesta* x (1971), 19–22.

85. Colvin *et al.*, op. cit., 760.

86. Devon, op. cit., 171.

87. Ibid., 144.

88. Ibid., 187.

89. Tout, op. cit., vol. 4, 327, 347.

90. Ibid., vol. 5, 255, without a precise reference. I have looked at John de Eston's accounts (P.R.O. E 101/387 (22–3), 388 (7), 389 (12, 7) but not found these particular payments, so do not know if a name is given.

91. J. Nichols, *A Collection of all the Wills . . . of the Kings and Queens of England* (London, 1780), 71.

92. Devon, op. cit., 213. E. Rickert, 'King Richard II's books', *The Library*, fourth series, xiii (1932–3), 144–7. R. F. Green, 'King Richard II's Books Revisited', *The Library*, xxxi (1976), 235–9. See also above, pp. 32–3.

93. M. V. Clarke, *Fourteenth-Century Studies* (Oxford, 1937), 122.

94. Devon, op. cit., 259.

95. T. Borenius, E. W. Tristram, *English Medieval Painting* (London, 1927, repr. New York, 1976), 27, but no proper reference is given.

copy of his poems which Froissart presented to Richard II was illustrated.[96]

Henry IV apparently gave Isabella, Richard's queen, a missal and his three sons Thomas, John and Humphrey and his daughter Blanche each a missal, all these discharged from St. Stephen's Chapel, Westminster in 1403.[97] In the same year he pardoned John Pykeworth, chaplain, who had killed Gilbert Tailour of Bristol and stolen a gradual worth 6s 8d from St. Stephen's, Westminster and a manual worth 7s from Littlehenney, Essex.[98]

In 1419 Henry V gave five books received the year before by the Deputy Treasurer to the Charterhouse he had founded in 1414 at Sheen, Surrey.[99] These included a Bible, possibly that now in the Bibliothèque Mazarine mentioned earlier. In 1422 he commissioned a bible from John Hethe, a clerk of the Privy Seal.[100] Payments for binding books for Henry are also recorded.[101] Some of the books captured in France, the French Chronicles, he retained for himself after the capture of Caen in 1417, and the one hundred and ten volumes taken at Meaux in 1422, many of them law books, will have been illuminated.[102] In 1421 John Robard of London, scrivener, was paid for writing twelve books on hunting.[103] Could these perhaps have been copies of Edward of York's translation of Gaston Febus' hunting book, which had been dedicated to Henry? It seems likely that dedication copies of this text and also of Lydgate's *Troy Book* dedicated to the king will have once existed, and possibly further study of later illuminated copies would give an indication of what they were like.[104] Henry's two wills, that of 1415[105] and that recently discovered of 1421,[106] both mention a number of books, some of the bequests being repeated in the second will. For example Henry Beaufort, bishop of Winchester, and Thomas Langley, bishop of Durham, were to have

96. Froissart's account is quoted by R. F. Green, *Poets and Princepleasers. Literature and the English Court in the late Middle Ages* (Toronto, 1980), 64.

97. Smith, op. cit., 165.

98. *Calendar of the Patent Rolls, Henry IV, II, A.D. 1401–5* (London, 1905), 221.

99. Palgrave, op. cit., vol. 2, 97.

100. Devon, op. cit., 372.

101. K. H. Vickers, *Humphrey Duke of Gloucester* (London, 1907), 343.

102. *The first English Life of Henry V*, ed. C. L. Kingsford (Oxford, 1911), 92. K. B. McFarlane, *Lancastrian Kings and Lollard Knights* (Oxford, 1972) Appendix C.

103. Devon, op. cit., 368.

104. For Lydgate's see Bodl. MSS Digby 232 and Rawl. C 446, Pächt, Alexander, op. cit., vol. 3, nos. 868, 943, pls. lxxxiii, xc, and Manchester, John Rylands University Library, English 1, which all have presentation miniatures. For the *Master of Game* see Bodl. MS Bodley 546 and Douce 335, Pächt, Alexander, op. cit., vol. 3, nos. 923, 1000, pl. lxxxviii, xciii, and W. A. and F. Baillie-Grohmann, eds., *The Master of Game by Edward, second duke of York* (London, 1904).

105. *Foedera*, ix, 292.

106. P. and F. Strong, 'The last will and codicils of Henry V', *EHR*, xcvi (1981), 93, 100. For Frampton cf. Doyle, Parkes, cit. note 27, p. 192.

respectively a beautiful breviary in two volumes written by John Frampton, and a missal and a breviary. There were also bequests to the king's secretary, almoner, doctor and chaplains of a missal or breviary, each to be worth £10. This in itself suggests a considerable collection of liturgical books at the king's disposal. Other books were to go to the Charterhouse at Sheen and the Bridgettines at Syon, with the remainder to his son. In 1415 he gave some of a considerable amount of books confiscated from the executed Lord Scrope of Masham to the canons at Windsor.[107] These were four antiphonals, four graduals, a lectionary in two volumes and an ordinal. After Henry's death the countess of Westmoreland asked duke Humphrey to procure for her the return of a Chronicles of Jerusalem which the king had borrowed and never returned.[108]

Henry VI gave the majority, seventy-seven out of the one hundred and ten, of the volumes captured by his father at Meaux to King's College, Cambridge. In 1435 the Treasurer, Lord Cromwell, passed on two volumes of Chronicles from this collection to Richard Caudrey, Master of the College, and these were followed by other books of civil law, etc. The gift was confirmed in perpetuity in 1440.[109] In 1434 two books, a Hegesippus and a *Liber de observantia Papae* were lent to William Toly, secretary of Cardinal Beaufort.[110] In 1440 Henry VI gave twenty-seven books to All Souls College, Oxford, nine on canon and civil law, seventeen on theology and one on philosophy.[111] The king also seems to have intended to give duke Humphrey's books after his death in 1447 to King's College. In 1450 among the goods confiscated from Jack Cade was a primer with silver clasps.[112]

There is sufficient evidence here, though it is scattered and sporadic, to prove that a very great deal of the evidence as to royal artistic patronage in this period is lost. The service books and paintings from the royal chapels must have been numerous and presumably particularly vulnerable at the Reformation and under the Commonwealth, though in this connection it is noteworthy that the St. Stephen's Chapel paintings were not destroyed. In 1397 the inventory of Thomas of Woodstock's goods at Pleshey lists eighty-four volumes of Romances

107. C. L. Kingsford, 'Two forfeitures in the year of Agincourt', *Arch* 2nd series, lxx (1918–20), 82–3. M. F. Bond, *The Inventories of St George's Chapel, Windsor Castle, 1384–1667* (Windsor, 1947), 123.
108. *Foedera*, x, 317.
109. Palgrave, vol. 2, 154. McFarlane, above. Only one MS from the college's inventory of 1452 survives according to M. R. James, op. cit. (n. 45 above). The King also left £200 in his will to the College to buy books: Nichols, op. cit., 309.
110. Palgrave, op. cit., vol. 2,152.
111. R. Weiss, 'Henry VI and the Library of All Souls College', *EHR*, lvii (1942), 102–6.
112. Palgrave, op. cit., vol. 2,220.

and Histories ranging in value from 40s to 6d.[113] One of these is described as 'une large livre en Fraunceis bien enluminez de la Rymance d'Alexandre' valued at 16s 8d. It has been suggested that this may have been the most lavishly decorated of all Alexander books, written and illuminated perhaps at Bruges between 1338 and 1344 (Bodleian Library, MS Bodley 264).[114] In addition there were forty books listed as *pro capella*, these ranging in value from £10 to 20d. The king is surely likely to have owned books on a comparable scale, and the will of Henry V shows that he had considerable numbers of books to bequeath. Nevertheless if we compare both the surviving material and the literary records on the Continent, especially for the kings of France, but also for the dukes of Burgundy, Berry and Anjou, artistic patronage by the kings of England would appear to have been on a considerably smaller scale. Charles V owned about one thousand manuscripts of which about one hundred have been identified as surviving, Philip the Bold of Burgundy about two hundred, Berry about three hundred of which about ninety to one hundred have been identified.[115] Charles V had a librarian, Gilles Mallet, and his books were kept in a special room at the Louvre assigned for the purpose in 1367. Other Continental patrons of the later fourteenth and early fifteenth centuries, the Visconti dukes of Milan,[116] the Emperor Charles IV in Prague and his son King Wencelas of Bohemia[117] were similarly active as patrons of both painters and illuminators. In the fifteenth century the discrepancy is perhaps even more obvious if one compares Charles VII of France, Philip the Good[118] and Charles the Bold of Burgundy to Henry VI and Edward IV. In Italy there are the great collections and libraries of the kings of Naples, the dukes of Milan, the Gonzaga at Mantua, Federigo of Urbino, the Medici at Florence and the Popes, especially Pius II and Sixtus IV.[119]

If, with all the necessary reservations as to the incompleteness of the evidence, it nevertheless seems that the kings of England were not as active as their Continental counterparts, especially the kings of France, then different explanations and combinations of factors suggest themselves. Comparative lack of financial resources is one

113. Viscount Dillon, 'Inventory of the Goods and Chattels belonging to Thomas, Duke of Gloucester', *Archaeological Journal*, liv (1897), 290.

114. Pächt, Alexander, op. cit., vol. 1, no. 297, pl. xxiii.

115. Meiss, op. cit. (note 65 above) 287.

116. E. Pellegrin, *La Bibliothèque des Visconti et des Sforza, ducs de Milan, au XVe siècle* (Paris, 1955) and *Supplément* (Florence, 1969).

117. J. Krasa, *Die Handschriften König Wenzels IV* (Vienna, 1971). Swoboda, *cit.* note 8 above.

118. Exhibition, *Le siècle d'or de la miniature flamande. Le mécenat de Philippe le Bon*, Brussels, 1959.

119. For literature see J. J. G. Alexander, *Italian Renaissance Illuminations* (New York, 1977).

possible explanation. It would also be necessary to take into account the personal characteristics of the various kings. No English king, not even Henry VI, seems to have had the interest in books and learning of Charles V. The fact that in Paris court and university existed in the same city was bound to make Paris a great centre of book production. Another factor would be the English monarchy's view of its role and the image it wished to present. Was the French kings' view of his position and status different at any particular moment? The duke of Bedford and Henry VI seem to acquire *de luxe* manuscripts precisely at the moment of the union of the two crowns and Bedford's purchase of the French royal library may have been due not so much to a love of learning and books for their own sake as in order to acquire a prestige possession of the French crown. As the union collapsed the library was allowed to be dispersed.

With regard to the artistic evidence, two last points should be made. First, at any particular period, reiterating all the necessary *caveats* as to survival, the finest quality surviving works are not those associated with royalty. In the first half of the fourteenth century the outstanding English illuminated manuscripts are mostly made for East Anglian patrons, whether monastic, secular clergy or local nobility and gentry. The Lutrell Psalter (BL Add. 42130) is the type *par excellence* of these luxurious books.[120] In the late fourteenth century a new style is imported from the Netherlands which revives English book painting, but even though the Scheerre atelier works for Bedford and possibly for Henry IV and Henry V (depending that is, on whether they were directly involved in the choice of illumination for the Cowcher Books and the Hoccleve respectively), there is no positive evidence that these foreign craftsmen came in response to royal initiative in the first place. Henry VI employed William Abell, an artist of no great gifts, who worked mainly for patrons in the City of London. Henry VI's best manuscripts were second-hand like his Psalter or gifts like the Talbot Romances.

Many of the best manuscripts owned by the kings of England were French and came by gift or marriage. Edward IV spent a great deal of money on his books from Flanders, but he certainly did not secure the best artists available, as did his sister Margaret of York. Two of the outstanding Flemish Books of Hours of this period were owned by Lord Hastings, though it is possible that one may have been intended originally for either Edward IV or Edward V (Madrid, Museo Lazaro Galdiano, and BL Add. 54782).[121] And the best English work of this period *c.* 1480, is the so-called Beauchamp Pageants, a manuscript

---

120. Rickert, op. cit. (n. 36 above), 133–4.
121. G. I. Lieftinck, *Boekverluchters uit de omgeving van Maria van Bourgondie c. 1475–c. 1485* (Brussels, 1969), 126ff., 178ff. Exh., *Richard III*, no. 1, pls. 14–6.

with drawings of the life of Richard Beauchamp, earl of Warwick, who died in 1439 (BL Cotton Julius E IV).[122] On surviving evidence at least the king did not even get the best.

Secondly, if we take a European view, English painting has been at various periods in the Middle Ages an innovative, imaginative and influential as that of other European countries, for example in the Anglo-Saxon period of the tenth to eleventh centures, or again in the twelfth century. English book painting, like English architecture, was also of outstanding quality and creativity in the late thirteenth and early fourteenth century, the period of so-called Decorated architecture. It is significant that a number of fine manuscripts produced at the end of the thirteenth century are for Edward I and his brother Edmund of Cornwall, and these may have contributed to the early stages of this flowering.[123] But thereafter in the later fourteenth and the fifteenth centuries it would be hard to argue that English art was of European importance. The foreign artists or works of art that come to England come to fill a vacuum. Scheerre is the predecessor of Horenbouts, Holbein and Van Dijk. The Wilton Diptych alone, if it is English, is an exception to these remarks, warning us yet again to be cautious. Later in the fifteenth century, considering what was available in England, it is not surprising that Edward IV bought books from Flanders. Patronage and artistic creation must be interrelated. The problem for English artists was in accepting the implications of the new space construction from Italy and the new naturalism from the Netherlands. Greater royal patronage might have helped them, but from the point of view of the patron clearly more exciting things were happening elsewhere. A final conclusion would be that, as far as the evidence permits us to see, royal discrimation was not particularly outstanding, but neither for much of the time was native talent.[124]

122. K. L. Scott, *The Caxton Master and his patrons* (Cambridge Bibliographical Society Monograph No. 8, 1976).

123. Rickert, op. cit., 112–13, 124.

124. I should like to thank Dr Richard Davies for guidance on historical sources during the research for this paper.

9

English Books In and Out of Court from Edward III to Henry VII

A. I. Doyle

It has been a common mistake to suppose that one can reach any reliable conclusions about books and their users in the fourteenth and fifteenth centuries by confining one's view to books in one language only, so I am conscious of engaging in a treacherous investigation. Nevertheless, I am going to try to see what grounds there are for thinking that particular English books were made for, owned or used by people 'at court' in one or other of the senses of that phrase, ranging from the blood royal through members of the nobility and gentry to others who can be shown to have been, at a relevant time, in attendance or service in the entourage of the sovereign or in one of the magnates' households closely connected with it. (I should say I am not going to deal with Scotland). I want to ask if there is sufficient evidence for believing that these social circles, or any of them, had a dominant or distinctive influence on the character, quantity or quality of the manufacture of books in English, in comparison with the evidence for the other classes of owner and user, groups and individuals not clearly or closely connected with any sort of 'court'.

Certainly for most and probably for all the English monarchs of the period under discussion we know (from surviving manuscripts or records) of more books which belonged to them in French or Latin than in English, and the same is true for most of their noble and gentle contemporaries. The commonest such possessions for members of all literate classes were books of hours and devotions, overwhelmingly in Latin, and for the more elevated ranks of society French books of entertainment and edification continue to take a leading place from the late fourteenth into the early sixteenth century. Professors Robbins and Pearsall have attempted in recent years to correct the tendency of Anglicists to underestimate what the latter has called 'the tenacity of French', and he has also well said: 'It is an innocent assumption on the part of literary scholars that associates literary activity at the court necessarily with the person of the king'.[1]

Dr Green's *Poets and Princepleasers: Literature and the English Court in the Late Middle Ages* has dealt not only with the education of the 'court' and the situation of authors at it, but also with the types of book which occur most frequently in lists and survivals of royal and noble libraries, and the choice of subjects of new composition and translation, in both French and English, emphasising the importance of literature of political interest rather than that of courtly love.

Another thing we must not ignore is the small number of individuals involved, in contrast with modern circumstances of literary circulation, and their complex inter-relationships by descent and marriage, when we try to trace the ways in which knowledge and ownership of books may have been transmitted; nor should we forget the geographical mobility of people of the book-owning levels. I am inclined to believe that everybody who was anybody in England in the late middle ages, and especially those 'at court', had kinship or alliance of one degree or another with everyone else, and we therefore need to beware of giving exclusive rather than alternative explanations of effects based on such links. And to rectify our focus on the royal court in the metropolis and its vicinity, we ought constantly to compare the evidence of book-production and dissemination, not only in different walks of life but also in distant cities, counties and households. While it is possible and may be necessary to generalise from examples picked from over the nearly two centuries of our survey, it can be very misleading to disregard chronology, since linguistic, intellectual, economic and technical changes were affecting book-production throughout the period. Consequently I feel obliged to look at the scene broadly in order of date, if we are to decide what part the court may have played in the unquestionable changes in the demand for and supply of English books.

I know of no Middle English manuscript definitely connected with Edward III or his closest associates. The outstanding candidate could be the Auchinleck anthology of romances, probably of metropolitan provenance early in his reign, which I feel, in view of its bulk, considerable cost, and the absence of anything contemporary of comparable characteristics, to have been more likely an exceptional effort than the sole survivor of routine commercial production which Mrs Loomis suggested. Its contents have been judged to be adapted for less

---

1. R. H. Robbins, 'The vintner's son: French wine in English bottles', in W. W. Kibler (ed.), *Eleanor of Aquitaine: Patron and Politician* (Austin, 1976), 147–72; D. Pearsall, 'The 'Troilus' frontispiece and Chaucer's audience', *Yearbook of English Studies*, vii (1977), 68–74: 'We might do well to look beyond the entourage of king and nobility . . . to the multitude of household knights and officials, career diplomats and civil servants, who constitute the "court" in its wider sense, that is, that national administration and its metropolitan milieu'.

sophisticated tastes than those implied by the French sources and their translation to be scarcely requisite for the courtly reader or listener of that time, and so perhaps intended for a wealthy bourgeois public. Those Londoners who lent large sums of money to the king for his wars, though not 'courtiers', must have been called to court, and cannot have been unacquainted with French, or with Anglo-Norman literature, but they and their families, and equally some at court, could have welcomed or commissioned the Auchinleck enterprise. Chaucer's putative acquaintance with it is similarly ambiguous, since it could have come about either in the city or at court within his career.[2]

That the expression of more or less refined feelings is not by itself a criterion of proximity to the throne of a book is proved by Harley 2253, the trilingual anthology of verse and prose dated by N. R. Ker to the same decade as Auchinleck, the 1330s, written by a clerical scribe connected by him with Herefordshire and the Mortimer family and recently identified by Professor Carlton Revard in a number of Ludlow deeds between 1314 and 1349, so tending to confine his activity, but not of course his employers or sources, to an even narrower provincial context, though at this era not so remote from the main streams of courtly society as it may have been later.[3] It is surely significant too that the only known copy of the alliterative romance *William of Palerne* which makes a bow to Humphrey Bohun, earl of Hereford, before 1361, is probably of Gloucestershire provenance in the third quarter of the century and that, like Harley 2253, it is written in a proficient anglicana of literary quality, such as is employed for the earlier extant copies of *Piers Plowman*, notably Trinity College, Dublin, 212, which has the ascription to Langland and the account of his parentage in the same hand as Latin historical notes on the Welsh Marches to the mid-fourteenth century.[4] Members of the Mortimer, Bohun, Beauchamp and other families, and their retainers, must have moved more or less frequently between their country seats and the royal court (wherever that might be, decreasingly outside the neighbourhood of the capital), but their literary interests and provision for them were not necessarily or primarily from metropolitan

2. D. Pearsall & I. C. Cunningham (intro.), *The Auchinleck Manuscript: National Library of Scotland Advocates' MS 19.2.1* (London, 1977), summarise the state of present opinion and observation: the latter could be improved upon.
3. N. R. Ker (intro.), *Facsimile of British Museum MS Harley 2253*, EETS OS 255 (1965); C. Revard, 'Richard Hurd and MS Harley 2253', *N & Q*, cciv (1979), 199–202.
4. King's College, Cambridge, MS 13: see M. Görlach, *The Textual Tradition of the South English Legendary* (*Leeds Texts & Monographs*, new series 6, 1974), 87–8; G. Guddat-Figge, *Catalogue of Manuscripts containing Middle English Romances* (München er Universitäts-schriften, Texte u. Untersuchungen zur Englischen Philologie 4, 1976), 84–85. Cf. E. St John Brooks, 'The *Piers Plowman* manuscripts in Trinity College, Dublin', *The Library*, fifth series, vi (1951), 141–53; G. Kane, *Piers Plowman: the Evidence for Authorship* (London, 1965), 26–32, pl. i–ii.

sources in the fourteenth century. As in the west midlands, so in the north, authorship and copying were well established at a period when it is still difficult to identify metropolitan products (or at least it has yet to be properly done). The extant manuscripts, by their language, suggest that the share of the capital in the making of copies of books in English may have been subsidiary to that of the provinces until the end of the century, and that the role of the court (whether at Westminster or elsewhere) might have been more as a meeting-place than a market for literary traffic in the vernacular previously.[5]

To take another celebrated case, BL MS Cotton Nero A.X. Although it may date from after the death of Edward III, the Garter motto at the end of *Sir Gawain* and of the volume connects one or both aptly with the culture of the royal court, yet the language of the poems and of their copyist can be placed very narrowly on the borders of Cheshire, Derbyshire and Staffordshire, and the execution of the book contrasts in several respects with the quality of its contents. The materials are poor, the preparation rough, the size (even before cropping) cramped, the handwriting uneven and betraying that its scribe was happier with anglicana than the textura he or his employer felt was called for, while the full-page coloured drawings are unlike most other manuscript illustration done in England in the same period.[6] The never-ending speculation concerning the origin of these poems (and, by implication, of the manuscript) has tended to seek authors and patrons in noble or gentle households based in the north-west midlands yet in contact with the royal court, a reaction against a former propensity to place the Cotton volume and Chaucer at opposite cultural poles. In fact we do not know that Nero A.X. was never copied in the metropolis or even for people of different dialects. Alliterative poetry was copied outside its native areas, and in the metropolis, by the end of the century, as is certain in the case of *Piers Plowman*. The adoption of a metropolitan spelling by copyists for texts of diverse origins is an important sign of the shift towards centralisation of book-production in English, or the predominance of the capital, which is not however solely a response to the presence of the court.[7]

5. M. L. Samuels, 'Some applications of middle English dialectology', *ES*, xliv (1963), 81–94, adduces only one small group in his type II after Auchinleck, as representing the language of the London area in this period.

6. I. Gollancz (intro.), *Pearl, Cleanness, Patience and Sir Gawain reproduced in Facsimile from the MS Cotton Nero A.X in the British Museum*, EETS ES 162 (1923); cf. E. Salter, 'The alliterative revival, II', *Mod.Phil.*, lxiv (1967), 233–6; G. Mathew, *The Court of Richard II* (London, 1968), 166.

7. Cf. A. O. Sandved, 'Prolegomena to a renewed study of the rise of standard English', and M. L. Samuels, 'Spelling and dialect in the late and post-medieval English periods', in M. Benskin & M. L. Samuels (eds.)., *So Meny People Longages and Tonges: Philological Essays in Scots and Mediaeval English Presented to A. McIntosh* (Edinburgh, 1981), 31–42, 43–54; also 66, 89.

I should like to compare with Nero A.X. the much more accomplished text-hand and miniatures of the alliterative Alexander extract in Bodley MS 264, added to that earlier French romance not long before or after the making of the Cotton manuscript and probably before the larger French prose additions in Bodley, with miniatures by Johannes, and border illumination also in the fashion of the early fifteenth century, which I think it is safe to say was practised chiefly if not exclusively in metropolitan contexts, though one must of course allow for the mobility of artists and craftsmen. The west midland English of the exemplar of the *Alexander* may have been modified by the copyist, but the style of its miniatures is more archaic than that of Johannes and his associates, and so possibly provincial. It has been guessed that Bodley 264 was one of the books at Pleshey left by Thomas of Woodstock, duke of Gloucester, uncle of Richard II, at his death in 1397, and his wife was a Bohun, whose antecedents might account for the cast of the English additions.[8] For not dissimilar miniatures of 'provincial' character we may look at those in the Vernon manuscript (Bod.poet.a.l), produced together with the largely parallel Simeon manuscript (BL Add.22283) about 1390–1400, by scribes of north Worcestershire orthography.[9] In contrast with all the manuscripts I have mentioned so far, the contents of Vernon and Simeon are entirely religious and moralistic, verse and prose. The unusual size and comprehensiveness of these collections imply exceptional knowledge, resourcefulness and expense devoted to their compilation and execution. One of the illuminated borders of Vernon includes a blank escutcheon, evidence that an armigerous owner or donor was anticipated. Events, such as a death, could have prevented its completion, as not infrequently happened in the course of such lengthy commissions in the middle ages. While one of the pictures and the contents list suggest that Vernon may have gone to a religious community, Simeon was never quite finished, which argues again for some changes of intention, or of utilisation. We do not know how far any commercial enterprise was involved, as distinct from execution, but it is pretty

8. M. R. James (intro.), *The Romance of Alexander: a Collotype Facsimile of MS. Bodley 264* (Oxford, 1933), includes English only on fol. 67 in a rubric; for verse see F. P. Magoun (ed.), *Gests of King Alexander of Macedon* (Cambridge, Mass., 1929), 8–14, pl. ii; O. Pächt & J. J. G. Alexander, *Illuminated Manuscripts in the Bodleian Library*, III (Oxford, 1973), 70, no. 792–3, pl. lxxv; cf. G. M. Spriggs, 'Unnoticed Bodleian manuscripts, illuminated by Herman Scheerre and his school', *Bodleian Library Record*, vii (1964), 194n.

9. Pächt & Alexander, op. cit., iii, 61–2, no. 676, pl. lxx–lxxi; A. I. Doyle, 'The shaping of the Vernon and Simeon manuscripts', in B. Rowland (ed.), *Chaucer and Middle English Studies in Honour of Rossell Hope Robbins* (London, 1974), 328–41; R. E. Lewis, 'The relationship of the Vernon and Simeon texts of the *Pricke of Conscience*', in M. Benskin & M. L. Samuels (eds), *So Meny People Longages and Tonges* (Edinburgh, 1981), 251–64.

certain that it must have been based in the west midlands. Yet a tiny inscription in Simeon, readable as 'Joan boun' led Miss H. E. Allen to attribute its ownership to the countess of Hereford, mother-in-law of Thomas of Woodstock and of Henry Bolingbroke, who spent much of her later life in the east. Supposing the manuscript were in fact made for her, or someone of similar tastes and status, she may be said to have retired from the court, and the ethos of the volume (including the treatise of Sir John Clanvowe quoted by Professor Scattergood) could be thought antipathetic to courtly values. In Richard II's reign and court, however, there is no doubt that English religious prose of pronouncedly serious character did become fashionable, not least in the form of the Lollard scriptural translations. A later Lollard alleged that Queen Anne of Bohemia (Richard's consort from 1382 to 1394) had what must have been the long or the short set of glossed gospels in English, and was commended for it at her funeral by Archbishop Arundel (brother, by the way, of Joan Bohun).[10] A copy of the short set, not much (if at all) later, with historiated initials, shows what it may have been like. A long-current Latin page design has been rendered in English, and could most easily stem from Oxford, where the work was probably compiled.[11]

If Queen Anne was presumably always at court, Thomas of Woodstock was turbulently in and out of it. BL MS Egerton 617, 618, of the early version of the Wycliffite bible has his arms as part of the original illumination and is mentioned in the list of his books in 1397, besides two other books of gospels in English – perhaps the glossed ones.[12] The massive size, lavish illumination and large text-hand of the bible, in two volumes, must be meant for display and use on a lectern (like Vernon and Simeon), and it has rubrics and a calendar for the lessons at mass from the New Testament, just as many copies of the latter alone do, to help conscientious worshippers. These full English bibles are not common and must have been very costly. Another of the early version, in one volume, Wolfenbüttel, Herzog-August Bibliothek, MS Guelf.Aug.A.2, with illumination rather later in style than Egerton and historiated initials like the glossed gospels, bears the name and

10. M. Deanesly, *The Lollard Bible and other Medieval Biblical Versions* (Cambridge, 1920), 445, but cf. Sherborne above, n. 30.

11. BL MS Add.41175 was shown; cf. Bod.143 in S. L. Fristedt, *The Wycliffe Bible, Part I* (*Stockholm Studies in English* 4, 1953), 129, pl. xvi.

12. The illumination is undoubtedly late fourteenth-century, including the arms, *pace* S. L. Fristedt, 'A weird manuscript enigma in the British Museum', *Acta Universitatis Stockholmiensis: Stockholm Studies in Modern Philology*, new series 2 (1964), 116–21, with plate; see also F. G. Kenyon (ed.), *Facsimiles of Biblical Manuscripts in the British Museum* (London, 1900), pl. xxiv; G. F. Warner (ed.), *Schools of Illumination* iv (London, 1922), pl. 2; R. Garnett, *English Literature: an Illustrated Record* (London, 1903), i, pl. opp. 218; Palaeographical Society, *Facsimiles of Manuscripts* (London, 1873–83), no. 171.

a motto of Thomas of Lancaster, son of Henry IV, apparently between 1399 and 1412.[13] It may be that the closer inspection of Wycliffite scriptural, sermon and polemical manuscripts, now being conducted by Hudson, Lindberg and others, will discover more which belonged soon after their making to identifiable and localisable individuals (or institutions) and so help to detect whether they were made mostly in one centre or in several (Oxford, London, Northampton, Leicester, or private workshops). Although the prototypes of these books were probably written at Oxford and other places in the midlands, their multiplication could have got going in the metropolis in the 1390s and have gone on there even after 1408 (the year of Arundel's restrictions), that is in the same two decades when the evidence of other books and the records of the craftsmen indicate that production in the vernacular was expanding, and beginning to be concentrated there. How much did this development derive from or depend on a growing market at court as distinct from, or more than, one in the city or from the provincial visitor? For ostensibly Lollard works, if not the plain scriptures, the support at court must have been hesitant or covert by the turn of the century, and we must ask ourselves at this point how far members of Parliament composed temporarily part of the court in the wider sense. The so-called Lollard knights, most of whom were at some time associated with the court of Richard II in a narrower sense, were obvious purchasers of such books, but perhaps rather to take home to their country seats than to use at court.[14] Although Sir John Oldcastle's career is the extreme, his gravitation between Herefordshire and the metropolis is representative, and it is in connection with his rising in 1414 that sympathisers are recorded in the London book-crafts.[15] The innumerable copies of the New Testament in English which must have been produced in the late fourteenth and early fifteenth century (to judge from the survivals), to common patterns, in similar text-hands and with decoration of professional standards, were surely in the majority London work. The multiplication of them can hardly have been surreptitious, even after 1408, and the market must have been a wide one to occasion it.

The transition, from individual commissioning of English books for people closely associated with the court, to more repetitive production for which courtiers can be shown to have been only one class of customer, may be seen in the early copies of Gower's *Confessio Amantis*. The Ellesmere manuscript (Huntington Library EL 26.A.17) of the

13. W. Milde (ed.), *Mittelalterliche Handschriften der Herzog August Bibliothek: 120 Abbildungen* (Frankfurt am Main, 1972), 182–3.

14. See K. B. McFarlane, *Lancastrian Kings and Lollard Knights* (Oxford, 1972), 139–226.

15. K. B. McFarlane, *John Wycliffe and the Beginnings of English Nonconformity* (London, 1952), 166, 180.

second version of the poem, dedicated to Henry Bolingbroke as earl of Derby in 1393, was probably made for him, on the evidence of illuminated emblems, including the swan of Bohun, family of his first wife, and was presumably a presentation from the author.[16] It is written in what Malcolm Parkes would call a bastard anglicana, of the highest degree of formality, contrasting with the rather rough-and-ready text-hands of many Lollard books. Nothing quite at the same level as the beginning of this is found in the other early copies of Gower's works in English, Latin and French which, from the character of the corrections and recurrent hands, must have been prepared under his supervision or direction, though they show a similar concern for and styles of calligraphy.[17] J. H. Fisher suggested a scriptorium at Southwark Priory, Gower's home in his later years, for these manuscripts, but corroboration is wanting and it is as likely that he employed some of the secular clerks with whom he had come in contact and of whom there were many expert in comparable anglicana and secretary scripts, across the river in Westminster or London. The Ellesmere illumination most resembles that of two books destined for Richard II, Roger Dymmok's *Liber contra Duodecim Errores Lollardorum* (c. 1395), Trinity Hall, Cambridge, MS 17, and a copy of the *Ordo Coronacionis* now at Pamplona.[18] The next generation of copies of the *Confessio Amantis*, only a little later and starting within the author's lifetime (i.e. before 1408), to judge from their illumination, which includes miniatures in the styles of Johannes and Scheerre and vinet-features of the early fifteenth century, although differing from copy to copy, shows more standardisation, particularly repetitions by one scribe. MS Christ Church, Oxford, 148 of the first version has original arms of England and France modern, so not before 1405, with what look like Thomas of Lancaster's labels, so before his death in 1421, and MS Bodley 294 of the second version has the inscription, after 1414, of his brother, duke Humphrey of Gloucester. Both were written by the most prolific copyist of middle English books of this period yet identified, the quantity and quality of whose output (including seven copies of the *Confessio*) leaves no doubt that he was

16. G. C. Macaulay (ed.), *The English Works of John Gower*, i, *EETS* ES 81 (1900), clii–iii; *A Handbook to the Huntington Library Exhibition* (San Marino, 1978), 15. See plate 15.

17. Cf. Bodley MS Fairfax 3, Macaulay, op. cit., frontispiece. John H. Fisher, *John Gower* (London, 1965), 116–17, 123–7, 303–7, did not take the palaeographical considerations far enough beyond Macaulay's; I offered a number of additional observations in the Lyell Lectures at Oxford in 1967, and a group of younger scholars under Professor Pearsall's guidance is now attempting a more thorough examination of text, language and presentation of all the manuscripts.

18. See A. Steel, *Richard II* (Cambridge, 1941), pl. opposite p. vi; the Pamplona MS is only referred to by W. Ullmann (ed.), *Liber Regie Capelle* (Henry Bradshaw Society, 92, 1961), 23n., as deriving from the Lytlington missal of Westminster textually.

employed commercially in the metropolis.[19] His and related books by other scribes must have been expensive and fashionable enough for the court to have provided the initial demand, but how far did they continue to work chiefly for such circles? Early evidence is sparse: the paucity of armorial insignia is not conclusive, but the ownership of these books later in the century by country gentry and London citizens perhaps means that their forebears were as active in acquiring them as their betters.

At the stage immediately after (or even before) a new composition or translation had been presented to a patron by its author, people in close touch with either of them were obviously at an advantage if they wanted access to an exemplar in order to get a copy made for themselves. At the court in Westminster there were plenty of clerks at hand to do it as a part-time job with the minimum inconvenience to the exemplar-owner, and so too in other milieux, to a lesser degree. Limners and miniaturists of excellence were, however, probably not so common and had to be hired separately, unless a stationer were commissioned to arrange copying, decoration and binding. If the latter could procure an exemplar, whether from the author (or his heirs) or an existing owner, he could also develop further demand by investing in handsomely decorated copies in advance of firm orders so that it would be easier, even for a would-be purchaser at court, to go straight to a stationer than to arrange for anything more than a plain copy for himself. Once a work was being fairly frequently copied and offered through the metropolitan book-trade, the courtier's advantage had gone, for members of other classes had equal access to it. Insofar as the enthusiasm for new works in English arose near the centre of the court about the turn of the fourteenth into the fifteenth century and spread through its outer circles, fringes or satellites and beyond, it must have led to the expansion or modification of the London book-trade, which was in the best position to serve it and as its records and extant books suggest did happen. Yet the court does not seem to have been dependent on the London book-trade for all its books any more than the book-trade seems to have been dependent on the court for all its business. I think there is still too much diversity in the combinations of handwriting, texts and decoration amongst the books which have court connections. A considerable bulk and continuity of employment is requisite to create distinct uniformity of style, and such uniformities as can be discerned cannot be connected exclusively with the court. The scribe of the Hengwrt and Ellesmere *Canterbury Tales*

---

19. A. I. Doyle & M. B. Parkes, 'The production of copies of the *Canterbury Tales* and the *Confessio Amantis* in the early fifteenth century', in M. B. Parkes & A. G. Watson (eds.), *Medieval Scribes, Manuscripts & Libraries: Essays presented to N. R. Ker* (London, 1978), 163–210, esp. 177, 208.

presumably worked for Chaucer's literary executors, perhaps his son
Thomas and friends within the ambience of the court, and contributed
to the Trinity College, Cambridge, R.III.2 copy of Gower, along with
Thomas Hoccleve. The Gower belonged either to a receiver of the
duchy of Lancaster in the second quarter of the fifteenth century or to
his son, recorder of London and chief baron of the exchequer in the
third quarter.[20] The Ellesmere Chaucer carries twice in an early hand
the motto of the Pastons of Norfolk, of whom three generations spent
some time in or about the court in the same period.[21] If these are not
the original owners in each case, nevertheless it would be surprising
if they were remote. The three autographs of Hoccleve's own poems,
composed from early in the fifteenth century although copied in the
1420s, include dedications to a London stationer, the Town Clerk,
several of the royal dukes, Joan Bohun, countess of Hereford and Joan
Beaufort, countess of Westmorland, as well as allusions to a number
of other acquaintances at court and in offices of state, besides Chaucer
and Gower. The apparent presentation copy of Hoccleve's *Regement of
Princes* for Henry, Prince of Wales, 1412, BL MS Arundel 38, is not
in the author's hand but a more formalised one of the same type,
possibly a colleague's, with an outstanding miniature and border illumination of the Scheerre school.[22] At whose initiative and expense
was this done, the author's or the patron's? The circumstances may
have been less one-sided than the conventions implied. The situation
was presumably simpler without a living author, as in the case of
Pierpont Morgan (Campsall) MS M817 of *Troilus and Criseyde*, to
which what may have been the arms of Prince Henry were added in
a space for them;[23] the even showier writing of the last has no precise
parallel, probably because it was a tour de force by someone who
normally followed a plainer mode, not necessarily in books. As with
the Ellesmere Gower, here we may have exceptional products from
Westminster rather than London.

It would be wrong to suppose that by this time, the second or third
decade of the fifteenth century, English books of the highest quality

20. Ibid., 209.

21. In a hand certainly of the fifteenth century and probably of the first half, on f. i
verso and again on vii verso of the ruled medieval flyleaves, 'demeuz enmeuz', i.e. 'de
mieux en mieux': for the Paston use of this see H. N. MacCracken, 'Additional Light on
the *Temple of Glas*', *PMLA*, xxiii (1908), 132–5. The Pastons had fairly frequent correspondence with the 12th and 13th earls of Oxford, for one of whom a poem on the
flyleaves was written in the third quarter of the century: see J. M. Manly & E. Rickert,
The Text of the Canterbury Tales, i (Chicago, 1940), 155–9. They do not notice the motto.

22. See pl. 7.

23. R. K. Root, *The Manuscripts of Chaucer's Troilus* (Chaucer Society, 1st series 98,
1914), 5–6, pl. iii; *Autotype Specimens of the Chief Chaucer Manuscripts Part III* (Chaucer Society, 1st series, 62, 1880); B. Boyd, *Chaucer and the Medieval Book* (San Marino,
1973), pl. ix. cf. G. F. Warner, *Schools of Illumination*, part iv, pl.10, 12 for very similar
illumination to M817 and script of the Privy Seal type like Arundel 38.

were produced only in the metropolis, because of the talent and the wealth concentrated there. Bodleian Library Digby MS 233, a volume of generous proportions containing Trevisa's prose rendering of Giles of Rome's *De Regimine Principum* and Walton's of Vegetius *De Re Militari*, both done for Thomas lord Berkeley, before 1402 and in 1408 respectively, has large pictures and border illumination differing considerably from contemporaneous metropolitan work, though influenced by it, and the costume extremely fashionable.[24] The pictures purport to show the court of the dauphin Philip of France but could be that of prince Henry of England. Kathleen Scott has observed that a swan represented in one margin may again be the badge of the Bohuns, subsequently used by Henry IV and V, duke Humphrey and the dukes of Buckingham. The language is distinctly south-western and there are resemblances in that respect and in the details of illumination which tempt me to relate the Digby volume to certain other manuscripts, three of which are in one elegant hand, two of them copies of a prose Passion, the Gospel of Nicodemus and connected texts, the third Rolle's English Psalter;[25] also to Bodley MS.953, which is a historiated copy of Rolle's Psalter made for Thomas lord Berkeley and probably bequeathed by him in 1417 to the hospital of St Mary Magdalene near Bristol,[26] and to a book of hymns and hours made for Gloucester Abbey about the same time.[27] The initials of the Berkeley Psalter are inevitably less inventive than the pictures of Digby 233, yet the standard of execution is high and the writing superior. One may wonder if the manuscripts of this group are not Bristol products, as the most obvious regional centre for a book-trade, comparable with York or Norwich. The Berkeleys' patronage of authors and books may have been both a continuation of provincial traditions and an emulation of what they knew from the royal court.[28] Digby 233 could even have been a gift to Henry V as prince of Wales or king; after 1485 it was in the hands of lady Hastings and Hungerford, from a westcountry family but also daughter-in-law of Edward IV's lord chamberlain.

Henry V was patron of both Lydgate's *Life of Our Lady* and his *Siege of Troy* and several manuscripts of the latter have miniatures of its presentation, though a bearded king in one of them suggest some

24. Pächt & Alexander, iii, 72, no. 815, pl. lxx.

25. John Rylands Library, Manchester, MS Eng.895; BL MS Egerton 2658; Trinity College, Dublin MS 71.

26. Pächt & Alexander, iii, 63, no. 701, pl. lxx–lxxi; cf. E. F. Jacob (ed.), *The Register of Henry Chichele Archbishop of Canterbury 1414–1443*, ii, liv, 124.

27. Pierpont Morgan Library, New York, MS M99, formerly William Morris's; T. W. Williams, 'Gloucestershire mediaeval libraries', *Transactions of the Bristol & Gloucestershire Archaeological Society*, xxxi (1908), 124–5.

28. Cf. E. Salter, 'The alliterative revival, I', *Mod.Phil.*, lxiv (1968), 149–50.

distance of time or place.[29] The most lavishly illustrated copy, of the
second quarter of the century, Rylands Eng.1, has added full-page
arms of the Carent family of Dorset, one of whom was a squire of the
household of Henry VI,[30] and they occur in the same way in Yale
Univ.Lib.MS 281 of the *Life of Our Lady*, which has a note that it was
later given to a queen, perhaps Elizabeth Woodville or her daughter
of York, since another copy, Bodl.MS Hatton 73, has a note that it
belonged to Queen Margaret (probably of Anjou, not Scotland) before
more than one gentlewoman.[31] These instances of shifting ownership
within the court, even of royal possessions, throw more light on the
courtiers' attitudes than the monarchs'. As in the sixteenth century,
it was probably not unusual for royalty to give away to one subject
what it had not long received as a present from another: the inflow
and outflow of the fount of grace. Changes of monarch and dynasty,
descent and marriage must also have affected the ownership of books
which were at one time or another in royal possession, as there is no
evidence of a continuous library before Edward IV, who appears to
have been the first king to commission books in quantity, although
from abroad. The effects on book-production of such orders, in pro-
moting and sustaining a high level of craftsmanship, as found at the
courts of France and Burgundy during our period, were very different
from those where, as in England, monarchs and magnates seem to
have mostly accepted books as gifts, often of high quality, but commissioned diversely by authors and others. Occasional orders were
less likely to result in uniformity of style than habitual ones, and
where we can discern settled styles they are not necessarily dependent
on the court, as I have already argued of one western group. The
presumable presentation copy of Lydgate's lives of SS. Edmund and
Fremund, BL MS Harley 2278, made shortly before or after the young
Henry VI's visit to Bury St Edmunds in 1433, is the work of a distinct
school of scribes, miniaturists and illuminators apparently operating
in that neighbourhood for thirty years or more, chiefly on Lydgate's
poems, sometimes so ambitiously as to suggest wealthy patrons, yet

29. Bodl. MS Rawl.C.446: Pächt & Alexander, iii, 82, no. 943, pl. xc. Digby 232,
ibid., 76, no. 868, pl. lxxxiii. BL Cotton Aug.A.IV and Rylands Eng.1 have him as
clean-shaven.
30. V. J. Scattergood, *Politics and Poetry in the Fifteenth Century* (London, 1971), pl.
3, shows the presentation; J. J. G. Alexander, 'William Abell "Lymnour" and
15th-century English illumination', in A. Rosenauer & G. Weber (eds.), *Kunsthistorische Forschungen Otto Pächt zu ehren* (Salzburg, 1972), 169, judges the arms to be
by the main artist (not Abell). For the Carents see J. C. Wedgwood (ed.), *History of Parliament: Biographies of the Members of the Commons House 1439–1509* (London, 1936),
154–6.
31. F. Madan *et al.* (ed.), *A Summary Catalogue of Western Manuscripts in the
Bodleian Library at Oxford*, ii, pt. i (Oxford, 1937), 850–1, no. 4119.

independently of contemporary metropolitan production,[32] just as the illustrated collection of Chaucer's poems, Cambridge University Library Gg.IV.27, had also probably been made in East Anglia rather earlier in the century.[33]

Corpus Christi College, Cambridge, MS 61 of Chaucer's *Troilus*, with the famous frontispiece, is the clearest attempt to emulate the standard and style of early fifteenth-century books for the French court; but the abandonment of its other illustrations, and the absence of other work by the same artist, are indicative of insufficient support. Henry V's unexpected death might be an explanation, even though he may have had the Pierpont Morgan manuscript of the same poem, previously mentioned. The Corpus copy bears the refrain of Lydgate's prayer for king, queen and people in the hand of John Shirley who, as secretary to Richard Beauchamp earl of Warwick, had been with the latter and Henry V in France;[34] when the earl became 'tutor' of the infant Henry VI, in the later 1420s, the king was surely too young for *Troilus*, and subsequently perhaps too pious! Beauchamp and Shirley must have known the French and Latin books the duke of Bedford bought or commissioned at Paris, and the high-points of English illuminated service and devotional books of the same time. Yet the only English book of Beauchamp's I know is Trevisa's *Polycronicon* (translated for his father-in-law, lord Berkeley), BL MS. Add. 24194, a metropolitan commercial product with very modest illumination of his arms, of the same type as Thomas of Lancaster's and duke Humphrey's Gowers, from the first decade of the century.[35] If there was a court style for English books, it was this, with variations in later decades, but the evidence is not enough to connect it exclusively or predominantly with original owners of that kind. If we look at the manuscripts of comparable quality of the 1420s, 1430s and 1440s which seem by writing, language and illumination, to be commercial and metropolitan, some of the finest were apparently made for men like Sir Thomas Chaworth of Nottinghamshire and Sir Edmund Rede of Oxfordshire, more active there than at court, where they must have appeared, of

32. See M. Rickert, *Painting in Britain: the Middle Ages* (London, 1954), 202, pl. 175; P. Lasko & N. J. Morgan (eds.), *Medieval Art in East Anglia 1300–1520* (London, 1974), 46, no. 66; British Library, *The Benedictines in Britain* (1980), pl. iii. I discussed the evidence for the school in the Lyell Lectures, 1967, and K. L. Scott has forthcoming an article on another copy of Lydgate's *Edmund & Fremund*.

33. M. B. Parkes & R. Beadle (intro.), *A Facsimile of Cambridge University Library MS.Gg.4.27*, III (Cambridge, 1980), 6–7, 63–4.

34. M. B. Parkes & E. Salter (intro.), *A Facsimile of Corpus Christi College, Cambridge, MS.61* (Cambridge, 1978), 10–11: it is not noted there that the queen in Lydgate's poem is Henry's mother, Catherine, in 1429, and could be so 1422–37.

35. C. Babington (ed.), *Polycronicon Ranulphi Higden* ii (RS, 1869), frontispiece; Doyle & Parkes, op. cit., 206–8.

course, as sheriffs and MPs, from time to time.[36] In contrast BL MS.Royal 17. D.VI, the *Regement of Princes* and other poems of Hoccleve, has the arms of William, lord Arundel only added (between 1438 and 1462). It was he who in 1483, via a gentleman of his household, was patron of Caxton's *Golden Legend*, taking a number of copies, presumably to give away rather than to sell. The Royal manuscript has served as a sort of *album amicorum* for members of a number of noble and gentle families in the later fifteenth century, suggestive of the intercourse of a large household if not the royal court.[37] Edmund, lord Grey of Ruthin, of a comparably long courtly career to Arundel, commissioned the exceptional illustrated copy of Nicholas Love's *Life of Christ*, Edinburgh, National Library of Scotland, Advocates' MS.18.1.7, in which he and his wife appear, by a scribe retentive of some provincialisms, followed by a conservative artist and illuminator, in the 1440s or 1450s, but there is no reason why that should not have been possible in the metropolis along with newer modes.[37a]

Let us return to John Shirley. Professor Green has rightly recognised that there are no adequate grounds for the belief of some scholars that he conducted a commercial scriptorium or book-shop.[38] The manuscripts certainly in his own hand are very plain productions, with no more than rudimentary decoration and mostly on paper, unlike the higher-quality books of his time. His contents-lists, headings and marginal comments, addressed familiarly but obsequiously to 'yee so noble and worthi princes and princesses other estatis or degrees whatever yee beo that have disposition or pleasaunce to rede or here', 'my frendes', 'my lordes', 'dere sirs', 'this companye', 'youre grace', 'youre gentylnesse' are evidence for the alternative hypothesis of a sort of circulating library, with a clientele however of courtly status and perhaps more as a hobby than a business. Books not copied for the

36. BL MS Cotton Aug.A.IV of Lydgate's *Troy Book* and Columbia University Library, New York, MS Plimpton 263 of Trevisa's Bartholomeus Anglicus *De Proprietatibus Rerum*, neither amongst those mentioned in his will, 1458, but both on an exceptionally large scale with his arms (after 1411) in the original illumination: see G. A. Plimpton, *The Education of Chaucer* (London, 1935), pl. v, for the latter. Cf. Wedgwood, *History of Parliament, ut supra*, 175–6. BL MS Harley 3490, Gower's *Confessio Amantis* and the *Speculum Ecclesie* of St Edmund Rich, has the arms of Sir Edmund Rede c. 1438–70, and may be one of the two Gowers mentioned in his will, 1489; Wedgwood, 711–12. He was styled a king's servant in 1447, but that need not have meant the same throughout a man's career. The Boarstall cartulary was made for him in 1444 or so, less lavishly, and BL Cotton Nero C.III about the same period in similar style to the Gower. All three have many coats of arms besides his own.

37. G. F. Warner & J. P. Gilson, *Catalogue of Western Manuscripts in the Old Royal and King's Collections* ii (London, 1921), 251–2; iv, pl. 101; Jerome Mitchell, *Thomas Hoccleve* (Urbana, 1968), frontispiece (presentation and armorial).

37a. See Alexander in Rosenauer & Weber, op. cit., 169–70, pl. 9. There is a full-page armorial, as in the same artist's Rylands Eng. MS 1.

38. *Poets and Princepleasers*, 130–3.

most part by him but inscribed or annotated give glimpses of a broader range of relationships in church, court and city, where his neighbours of St Bartholomew's Close for at least the last twenty years of his long life included also notable representatives of each walk of life.[39] The form of some of his ex-libris implies that, like Jean Grolier, he regarded his books as 'et amicorum'. The most significant for us is Ellesmere MS 26 A 13 in the Huntington Library. This, containing poems of Lydgate and Hoccleve's *Regement* in a bastard anglicana and another section which need not have been with it in Shirley's lifetime, is preceded by four leaves in his hand of extracts from Lydgate and Chaucer and an engrossed inscription coupling the names of Margaret and Beatrice above his own, and at the end of the *Regement* is 'Iste liber constat Aluredo Cornburgh de Camera Regis', the last five words being apparently by Shirley.[40] Avery or Alfred Cornburgh was a yeoman of the King's Chamber, at the beginning of a long career there when this must have been written, not after 1456. Margaret and Beatrice were, it seems, the daughters of Alice Lynne, the wealthy widow of a London woolman and grocer, of whom Margaret became Shirley's second wife between 1421 and 1441 and Beatrice married Cornburgh as her second husband between 1459 and 1467. A Cornishman by origin, settled in Essex, ending as Under-Treasurer of England and Keeper of the Great Wardrobe to Henry VII, Cornburgh is also recorded as an ironmonger of the city of London and he was a dealer in tin.[41] Court and city were not unconnected economically, socially or culturally. One prolific scribe, who after Shirley's death, in the reign of Edward IV, used some of his manuscripts as exemplars for plain paper books, may have worked for a London stationer.[42] Others were

39. A. I. Doyle, 'More light on John Shirley', *Medium Aevum*, xxx (1961), 93–101, for biographical details, which now require correction and supplementation; cf. C. D. Ross, 'The household accounts of Elizabeth Berkeley, countess of Warwick, 1420–1', *Transactions of the Bristol & Gloucestershire Archaeological Society*, lxx (1951), 81–106; R. F. Green, 'Three fifteenth-century notes', *ELN*, xiv (1976), 16–17.

40. See Plate 17. The first three words, in rubricated textura, might have been meant like a blank escutcheon or bookplate, for an unknown purchaser. Shirley seems to have written Cornburgh's name previously, perhaps in plummet, under the present ink. There can be little doubt of the duct, forms and mannerisms of the hand. The writing of the *Regement*, and its conspicuous corrector's markings, are not in any other manuscript connected with Shirley, so far as I am aware. Was it an appropriate present for a career at court? 'Aure kornbrou' in another hand is on f. iv recto with sketches of a griffin passant (Lynne) and a boar (Cornbrough).

41. Wedgwood, *History of Parliament*, 223–4 (mistaken about wife's parentage: her will, their tomb etc. make it certain).

42. A. I. Doyle, 'An unrecognized piece of *Piers the Ploughman's Creed* and other work by its scribe', *Speculum*, xxiv (1959), 428–36; R. F. Green, 'Notes on some manuscripts of Hoccleve's *Regiment of Princes*', *BLJ*, iv (1978), 39–41. Another volume by the same hand, of Medica, Trinity College, Cambridge, MS R.14.52, of which parts are signed 'Quod Multon', one dated 1458 but in fact probably later, indicate a connection with John Multon, stationer of London which is confirmed by his will, 1475 (Commissary Court of London, reg. 6, f. 178v).

used by very amateurish-looking copyists. By this period of the fifteenth century the possible range of standard of book-production was wide, even within paid work, and the cases in which we have specific knowledge of origination near the court do not fall into one category.

The nearest analogue in textual importance to Shirley's anthologies of Chaucer's and Lydgate's minor poems is Bodleian Library MS Fairfax 16, of middling quality membrane, writing and decoration except for its added full-page picture of Mars and Venus with an armorial now attributed to John Stanley of Battersea, Usher of the Chamber and Serjeant of the Armoury 1431–60, towards the last date.[43] The exemplars of this and related volumes presumably came (surprisingly late, it seems) from Chaucer's literary executors or heirs (his son Thomas or grand-daughter Alice duchess of Suffolk perhaps), as Shirley's gossipy rubrics imply his must have done. From Shirley's readers could come purchasers like Stanley. Between 1450 and 1461 Sir John Astley had his arms and other items added to copies of Walton's Vegetius and Scrope's *Othea*, later bound up in one volume, now Pierpont Morgan MS M.775. This copy of the *Othea* is dedicated to a 'hye princesse', unlike others for the duke of Buckingham and Sir John Fastolf, and its derivation, like Astley's career, with little doubt lay at court.[44] In its turn Astley's volume served as an exemplar when in 1467 or 1468 Sir John Paston, also a knight of the body to Edward IV, commissioned a miscellany, not on membrane in a bastard anglicana and with illustrations and armorials, like the Pierpont Morgan manuscript, but on paper in a current secretary with simple flourishing, from William Ebesham, a free-lance scribe, perhaps partly because he was off and on at Westminster, most conveniently for all concerned, though moving backwards and forwards to Norfolk, like his employer.[45] We get other glimpses of how the court was not detached from city and country in these matters in a letter of John Paston the younger at home to his brother Sir John in London in 1472:

> Also I prey yow to recomand me in my most humbyll wyse on-to the good lordshepe of the most corteys, gentylest, wysest, kyndest, most compenabyll, freest, largeest, and most bowntefous knyght, my lord the Erle of Arran, whych hathe maryed the Kyngys sustyr of Scotlon . . .

43. J. Norton-Smith (intro.), *Bodleian Library MS.Fairfax 16* (London, 1979). While Tanner 346 is not dissimilar in date, script and quality, Bodley 638, the other manuscript of E. P. Hammond's 'Oxford group' is much inferior and later: cf. *Manuscript Tanner 346, a Facsimile*, intro. P. Robinson (Norman, 1981), xxiv.

44. Viscount Dillon, 'On a MS. collection of ordinances of chivalry of the fifteenth century, belonging to Lord Hastings', *Arch.*, lvii (1900), pt. i, 28–70; Stephen Scrope, *The Epistle of Othea Translated from . . . Christine de Pisan*, ed. C. F. Bühler, EETS OS 264 (1970), frontisp., xv–xvi, xviii–xxi.

45. A. I. Doyle, 'The work of a late fifteenth-century scribe, William Ebesham', *BJRL*, xxxix (1957), 298–325; I am indebted to G. A. Lester for confirmation that BL MS Lansdowne 285 is derived directly from the Pierpont Morgan texts in common to both.

He is lodgyd at the George in Lombard Strete. He hath a book of my
syster Annys of the Sege of Thebes. When he hathe doon wyth it he
promysyd to delyuer it yow. I prey yow lete Portlond brynge the book
hom wyth hym. Portlond is loggyd at the George in Lombard Stret also.

And in the sadly defective list of Sir John's books, between 1475 and
1479, he mentions a romance and chronicle volume 'had off myn
ostesse at the George'.[46] The inn may often have been as important in
this traffic as the palace.

The most expensive copies of Gower's, Chaucer's and Lydgate's major poems from the third or fourth quarter of the fifteenth century,
approximately, fall into groups defined by common scribes and styles
of decoration it is reasonable to suppose metropolitan and commercial,
but for their first purchasers only a minority have clear clues, just as
in the case of the early fifteenth-century parallels.[47] BL Royal 18 D II,
begun for Sir William Herbert and his wife after 1455 and completed
after 1476 for his son-in-law earl of Northumberland, 18 D IV for John
Tiptoft earl of Worcester and his wife after 1446, are instances for
noblemen of fluctuating fortunes at court.[48] It cannot be assumed that
these predominate. Two of the English books with the best pen illustrations of the reign of Edward IV, Trinity College, Cambridge,
MS.R.3.21, and Bodley MS.283, (those in the latter being attributed
by Kathleen Scott to the same artist as in Caxton's Ovid), are inscribed
contemporaneously by and were very probably made for Roger Thorney, mercer of London and Thomas Kippyng, draper, respectively.[49]
Dr Scott has suggested that her Caxton Master 'moved on' from them
to more courtly patrons after the death of Edward IV, rather than vice
versa. The Ovid manuscript, 1480, one of the few English imitations
of the Burgundian style of book, is unattached, while the more ambitious Lambeth Chronicle bears arms probably of an alderman of
London, later Lord Mayor.[50]

46. *Paston Letters and Papers of the Fifteenth Century*, ed. N. Davis, I (Oxford, 1971),
574–5, 516–18.

47. BL MS.Royal 18.D.VI, Lydgate's *Troy Book*, has presentation verses by lord
Audelay to Henry VII or VIII, but obviously added to match as well as possible. One or
other of the Audelays owned a number of English manuscripts, including BL Harley
2278, Lydgate's *Edmund & Fremund*, presumably after Henry VI's death.

48. Warner & Gilson, *Catalogue*, ii, 308–1; iv, pl. 105: the *Sieges of Troy* and *Thebes*,
and the *Fall of Princes*, respectively.

49. Kathleen L. Scott, *The Caxton Master and his Patrons* (Cambridge Bibliographical Society Monograph 8, 1976), 45–6, 69.

50. Lambeth Palace Library MS.6: see M. R. James, *A Descriptive Catalogue of the
Manuscripts in the Library of Lambeth Palace* (Cambridge, 1932), 15–18. P. W. Parshall,
'A Dutch manuscript of c. 1480 from an atelier in Bruges', *Scriptorium* xxiii (1969),
334–5, pl. 113b, relates the miniatures to the atelier of the Bruges Master of Edward
IV c. 1480–1500. The soignée lettre bourguignonne of the text however appears to be
at ease in its spelling, even with *thorn* and *yogh*, while the instructions to the artist are
in a French hand as well as language.

That Caxton set up his press at Westminster rather than London indicates that he expected to find there not only patrons but also a general market for books in unprecedented quantity, both long-established English works and new translations. His printed products did not in fact physically rival the stylish manuscripts of the Burgundian court, by the content of which some were strongly influenced, or even the attempts of his first partner at Bruges, Colard Mansion, still less those of Antoine Vérard at the end of the century in Paris, who supplied Henry VII as well as Charles VIII with personalised over-painted books printed on vellum.[51] Although it was not very long before Caxton included woodcut illustrations, scarcely any of his books are found on vellum or with the illumination of initials and borders, and few with even the cheaper standard penwork flourishing, both of which are common in continental incunabula.[52] Evidently from the number of manuscripts which survive without either type of decoration, it was a dispensable extra, and perhaps English book-buyers have always been stingier than their neighbours d'outre-Manche, even when they are conscious of and envious of the others' accomplishments. There is thus little to show that Caxton's was in any way a luxury trade in printed books, or that they were sold chiefly to courtiers rather than citizens, churchmen or countrymen. His prefaces about his royal and noble patrons were, as Professor Blake has emphasised, meant to sell the books to socially-conscious courtiers and non-courtiers alike, besides encouraging further patronage, yet those copies which have been attributed to individual owners of the highest ranks are mostly run-of-the-mill.[53] Earl Rivers' version of the *Dicts and Sayings of the Philosophers* was copied, from a different exemplar than that used for the printed edition, by an accomplished clerical scribe and completed about a month later than it in 1477, probably as a Christmas presentation to Edward IV as shown in the well-known

51. See G. D. Painter, *William Caxton* (London, 1976), 72–81; S. Hindman & J. D. Farquhar, *Pen to Press: Illustrated Manuscripts and Printed Books in the First Century of Printing* (College Park, 1977), 123–5, 135–7.

52. The *Sarum Horae* on vellum, in the Pierpont Morgan Library, New York, printed between 1476 and 1478, possibly at Bruges, has illumination in the Flemish style, not English; and so are the initials of the Ovid manuscript (Pepys Library, Magdalene College, Cambridge), which is on paper. For the former see British Library Reference Division, *William Caxton: an Exhibition* (London, 1976), 41; for the latter *The Metamorphoses of Ovid Translated by W. Caxton*, 2 vols (New York, 1968).

53. The Huntington Library *Recuyell of the Histories of Troy*, 1474, with the unique frontispiece, has an early attribution to Queen Elizabeth Woodville: see Painter, *William Caxton*, frontisp., 63: the Thomas Shukburghe junior who signs it was possibly the man of the same style who appears in additions to Harvard University Law School MS.43, very likely a London draper. The former Holford *Godfrey of Boloyne*, 1481, now in the Rosenbach Foundation, Philadelphia, is attributed to Edward IV by a 16th/17th-century hand; the only contemporary inscription is that of Roger Thorney, the London mercer, owner of other English books.

miniature.[54] This was sticking to tradition in more than one way, for it looks as if it was at the author's initiative and a scribe of special talent takes the place in the foreground, not the printer and publisher. The latter's job, the manufacture and dissemination of further copies, was conceived as quite distinct still.

When manuscripts were specially made for presentation to someone of eminence, by authors wanting rewards or others after favours, the standards of execution were likely to be as high as the donor could afford and procure. The display of such gifts in court and household must have sometimes inspired emulation, or inclined the recipients and their friends to commission similar books. Gifts to the monarch or other potential patrons were a custom of court life, and theirs in return, which could, but would not necessarily promote literary circulation. Book-selection at all times, whether by individuals or for institutions, involves a large element of well-meaning or wishful thinking, not uncommonly disappointed in the event. If the taste for books in English of particular kinds did not catch on there widely or quickly enough to occupy the suppliers fairly steadily, a distinctive 'court style' was unlikely to develop, nor was it when the alternative markets were larger. The court in England was not insulated and inward-looking, and it was far from self-sufficient in exemplars or executants of books. People moved in and out of it frequently and freely and did not expect to find their books in one place and that, so far as it tended to happen, would be London, not Westminster.

Although the tendency of this cursory treatment of selected examples has been to doubt a uniquely distinguishable influence of the royal court on the character of book-production in English, and to emphasise alternative centres, I want to emphasise the interim and fragmentary nature of my observations. The foregoing survey is not a thorough comparision of all the books, even in English, which can be connected with the court in the period. Until the sorting-out of the oeuvre of scribes, limners and minaturists has gone a good deal further, and the early ownership of many manuscripts has been better investigated, I shall not be confident that I have not misrepresented the state of affairs; and if the present exercise has been of any value it has been in raising questions I have not had time to pursue, some of a contradictory effect.

---

54. Lambeth Palace Library MS 265: James, *Descriptive Catalogue*, 412–4; Painter, pl. iia. If the figure in the foreground on his knees with Rivers is the scribe, Haywarde, he was a cleric, from his garb perhaps a member of a college; and St James in the Fields, where he wrote, may be the hospital of that name at Westminster. Cf. *VCH* London I (1909), 545. It cannot be Guillaume de Tignonville, the original author, unless the miniaturist misunderstood the status of the Provost of Paris!

10

Music and Poetry at Court: England and France in the Late Middle Ages

Nigel Wilkins

Anglia et Francia,
Cunctaque imperia
Orbis per climata:
Benedicite Deo.

(Fifteenth-century carol)

My theme is the constant interchange and cross-influence which took place in music and poetry in the late middle ages between England and France.

The general conditions for such contact were, of course, very good. Quite apart from the still widespread use of French among the English nobility and the English possession of large territories on the Continent, Anglo-French marriages kept the common culture alive. Kings from Henry III and Eleanor of Provence to Henry VI and Margaret of Anjou, dukes such as Bedford with Anne of Burgundy or the duke of Burgundy with Margaret of York . . . even Chaucer's wife Philippa, it has been surmised, was a lady-in-waiting like her mistress Queen Philippa from Hainault, and thus French-speaking.

The drawn-out conflict of the Hundred Years War, if anything, reinforced mutual contacts and influences with the frequent presence of the English in large numbers south of the Channel, the continual to-and-fro of ambassadors and proclamations. Certain moments in these campaigns stand out from the general troubled and complex background as particularly favourable to cultural exchange, and these could with profit be considered more closely. I have in mind in particular: the circle of Walloon artists and men-of-letters which gathered around Queen Philippa in the English court; the celebrated captivities of Jean le Bon, king of France, after Poitiers in 1356, and of the duke Charles d'Orléans, after Agincourt in 1415; the regentship of the duke of Bedford in Paris (1422–35). Around these points, we shall see, considerable networks of many kinds stretch out, including networks of musical and poetic contact. I propose here to deal for the most part with the outstanding poets and musicians of the period. Records of contact on the humbler level of minstrelsy, whether of foreign minstrels in England, or of English and Scottish minstrels abroad, are to be found in such profusion that a very extensive inventory would be needed to list them all.[1]

It should be noted that very little purely instrumental music survives from this period. Secular music thus mostly consists of songs: lyric texts set to music, in France mostly in *ballade, rondeau* and *virelai* forms, generally for solo voice with a small number of accompanying instruments. These are never specified in the sources, but certainly were such as small harp, fiddle, lute, rebec or psaltery. Due to the swift technical advances made in the composition of polyphony in the fourteenth century, however, as we see above all in the works of Philippe de Vitry, Guillaume de Machaut and the later so-called 'ars subtilior', a divorce took place between the traditionally allied arts of poetry and music. Many major poets emerged, such as Froissart, Deschamps, Christine de Pisan, Chartier and Charles d'Orléans, using the musical forms for their verse but having to be content with this *seconde rhetorique* unless some independent musician chose them for setting. In a context where some manuscripts give song texts alone but omit settings which certainly existed, where apparently non-musical poets such as Chaucer are praised for their 'songs', and where the practice of *contrafactum*, or the fitting of a new text to already existent music, was extremely common, it will be understood that there is at times uncertainty as to whether a poem in lyric form was originally set, or could have been set, or was later set to music. Hence the need firmly to include poetry in our discussion. In England very few polyphonic settings of this type with English words have survived,[2] though we do have the rich repertory of fifteenth-century carols[3] and the later music from the court of Henry VIII.[4] The obvious taste for the French

1. See references particularly in: H. Anglès, 'La musica anglesa dels segles XIII–XIV als Països Hispanics', in *Analecta Sacra Tarraconensia*, ii (1935), 211–34; C. Bullock-Davies, *Menestrellorum Multitudo* (Cardiff, 1978); M. C. Gómez Muntané, *La Música en la casa real catalano-aragonese 1336–1442*, (Barcelona, 1979); W. Grattan-Flood, 'Entries relating to music in the English patent rolls of the fifteenth century', in *The Musical Antiquary*, iv (1912–13), 225–35; J. Marix, *Histoire de la musique et des musiciens de la cour de Bourgogne sous le règne de Philippe le Bon* (Strasbourg, 1939); A. Pirro, *La musique à Paris sous le règne de Charles VI* (2nd. ed., Paris, 1958); R. Rastall, *The Minstrels of the English Royal Households, 25 Edward I - Henry VIII: an Inventory, Royal Musical Association Research Chronicle*, iv (1967); *Register of the Black Prince* (London, 1930–3); N. Wilkins, *Music in the Age of Chaucer* (Cambridge, 1979).

2. See E. Dobson & F. Harrison, *Medieval English Songs* (London, 1979).

3. Ed. J. Stevens, *Medieval Carols, Musica Britannica*, iv (London, 1958).

4. Ed. J. Stevens, *Music at the Court of Henry VIII, Musica Britannica*, xviii (London, 1962).

style of poetry and music in the late fourteenth and early fifteenth centuries is, however, very well attested in the works of Chaucer, Gower and Lydgate,[5] and there also exist 'mixed-repertory' sources from the period, and examples of *contrafactum*, which we must examine later.

Music was a very basic ingredient in life in the middle ages, at all levels and on all conceivable occasions. One of the best examples to demonstrate both the widespread concern for the cultivation and enjoyment of music and poetry and the firm background of Anglo-French cultural contact before the Hundred Years War is the society of the Pui which existed in London in the late thirteenth and early fourteenth centuries. This was a brotherhood of French and English traders in London. Like many a guild it served social and charitable purposes, but also, in the French tradition, was a forum for musical and poetic contest. In 1299 Sir Henry le Waleys, who had been mayor of both Bordeaux and London, granted to the brethren of the Pui 'five marks of yearly quit-rent, toward the support of one Chaplain celebrating divine service in the new Chapel at the Guildhall of London'.[6] The very full statutes of the Pui[7] give us invaluable insight into the activities of such gatherings, and it is surprising that the document is so little referred to in literary histories. In particular, for our present purposes, we may note the regulations appointing the retiring 'prince' of the Pui, together with the newly-elected 'prince', as judges of the best song; a crown is to be presented to the winning entrant:

Et doivent jugier le meillour des chançons, a lour escient. . .
Et le meillour des chauçons doit estre corouné . . .[8]

All members of the Pui are required to promote *chaunsouns reales* to the best of their ability, this being the main purpose of the *feste roiale du Pui*, and above all the prize-winning song, which is to be especially copied out and for one year suspended beneath the arms of the new Prince in the Banquet Hall. No singer is to perform on the annual feast day if the previous winner has not been duly honoured in this way. The judges must include men knowledgeable in music as well as in verse, and no entry can be considered to be a true *chaunçon reale* if it has no melody:

E qe il ieit a les chauçouns juger eslu .ii. ou .iii. qi se conoisent en

5. For a general background to the music of this period, see: N. Wilkins, op. cit.; I. Cazeaux, *French Music in the Fifteenth and Sixteenth Centuries* (Oxford, 1975); J. Caldwell, *Medieval Music* (London, 1978).

6. H. Riley, *Memorials of London and London Life in the Thirteenth, Fourteenth and Fifteenth centuries* (London, 1868).

7. Ed. H. Riley, *Munimenta Gildhallae Londoniensis: Liber Custumarum*, ii (*RS*, 1859–62), 216–28.

8. Ibid., 217.

chaunt et en musike, pur les notes et les poinz del chaunt trier et examiner, auxi bien com la nature de la reson enditée. Kar saunz le chaunt ne doit om mie appeler une resoun endité chançoun, ne chaunçoun reale courounée ne doit estre saunz douçour de melodies chaunteé.[9]

Puis, with their princes, just like minstrel guilds with their kings, are, of course, a reflection of the real thing. Noblemen could participate in the proceedings of Puis, but kings of minstrels mostly performed for noblemen, and we have to accept that the vast majority of the music which has survived from the late middle ages is true court music, by which I understand music designed and performed for entertainment and ceremonial in noble and ecclesiastical, as well as royal circles. Only in such courts were patrons of sufficient sophistication to be found, with very few exceptions, and only there could funds be provided for expensive manuscript copying and the assemblage of precious written repertories. Most popular or folk music, by its very nature, is oral in tradition or improvisatory in character, and so fails to survive. Records of bourgeois or popular musical activity are far outnumbered, naturally, by descriptions of musical performance in noble settings, and in addition courts have so often left us extensive and informative payment accounts. In the realm of church music, although much which survives is of monastic or cathedral origin, some comes from court chapels: a very celebrated example is the Old Hall manuscript, now BL Add. 57950,[10] which contains late fourteenth- and early fifteenth-century music from the English Chapel Royal. We should also note the possibility of church musicians, principally employed to sing, composing and performing entirely secular items for court entertainment: the period offers many such examples, among the most celebrated of which are Machaut and Dufay, and a valuable attestation of this practice is given in a letter written in 1389 by king John I of Aragon which specifically refers to singers in the papal church at Avignon as the best composers of motets, *ballades*, *rondeaux* and *virelais*.[11]

The essential rôle of music in flamboyant court celebrations may be illustrated by the Anglo-French occasion of the wedding of Henry V of England to Catherine of France on 2 June 1420 at Troyes. On 1 July 1415 Henry V's twenty-eight chapel singers had sung for the French envoys come to negotiate the marriage;[12] in 1418 six singers

---

9. Ibid., 224–5.

10. Ed. A. Hughes & M. Bent, *The Old Hall Manuscript, CMM* 46, (American Institute of Musicology, 1969).

11. M. C. Gómez Muntané, *Conèixer Catalunya: La música medieval* (Barcelona, 1980), 94.

12. J. Marix, op. cit. 148.

were brought from England for the king's chapel in France.[13] From
the signing of the treaty at Troyes in April 1420 Henry had remained
there, surrounded by chaplains and instrumentalists. On several occasions the duke of Burgundy, Philippe le Bon, made payments to the
English king's heralds and minstrels, and to those of other English
lords there present. The coach carrying the two queens, driven by
coachmen liveried in scarlet striped with gold, was preceded by a huge
assembly of trumpeters and the like:

> et par devant ce chariot se demenoit grand melodie de trompettes, cla-
> rons, menestrès et de moult d'autres instruments a cents et a
> milliers. . .[14]

During the celebrations the new queen, Catherine, played the harp.[15]

The most elaborate musical occasion of all must have been the
celebrated Feast of the Pheasant in Lille on 17 February 1454, which
was a gathering of the Knights of the Order of the Golden Fleece
(Toison d'Or). This included, in the banquet hall, a model church with
sounding bells and four singers who also played organs; an enormous
pie containing twenty-eight *live* performers on divers instruments;
two trumpeters playing a fanfare while riding a horse which entered
the hall backwards; a twelve-year old boy singing astride a handsome
stag, which miraculously provided a tenor voice; a noble lady simply
attired in white satin and representing Holy Church, who sang a
piteous lament on the back of an elephant, led in by a giant! The
whole entertainment was very extended and highly organized into a
pattern of surprises and contrasts.[16] Similar entertainments, including
a lion singing in two voices and a quartet of flute-playing wolves, were
seen in 1468 at the wedding between Charles le Téméraire and
Margaret of York.[17] Olivier de la Marche states that Charles composed
songs, though he had a poor voice:

> . . aimoit la musique, combien qu'i eust mauvais voix, mais toutefois il
> avoit l'art, et fist le chant de plusieurs chanssons bien faictes et bien
> notées.[18]

The nobility were sometimes introduced to the practice of music at an
early age. The fifteen- and twelve-year old Charles VI of France and
his brother Louis, for instance, were given musettes and some small-
size instruments on 25 March 1383:

13. A. Pirro, op. cit. 31.
14. *Chronique manuscrite de la Haye*, after J. Marix, op. cit., 24; see also *Le Livre des Trahisons de France envers La Maison de Bourgogne*, ed. K. de Lettenhove (1873), 156.
15. A. Pirro, op. cit., 31.
16. J. Marix, op. cit., 37–43.
17. Ibid., 43, 106.
18. Ibid., 19.

Maistre Johan Boutier, secrettaire de monseigneur de Valois, pour l'argent qu'il a baillie au Roy et a mondit seigneur de Valois pour acheter des musettes et autres petis instruments. . .[19]

Louis d'Orléans was to become a lavish patron of minstrels, and his wife Valentina Visconti was fond of playing the harp. Their son Charles d'Orléans also played this instrument,[20] as did Charles VI's daughter Isabelle, who became an English queen.[21] Charles V of France had been said by Christine de Pisan to be so knowledgeable in music that no–one dared play wrong notes in his presence.[22] In England Richard II is known to have been devoted to poetry and music; we recall his enthusiastic reception of Froissart's book of love poems, his patronage of Gower, or scenes such as those during his presence at Milford Haven, described by the French visitor at court, Jean Creton:[23]

Mainte trompette y povoit on oïr,
De jour, de nuit, menestrelz retentir.[24]

It seems likely that Henry IV was the 'roy Henry' represented by a *Gloria* in the Old Hall manuscript. When he entered London after the deposition of Richard II, the Mayor and Commons came out to meet him 'a grant quantité d'instrumens et de trompetes'.[25] Henry VIII's musical talents are particularly well known.[26] Earlier, we may note that Henry of Lancaster, in the pious work of his later years, *Le Livre de Seyntz Medecines*,[27] confesses to a weakness for vocal and instrumental music.[28] John of Gaunt, incidentally, provided French statutes for the only known minstrels' guild in fourteenth-century England, at Tutbury.[29] Of Sir John Montagu, earl of Salisbury and Knight of the Garter, we read:

19. L Douët d'Arcq, *Comptes de l'hôtel des rois de France au XIVe et XVe siècles* (Paris, 1865).

20. P. Champion, *Vie de Charles d'Orléans* (2nd ed., Paris, 1969), 477–8.

21. Her harp was repaired in 1405: see A. Pirro, op. cit., 26.

22. *Livre des fais et bonnes moeurs du sage roy Charles V*, ed. S. Solente (Paris, 1936–41).

23. Creton included in his history a Ballade critical of Henry IV, 'O tu Henry, qui as en gouvernance', and also composed further *ballades* contained in the MS Paris, BN., n.a.fr.6223.

24. *Metrical History of the Deposition of King Richard II*, ed. J. Webb, in *Arch.*, xx (1824), 297.

25. Ibid., 178, 377.

26. For an inventory of English royal minstrels, see R. Rastall, op.cit.; also *Liber Quotidianus . . . 1299–1300*, ed. J. Nicols (Society of Antiquaries, London, 1787), 163, 166, 168, 323.

27. Ed. E. Arnould, (Oxford, 1940).

28. Ibid., 10, 22.

29. N. Wilkins, op. cit., 140.

Et si faisoit balades et chançons
Rondeaulx et lais.[30]

Christine de Pisan, whose discernment in poetry and music we cannot
doubt, called him 'gracieux chevalier, aimant ditiez, et lui même
gracieux dicteur'; almost certainly his verse was composed in French.
The poetess put such trust in him as to give him charge of her
thirteen-year old son Jean, who, 'assez abille et bien chantant', accompanied the earl to England in 1397. Following the deposition of Richard II and the execution of Salisbury, Henry IV seems with
appreciation to have read some of Christine's works, no doubt in
volumes which had belonged to Salisbury, and attempted to use the
son as a pawn to persuade Christine to come to the English court.
Only by deception was she able to secure his return, when she then
presented him to another noble amateur of poetry and music, Louis
d'Orléans:

Ja .iii. ans a que, pour sa grant prouesse,
L'en amena le conte tres louable
De Salsbery, qui mouru a destrece,
Ou mal païs d'Angleterre, ou muable
Y sont la gent. Depuis lors, n'est pas fable,
Y a esté, si ay tel peine mise
Que je le ray non obstant qu'a sa guise
L'avoit Henry, qui de là se dit hoïr.[31]

One of the most complete sources of information we have about the
function of music and musicians in an English royal court is the
much-quoted *Household Book of Edward IV*, compiled in 1471–2.[32]
Kings of arms, heralds and pursuivants 'crye the Kinges largesse,
shaking theyre grete cuppe'[33] at feasts, while minstrels 'use trum-
pettes, some shalmuse and small pipes',[34] and are occasionally aug-
mented by 'strengmen' or outsiders;[35] a wait is allowed to eat in the
hall with the minstrels, and has to pipe the watch four times during
winter nights but three times in summer;[36] chaplains and clerks of
chapel must be 'men of worship endowed with vertuouse, morall and
speculatiff, as of theyre musike, shewing in descant clene voysed, well
relysed and pronouncyng, eloquent in reding, sufficiaunt in organez
playing, and modestiall in other maner of behaving';[37] the eight Chil-

---

30. *Metrical History* . . . , op. cit., 320.
31. Christine de Pisan, *Oeuvres poétiques*, ed. M. Roy, (SATF, Paris, 1886–96), i,
232–3; *cf.* also E. McLeod, *The order of the Rose* (London, 1976), 50–1.
32. Ed. A. Myers, (Manchester, 1959).
33. Ibid., 130.
34. Ibid., 131.
35. Ibid., 132.
36. Ibid., 132.
37. Ibid., 135.

dren of Chapel are in the charge of 'the mastyr of song assigned to teche them .. and he to draw thees chyldren all as well in the scoole of facet as in song, organes, or suche other vertuouse thinges'.[38] Interesting details concerning the later stages of the boys' training are given: 'And when they be growen to the age of .xviij. yeres, and than theyre voyces be chaunged, ne can nat be preferred in this chapell nor within this court, the numbyr beyng full, then, if they wull assent, the King assigneth every suche child to a College of Oxenford or Cambridge, of the kinges fundaciun, there to be in finding and study sufficiauntly tyll the King otherwise list to avaunce hym'.[39] The minstrels of the court may often have found their way into these favoured circles after a long apprenticeship. A rare insight into this kind of training is afforded by an entry in a recently discovered scrivener's book from Bury St. Edmunds, now in Cambridge University Library, MS Add. 7318. In an entry on fol.28v, dated *c*. 1461, we find an indenture in which Thomas Lorymer of Bury, harper, drew an apprentice, William son of Thomas Stevenyssone of Braburne in faraway Northumberland. The boy was apprenticed for seven years and was to receive in his final year a harp, a 'lowde pype' and a 'stille pype'.[40] A royal commission of 10 March 1456 requires Walter Halyday, Robert Marshall, William Wykes and John Cliffe 'to take boys elegant in their natural members and *instructed in the art of minstrelsy*, and to put them in the king's service at the king's wages, to supply the place of certain of the king's minstrels deceased'.[41]

Queen Philippa had come from Hainault to be Edward's III's bride in 1328. As is well known, a circle of Walloon men-of-letters enjoyed her patronage and protection in England. Most famous of all, of course, was the poet and chronicler Jean Froissart. His rôle in propagating French poetry and music, especially that of his master Guillaume de Machaut, must have been considerable. The literary links between Machaut, Froissart and Chaucer are demonstrably great.[42] Froissart's predecessor Jean le Bel, who had fought in Edward III's army in Scotland in 1327, had, it seems, a similar diversity of talents, for the flattering portrait of him drawn up by his friend Jacques de Hemricourt tells us that: 'He was gay and cheerful, and could compose songs

38. Ibid., 136.
39. Ibid., 137.
40. A. Owen, 'A scrivener's notebook from Bury St. Edmunds', *Archives*, xiv (1979), 20.
41. *CPR* 1452–61, 278; see W. Grattan-Flood, op.cit., 230; also C. Bullock-Davies, op. cit., 149–50.
42. See e.g. J. Wimsatt, *Chaucer and the French Love Poets* (Chapel Hill, 1968).

and virelays'. Most interesting of all among Philippa's protégés, though, from the musical point of view, was Jean de la Motte. Jean de la Motte is known today for three substantial verse works: *Li Regret Guillaume Comte de Hainaut*,[43] written in 1339 at the request of Queen Philippa, in memory of her father, who had died two years previously (the closing lines tell us: 'Ce songe contai a ma dame/Qui Jhesus sauve corps et ame,/Qui est roynne d'Engleterre'); two works composed in Paris in 1340 for Symon de Lille, Master Goldsmith of Philippe VI King of France, the Alexander romance of *Le Parfait du Paon*[44] (which contains an acrostic signature) and the pious *La Voie d'Enfer et de Paradis*.[45] Although no music known to be by Jean de la Motte survives today, he was listed in 1350 by Gilles li Muisis, in a celebrated passage in his *Méditations*, along with Philippe de Vitry and Guillaume de Machaut, as one of the prominent living poet-musicians of the time.[46] There seems to be a link between his royal patroness and his craftsman patron, for it is recorded that in 1323 Symon de Lille made 'joyaux et bijoux achetés a Paris pour la fille du Comte de Hainaut'.[47] There is a further link between Jean de la Motte and the famous musical theorist and composer Philippe de Vitry, in lyric form, in the curious exchange of six Ballades involving also Jean Campion.[48] These Ballades date from somewhere between 1328 and 1339. De la Motte tells of his unpleasant crossing to England ('Sur haulte mer, helas, que de nuisanches!')[49] but is reproached, almost as a traitor, by De Vitry, for going 'en Albion de Dieu maudite'.[50] De la Motte's line of defence is that he is not be be reproached, since he is not French, and in any case has never had any reward in France.[51] He uses musically flattering titles in addressing his critic:

O Victriens, mondains dieux d'armonnie,
Filz Musicant et peres Orpheus

and goes on to call him 'Angles en chant'.[52] The title 'Victriens dieus d'armonie' is taken up by the third participant in the debate, Jean Campion, who was a particularly cultured chaplain at Notre Dame in Tournai. His interest in music, and therefore perhaps in Jean de la Motte, is attested by a legacy of books he received in 1357 including

43. Ed. A. Scheler (Louvain, 1882).
44. Ed. R. Carey (Chapel Hill, 1972).
45. Ed. M. Pety (Washington, 1940).
46. See N. Wilkins, op. cit., 1.
47. M. Pety, op. cit., 11.
48. E. Pognon, 'Ballades mythologiques de Jean de la Mote, Philipe de Vitri, Jean Campion', *Humanisme et Renaissance*, v (1938), 385–417.
49. Ibid., 407.
50. Ibid., 409.
51. Ibid., 410.
52. Ibid., 410.

a *Romance of the Rose* and rolls of Motets and songs.[53] Gilles li Muisis also came from Tournai, and could well have mentioned Jean de la Motte in his *Méditations* because Jean Campion introduced his works to him.

The earliest reference we have to Jean de la Motte is from the *Comptes de la Chancellerie de Hainaut*, from 1326–7, before his departure for England, as a copyist of some stories:

> Pour transcrire plusieurs escris des darrains comptes que Gobers fist apres chou k'il eut compté, xx sols.[54]

It has generally been assumed that, after his time in Paris in 1340, he remained on the continent. However, a reference almost certainly to this poet-musician is to be found in the Wardrobe controller's book for 21 July 1343, which shows him being paid for entertaining the English king in a practical musical capacity, at Eltham:

> Johanni de la Mote menistrallo facienti menistralciam suam coram domino Rege in festo Pasche apud Eltham, de dono regis per manus proprias ultimo die Marcii xl s.[55]

Further evidence of Jean de la Motte's musical and poetic activities in the English court may well emerge from a close study of the appropriate account books of this period. Records of payments to the minstrels of Queen Philippa do not always specify names, such as those who in 1358 'were in her company with the prince at Waltham'.[56]

The works of this poet-musician, active in the English court, it seems, over a period of possibly twenty years, provide further evidence of his interest in the musical side of his craft. *Le Parfait du Paon*, albeit in pseudo-antique setting, contains a remarkable passage describing a court song contest, not far removed from the ceremonies described in the statutes of the London Pui, with a detailed account of the composing and copying of ballades, which are included in the text, the singing of them and performance on instruments such as flutes, shawms, organs, harps, gitterns, douçaines, flageolets, pipes, horns, trumpets, drums and fiddles.[57] Although, sadly, no music is given in the manuscript source, great emphasis is laid on the need for

53. A. de la Grange, 'Choix de testaments tournaisiens antérieurs au XVIᵉ siècle', *Annales de la Société historique et archéologique de Tournai*, ii (1897), 79.

54. M. Pety, op. cit., 6.

55. *PRO*, E 36/204, fol. 84v; see R. Rastall, op. cit., 19; I thank Dr Rastall for his assistance in verifying this point.

56. *Register of the Black Prince* (London, 1930–33), iv, 251; other French-speaking queens had their personal minstrels too, e.g. payments in 1299–1300 to Guillot de Psalteron, minstrel of Queen Margaret, *Liber Quotidianus . . . 1299–1300*, 7, 95; cf. R. Rastall, op. cit., 9, 14, 20.

57. N. Wilkins, op. cit., 2–3.

all entries in the contest to have a proper musical setting, just as it had been in the London statutes.

Il vous convient par force *a canter* esmouvoir. (984)

J'ai si grant haste au fere qu'elle n'est pas notée.
Et dist Buchiforas: 'N'est pas chose ordenée,
Balade vaut trop peu quant elle n'est chantée.'
Et respont Preamuse: 'Bien tost seroit werblée.' (1209–12)

In the dream framework of *Li Regret Guillaume Comte de Hainaut*, Jean de la Motte describes himself as composing in his sleep a love song which he might later enter in a contest:

En dormant melancolioie
A une cançon amoureuse,
Et par samblance grascieuse
Dis k'a .i. puis la porteroie
Pour couronner, si je pooie. (100–4)

He later tells how, while he was passing through some woods and trying to memorize his song, he heard the sounds of many loud instruments:

En ce biau lieu fu fais recors
De la cançon que je portoie.
Einsi que je le recordoie,
Viers le seniestre main oÿ
Retentir le grant bos foelli,
De trompes et de calemiaus,
Et d'arrainnes et de fretiaus,
De nacaires et de tabours,
De timbres dont li sons est dous. (140–8)

Following this he reaches a castle, relates what he has heard, and reveals his own talents as a minstrel:

S'oÿ ceens moult grant menée
Des cors, des trompes, des buisinnes;
Dame, ce sont les causes finnes
Par quoi ceste part aproçai,
Car .i. poi deduire me sai
De faire plaintes et clamours,
Brances d'armes et dis d'armours.
Pour çou vouloie chi entrer
Pour aucun boin fait recorder
Afin c'a tous peüisse plaire. (226–35)

In addition, this work contains thirty Ballades intended to be sung by each of the noble qualities lamenting the passing of Queen Philippa's father. There is much skill here in metrical variation, and certain lines provide a link to the greatest poet-musician of fourteenth-century France, Guillaume de Machaut, who was born in 1300. The first *ballade*, for instance, sung by Debonnaireté, has the same first line, 'On ne porroit penser ne souhaidier' and a similar refrain, 'Puis c'ai pierdu la flour de douçour pure', as a *ballade* by Machaut in his collection entitled *La Louange des Dames*.[58] Machaut's refrain reads 'Quant j'aim la flour de toute creature'. De la Motte's 14th ballade opening 'Cuer de marbre couronné d'aÿmant', reappears as the first of two refrain lines in Machaut's Chant Royal 'Amis, je t'ay tant amé et cheri'.[59] Although there is some room for uncertainty, it seems fairly clear that Machaut was indebted to De la Motte, rather than the other way about.[60] In addition, certain lines of De la Motte anticipate lines in songs by poet-musicians of the post-Machaut generation. A notable example of this is the fourth line of Ballade II in the set of six. The opening lines also contain musical allusions:

Dyodonas a ses cleres buisines,
Ne Orpheus li dieux de melodie,
Ne Musicans a ses chançons divines,
Ne Dedalus od sa gaye maistrie

– none of these divinities has the power to comfort the poet. A later Ballade by Taillandier begins 'Se Dedalus en sa gaye mestrie'.[61] Queen Philippa's protégé thus played an important rôle in the development of poetry and music in France, and his own songs must often have been heard in courts there as in the English court.

The noble French prisoners taken to England after Crécy and Poitiers, as is well known, were allowed to engage in many of the more pleasant aspects of court life while they waited for their ransoms to be paid, and the more distinguished of them maintained retinues, including musicians. Raoul de Brienne, comte de Guïnes and comte d'Eu,[62] for

58. Ed. N. Wilkins (Edinburgh, 1972).
59. Ed. cit., 47.
60. C.F.E. Hoepffner, 'Die Balladen des Dichters Jehan de la Mote', *Zeitschrift für romanische Philologie*, xxxv (1911), 153–66.
61. Ed. W. Apel, *French Secular Compositions of the Fourteenth Century*, CMM, 53 (1970), i, 207–8; cf. also N. Wilkins, 'The late medieval French lyric: with music and without', in *Wolfenbüttel Kolloquium*, (1980).
62. Jean d'Artois, comte d'Eu was captured with Jean II at Poitiers in 1356; Philippe d'Artois, comte d'Eu was invited to judge the *Livre des Cent Ballades* composed by his Seneschal Jean de Bordes when in captivity with Boucicaut in Egypt *c.* 1388; his son, Charles, comte d'Eu was captured along with Boucicaut and Charles d'Orléans at Agincourt in 1415. Boucicaut (d. 1421) and Charles d'Orléans took part in an exchange of rondeaux: ed. P. Champion, *Charles d'Orléans: Poésies* (Paris, 1956), ii, 353–5.

instance, was awarded the 'favour of the field' as best jouster at the Windsor Tournament in 1348 and the *Register of the Black Prince* lists in 1352 'Four pipes, silver-gilt and enamelled, made for the minstrels sent by the Count of Ewe from the parts of France', these being given to the prince's minstrels, along with a bagpipe, a cornemuse and a drum.[63] Account book payments in the Black Prince's household in 1352 mention minstrels named Hans and Soz and it has been conjectured that these may have been two of the four minstrels so provided.[64] It is curious to note the taste for an ensemble of four flutes, for which no known music survives; Philippe le Bon had sent a similar set of instruments to the Marquis of Ferrara in 1426, and they were seen again at the York-Burgundy wedding.[65]

Following Poitiers, lavish entertainments were provided for the new distinguished French prisoners as well as for David Bruce and Scottish lords still held in England. We read of tournaments at Smithfield in 1357, a night-time tournament at Bristol in January 1358, and especially the lavish Garter feast at Windsor in April 1358, when the Black Prince paid £100 to the heralds and minstrels.[66]

Within a short time of his arrival in England in May 1357, the captive king of France, Jean II, was installed with his son Philippe and their retinue in Windsor Castle. As Froissart tells us, hunting occupied much of their time:

> Si alloit voler, chasser, deduire et prendre tous ses esbatemens environ Windsor.[67]

Particularly interesting is the presence in the king's company of the chaplain Gaces de la Buigne, who taught the young prince falconry and composed for general instruction a verse hunting treatise, *Le Roman des Deduis*,[68] a worthy rival to the *Livre de la Chasse* of that noted patron of poets and musicians, Gaston Febus, comte de Foix. Gaces de la Buigne began his treatise in Hertford in 1359, when the French king was moved there, and completed it in France at a later date.[69] For our present purposes, the most striking section is where

---

63. Vol. iv, 73; in 1355 the instruments are again listed: 'two silver trumpets given to Ralph Dexestre and John Martyn respectively, and of four pipes, silver-gilt and enamelled, which the Prince has given to the four minstrels sent to him by the Count of Eu, and of a cornemuse, a pipe and a tabor, silver-gilt and enamelled, which the Prince has given to his own minstrels' (vol. iv, 157); see also R. Barber, *Edward, Prince of Wales and Aquitaine* (London, 1978), 92–3.

64. R. Rastall, op. cit. 21.

65. J. Marix, op. cit., 42.

66. R. Barber, op. cit., 154–5.

67. Froissart, *Chroniques*, ed. J. A. C. Buchon 3 vols (Paris, 1837), iii, 267.

68. Ed. A. Blomquist (Karlshamm, 1951).

69. Duc d'Aumale, *Notes et documents relatifs à Jean, roi de France et à sa captivité en Angleterre* (Miscellanies of the Philobiblon Society, ii London, 1855), 189–90.

the chaplain, who clearly was highly regarded in the French royal household within England, shows detailed musical knowledge in an extended comparison between the baying of hounds at the sight of their prey and the singing of the choir in the king's chapel:

Adoncques y a telle noïse
Qu'il n'est homs qui sur deux pieds voise
Qui onc oÿst tel melodie;
Car n'est respons, ne alleluye,
Et feust chantée en la Chappelle
Du Roy, qui là est bonne et belle,
Qui si grant plaisance face
Comme est ouïr une tel chace.
Les uns vont chantant le motet,
Les autres font double hoquet,
Les plus grans chantent la teneur,
Les autres la contreteneur;
Ceulx qui ont la plus clere gueule
Chantent le tresble sans demeure,
Et les plus petits le quadrouble,
En faisant la quinte surdouble;
Les uns font semithon mineur,
Les autres semithon majeur,
Diapenthe, diapazon,
Les autres dyathessaron.
Adonc le Roy met cor a bouche . . .[70]

Surviving account books for 1359 and 1360 give numerous details of the French king's musical concerns. His *Roy des menestereux*, a faithful companion in a difficult time, is particularly charged with negotiations for the making and purchase of a special clock.[71] Clement, *clerc de chapelle*, on the other hand is entrusted with moving and maintaining an organ, possibly a positive rather than the smaller portative type. The instrument was transported from London to Hertford[72] and back again to London. Skins, nails, glue and twine had to be purchased for repairs which were effected in three weeks by *Maistre Jehan, l'organier*, who travelled from London to Somerton. Extra charges were incurred for transportation and a helper for three days' pumping![73] In 1360 the king also received, as a gift from Edward III, a clavichord or *eschequier*; on his behalf his *Roy des menestereux* purchased a harp, and also visited Chichester to inspect *certains in-*

70. Duc d'Aumale, op. cit., 174; the passage is also quoted by J. Marix, op. cit., 15.

71. Duc d'Aumale, op. cit., 91, 103, 108, 112–13, 117, 132; L. Douët d'Arcq, *Comptes de l'argenterie des rois de France au XIVe siècle* (Paris, 1851), 209, 221.

72. Duc d'Aumale, op. cit., 120.

73. L. Douët d'Arcq, op. cit., 214, 221, 239–40; we have other instances of such concern for organ maintenance, e.g. the Duc de Berry in 1371, see N. Wilkins, op. cit., 134.

strumens.[74] It is intriguing to note that in February 1359 Jean II made payments to Maciet and Thomelin, minstrels of the king of Scotland.[75]

When Charles d'Orléans came to England in 1415 to begin his twenty-five year exile, few can have foreseen that he would come to compose some of the finest lyric poetry in Middle English.[76] In the late fourteenth century a network of Anglo-French poetic exchange had involved, among others, Machaut, Froissart, Deschamps,[77] Granson,[78] Chaucer and Gower.[79] Charles d'Orléans, who had already proved his poetic accomplishment in French and had exchanged verses with such as his unfortunate companion-in-arms at Agincourt, Jehan de Garencières,[80] entered into a comparable network[81] especially from August 1432 when he was put into the keeping of William de la Pole,

74. L. Douët d'Arcq, op. cit., 273, 248, 241; ibid., 382 records a purchase in 1393 of a harp case for the Queen, and in 1403 to Colin Julienne, *harpeur*, for repairing and restringing the harp of the *Royne d'Angleterre*.

75. Duc d'Aumale, op. cit., 106; little attention has been paid to poetic and musical consequences of the *auld alliance* at this early date. Scottish poetry contains some remarkable echoes of the French repertory, however; *cf.* the anonymous late fourteenth-century *rondeau* 'Passerose de biauté pure et fine/Et de bonté tres douche flour de lys' (ed. N. Wilkins, *A Fourteenth-Century Repertory from the Codex Reina*, *CMM* 36 (1966), and Dunbar's 'Sweit roise of vertew and of gentilnes, /Delytsum lilie of everie lustynes', ed. W. Mackay Mackenzie, *The Poems of William Dunbar* (London, 1932), 99.

76. Ed. R. Steele, *The English Poems of Charles d'Orléans*, EETS OS 215, 220 (1941, 1946).

77. Deschamps addressed a *ballade* of eulogy to Chaucer, 'O Socrates, plains de philosophie', ed. Q. de S. Hilaire & G. Raynaud, *Oeuvres complètes* (*SATF*, Paris, 1878–1903), ii, 138–40.

78. Chaucer's group of three Ballades entitled *The Compleynt of Venus* is an adaptation of Ballades by Oton de Granson: ed. A. Piaget, *Oton de Grandson: sa vie et ses poésies* (Lausanne, 1941), 209–13.

79. Gower wrote *Cinkante Balades* in French dedicated to Henry IV, and deliberately changes from the English of his *Confessio Amantis* to the French of his *Traité* and eighteen Ballades which follow in seven out of ten MSS: 'Puis qu'il dit ci devant en Englois par voie d'essample la sotie de cellui qui pour amours aime par especial, *dirra ore en françois* a tout le monde en general un traité selonc les auctors pour essampler les amantz marietz ...', J. Gower, *Complete Works*, ed. G. C. Macaulay (Oxford, 1899), i, 335–78, 378–92. Note also the northern translation by Quixley of Gower's *Traité*, 'probably the earliest Ballade sequence in English', H. Cohen, *The Ballade* (New York, 1915), 264–6.

80. Ed. Y. Neal, *Le Chevalier Poète Jehan de Garencières (1372–1415)* (Paris, 1953).

81. Note, by contrast, Alain Chartier's lady in his *Livre des Quatre Dames*, whose lover has been captured by the English at Agincourt and who wants to hear no more music:
1488.   Ne il n'est harpe, orgue ne doulçaine,
        Luz n'eschequier,
    N'instrument que on sceust appliquer,
    Que desormaiz ouÿr requier ... Ed. J. Laidlaw, *The Poetical Works of Alain Chartier* (Cambridge, 1974), 242.

third earl, later duke of Suffolk. At about this time Suffolk married Geoffrey Chaucer's grand-daughter Alice and at Wingfield and Ewelme provided a resort for cultured company, including especially the poet 'monk of Bury', John Lydgate, who had been a friend of Alice Chaucer's father, Thomas.[82] Although Charles d'Orléans wrote no music, he had great sympathy for it. In 1414 he had embroidered on his sleeves, using 568 pearls, the 142 notes of a *chanson*, 'Madame, je suis plus joyeux'.[83] As we have seen, he played the harp, and also the organ. When he eventually returned to Blois he was pleased to find 'son vieil psalterion enclos en ung estuis de bois'.[84] In 1413 a payment is recorded to his harper Jehan Petit-Gai.[85] At his marriage to Marie de Clèves, niece of Philippe le Bon, in Bruges, following his release in 1440,[86] the ceremonies included church processions chanting *Te Deum laudamus* 'a haulte voix et clere' and playing on silver trumpets, clarions, and many other instruments, so many that the town resounded from them.[87] Marie de Clèves shared his musical interests.[88] In 1449 three 'haulx menestrels anglois' played before her at Blois; in 1451, 1452 and 1457 the duke received English heralds sent by the duchess of Somerset.[89] Suffolk, for his part, also wrote *rondeaux* and *ballades* in the language of his captors,[90] in France in 1429, curiously in the château of Dunois, half-brother to Charles d'Orléans. One of this group, however, the *ballade* 'Dieux nous dona petit de vie', is described by Shirley as simply a poem which Suffolk highly approved of ('Theorlle mich allowethe in his witt'), while the Rondeau 'Lealment a tous jours mais', described as 'made by my lord of Suffolk whylest he was prysonnier in Fraunce', is in fact by Alain Chartier.[91] That

82. See E. McLeod, *Charles of Orléans* (London, 1969), 186–7.

83. A. Pirro, op.cit., 26 n.2.

84. P. Champion, *Vie de Charles d'Orléans* (Paris, 1969), 477.

85. L. de Lincy, *Recueil de chants historiques* (Paris, 1841), i, xxxiii.

86. An element of the negotiations was an exchange in *ballade* form between the dukes of Orléans and Burgundy: P. Champion, *Charles d'Orléans: Poésies*, i, 138–49.

87. J. Marix, op. cit., 30–1.

88. 'Volentiers elle entendait ses quatre chantres, les hauts menestrels anglais, les lombards, les guitarniers d'Orléans, son tambourineur Pierre Fleury', P. Champion, op. cit., 525.

89. P. Champion, *Charles d'Orléans: Poésies*, ii, 569.

90. In MSS. Cambridge, Trinity College, R.3.20, and BL Add. 34360. Pages 49 & 52 of the Cambridge MS, inadequately described in the *Catalogue*, 77, give Ballades by Eustache Deschamps, who is described as 'le plus grand poetycal clerk de Parys'. The first of these, 'Le monde va en amendant', is followed by a Lydgate English translation, 'This worlde is ful of stabulnesse'; the second, 'Qui veult son corps en santé maintenir', is found elsewhere, MS BL Lansdowne 699, in English translation also by Lydgate, 'Who will been holle and kepe hym from sekenesse'; see H. Cohen, op. cit., 262–264.

91. See H. MacCracken, 'An English Friend of Charles d'Orléans', *PMLA*, xxvi (1911), 142–180; MacCracken's suggestion that English poems in the MS Bodleian Library, Fairfax 16 are by Suffolk was refuted by Steele, op. cit., xxi–xxiii. The Compleynt 'Knelyng allon, ryght thus I may make my wylle' (Fairfax MS, ed. MacCracken, op. cit., 158–9) gives in the first stanza the acrostic KATERIN; cf. the Ballade by

Suffolk shared Charles' fondness for music is amply proven by the fact that during his time in France he had in his service from 1424 one of the greatest composers of the period, Gilles Binchois.[92] A curious document, the deposition of Guillaume Benoît, a former steward of Suffolk's, concerning his master's alleged involvement in a plot to assassinate the duke of Burgundy, tells how Suffolk, recuperating in Paris at the end of 1424, was in a highly emotional state over a slight said to have been given to his *dame*; in order to regain his spirits he had poetry by Garencières and other *diz amoureux* read to him, and also heard Binchois perform ('. . . je lui fey venir Binchoiz qui, par son command, *fist* ce rondel', in the circumstances, may be understood as *performed* rather than composed, as A. Pirro takes it[93]) a *rondeau* 'Ainsi qu'a la fois m'y souvient'.[94] It is interesting to note that Binchois, with unusual discernment, eventually set to music a *ballade* by Christine de Pisan and a *rondeau* by Chartier, as well as the *rondeau* 'Mon cuer chante joyeusement' of Charles d'Orléans;[95] indeed, two further settings of Charles d'Orléans' *rondeaux*, in an Escorial MS, 'Je ne prise point tels baisiers' and 'Va tost mon amoureux desir', may also be by Binchois.[96] The deposition also mentions that in 1425, when Suffolk was travelling in Hainault, Binchois was in his company and took the part of the duke of Burgundy in argument with some Norman brothers named Desquay.[97] This is interesting, for Binchois in 1430 joined the Burgundian court and remained there until 1456 as a member of the ducal chapel. It is in this setting that he is linked with his great contemporary Guillaume Dufay, in a passage in *Le Champion des Dames*,[98] where Martin le Franc, writing *c.* 1440, declares

---

Russell, 'Slombrying ryhgt choncefull ful of unkyndenes' (MS Cambridge, Trinity College, R.14.51, fol. 95) which apparently concerns Catherine de Valois, wife of Henry V; see H. Cohen, op. cit., 289–91.

92. J. Marix, op. cit., 176–89; cf. W. Rehm, *Die Chansons von Gilles Binchois*, (Mainz, 1957).

93. Op. cit., 35.

94. A. Desplanque, *Projet d'assassinat de Philippe le Bon par les Anglais* (Bruxelles, 1867), 70; this Rondeau, whether by Binchois or not, has failed to survive.

95. Binchois, ed. cit., No. 29; Charles d'Orléans text, ed. cit., ii, 573, incorrectly classed as a *ballade*.

96. See J. Marix, op. cit., 188; Escorial MS V.III.24.

97. A. Desplanque, op. cit., 72.

98. Ed. A. Piaget (Lausanne, 1968); the melifluousness of Dufay and Binchois, with that of Busnois and Ockeghem, is unfavourably compared by Jean Molinet with the singing of Sirens sent by Circe in *Le naufrage de la Pucelle*, in *Les Faictz et Dictz de Jean Molinet*, ed. N. Dupire (*SATF*, Paris, 1936), i, 89: 'Ces seraines donques, fringans et gentes, pretendans livrer la pucelle ès gueules des belues et endormir ses domestiques au son de leurs musettes, jouerent une chançon composée de tant de melodieuses consonances et proportions amesurées que les subtiles cantilenes, les artificielles messes et armonieux motetz de Ockeghem ne Du Fay, ne de Binchois ne de Busnois n'y porroient sortir comparaison.'

that both of them were on occasion overshadowed by the brilliant playing of blind harpers and fiddlers:

> Tu as les aveugles ouÿ
> Jouer a la court de Bourgogne,
> N'a pas certainement ouÿ
> Fut il jamais telle besogne.
> J'ay veu Binchois avoir vergongne
> Et soy taire emprez leur rebelle
> Et Dufay despité et frongne
> Qu'il n'a melodye si belle.

This same work contains a well-known passage in which both Dufay and Binchois are said to be deeply influenced by the English style or 'contenance angloise' of John Dunstable.[99] Dunstable, recognised as the outstanding English musician of this period, was, however, in the service of the duke of Bedford. Dunstable was probably a member of Bedford's chapel in France, since he is not listed in the register of the English Chapel Royal, and his compositions, about fifty-eight in number and mostly religious in nature,[100] are almost entirely preserved in continental sources. His one known setting of a French text, the *rondeau* 'Puisque m'amour m'a pris en desplaisir', was probably of verses by an independent poet, since they reappear in the MS Stockholm, Royal Lib. Vu 22, and in the later printed anthology of the *Jardin de Plaisance*. John Pyamour, like Dunstable from the generation following the Old Hall compilation, was master of the children of the Chapel Royal in 1420[101] but is also known to have served the duke of Bedford in France in 1427. The one extant motet by him, in advanced style, is preserved in the MS Modena, Est. lat. 471.[102] Later their countryman Robert Morton was a member of the Burgundian chapel, which he entered in 1457 in company with Hayne de Guizeghem, whose music

---

99. See S. Kenney, *Walter Frye and the 'Contenance angloise'* (New Haven, 1964); Dunstable, Binchois and Dufay are similarly grouped in Eloy d'Amerval's *Livre de la Deablerie* (Paris, 1508), and in Johannes Nucius' *Musices poeticae sive de compositione cantus* (1613).

100. *John Dunstable: Complete Works*, ed. M. Bukofzer, *Musica Britannica*, viii (London, 1953).

101. On 14 January 1420 he was commissioned 'to take boys for the said chapel, and bring them to the King's presence in his duchy of Normandy': CPR 1416–22. Henry V, ii, 270; see W. Grattan-Flood, op. cit., 225–35.

102. M. Bukofzer, *Studies in Medieval and Renaissance Music* (London, 1950), 77; the high quality of musician recruited by Bedford is well illustrated by the case of Robinet de la Magdalaine (*alias* Robert Pele). Born in 1415 near Rouen, he was a choirboy at Beauvais in 1422 and Rouen in 1424, when he entered Bedford's service. Following this he served Louis de Luxembourg, Archbishop of Rouen and Chancellor of France under the English King, and was taken to England in 1443. In 1446 he spent some months in Italy in the Papal Chapel, and was in the Burgundian Court from 1448–78; he may have been the author of one of the *Cent Nouvelles Nouvelles* (J. Marix, op. cit., 202–3).

was appreciated in the court of Henry VIII.[103] Both were virtuoso singers, and instrumentalists too according to the author of a song recording their visit to Cambrai:

> La plus grant chiere de jamais
> Ont fait a Cambray la cité
> Morton et Hayne . . .[104]

Morton set a number of French *chansons* and was named with Dunstable in the *Dialogus in Arte Musica* of the theoretician John Hothby, who died in 1487.[105] Tinctoris, who had been at the University of Louvain in 1471, also mentions Morton among those composers 'whose works are known everywhere, and whose sweet accents are heard in churches, in royal palaces as in private houses'.[106] Walter Frye is included in Hothby's list. He was probably at one time attached to Ely Cathedral, but his extant works, eight motets and *chansons*, are again known through continental sources, including some with English text in the Burgundian Mellon Chansonnier.[107] He appears to have made original settings of texts in both English and French, but the English songs, 'So ys emprentid', 'Myn hertis lust', and 'Alas, alas, alas', all also occur in *contrafactum* versions where the English is replaced either by a deformed French version, or by a totally different French text, or by a religious text in Latin. The principal reason for this must be the difficulty posed to continental scribes and audiences by the English language, though Frye's music was greatly prized. Conflicting attributions link Frye with Binchois and with John Bedingham, who set Charles d'Orléans' Rondeau 'Mon seul plaisir', though possibly first in the English version 'Mi verry joy'.[108]

It is not hard to see, given the conditions in the early years of the fifteenth century, how these musicians from each side of the Channel were able to meet, circulate and influence each other. Even choirboys were taken, along with chaplains and minstrels, to the scene of, if not into, battle.[109] Suffolk was probably associated with Bedford, together

---

103. J. Stevens, ed. cit., 3, 30.

104. MS Dijon, Bibl. mun. 515, fols. 155v–156r; J. Marix, op. cit., 206–7.

105. J. Marix, op. cit., 205–11.

106. C. E. H. De Coussemaker, *Scriptorum de musica medii aevi* . . . 4 vols. (Paris, 1864–76), iv, 200.

107. S. Kenney, op. cit.; S. Kenney, ed., *Walter Frye: Complete Works*, CMM 19 (American Institute of Musicology, 1960); S. Kenney, 'Contrafacta in the Works of Walter Frye', *Journal of the American Musicological Society*, viii (1955), 182–202.

108. See D. Fallows, *Two mid-fifteenth-century English Songs* (Oxford Early Music Series 28, 1977); the second song edited here is an anonymous setting of Lydgate's *Pryncesse of youthe*, from *The Temple of Glas*, from the Escorial MS.

109. In 1418 three choirboys of the duke of Burgundy's chapel were each given 12 fr. 'pour se monter et s'habiller afin de l'accompagner au voyage du Roy lequel il doit bientot faire contre les Anglois ses anciens ennemis', J. Marix, op. cit., 138.

with Gloucester, Salisbury and others in the 1424 plot against Burgundy; meetings over this and other matters, attended by the usual ceremonies, would give ample opportunity for such as Dunstable and Binchois to associate. More musicians came to Hainault after the death of Henry V[110] in 1424, with the duke of Gloucester, and probably took part in a solemn service in the cathedral of Cambrai.[111] Alliances between English and Burgundians account for much interchange and the presence in Burgundian inventories of choirbooks apparently of English provenance.[112] We read of meetings such as that between Bedford and Burgundy in Hesdin, to the full accompaniment of heralds, pursuivants and minstrels.[113]

The duke of Bedford resided as Regent in Paris from 1425, after the death of Charles VI.[114] He maintained a chapel there, in which the singers were divided into two 'nations', English and Burgundian.[115] Certain local musicians, it seems, did not prosper at this time. In c. 1422 the English confiscated the Paris house of Jean Verdelet, *menetrier du roi* since at least 1416.[116] In 1427 Jehan Facien, son of Jehan Facien l'aîné, king of minstrels in Paris, had his house 'assis en la rue St. Martin, ou pend l'enseigne de la fleur de lys rouge' confiscated; his father had also served the Burgundian court.[117] The English dean of the chapel complained that he could not understand the annual confession of those who spoke only French. Engaged for this purpose was Thomas Hoppinel, who was at that time *maître des enfants* at Notre Dame and had earlier held a similar post in the Burgundian chapel in 1419. Some of the English singers had previously served the king of England; in 1418 Bedford had six of them sent to him for his own chapel.[118]

110. After a solemn ceremony in Notre Dame in Paris, the King's body was transported through Rouen and Calais with chanting day and night of the Office of the Dead: Jean le Fèvre, *Chronique* (Paris, 1876–), ii, 66.

111. S. Kenney, *Walter Frye and the "Contenance angloise"* (New Haven, 1964), 12–13.

112. Ibid.

113. '. . . aux heraulx et poursuivans d'armes dudit monseigneur le regent .xl. livres, que monseigneur leur a semblablement donné; a ses trompettes et menestrelz, semblablement .xxxvi. livres, .x. solz.': Burgundian Accounts, after A. Desplanque, op.cit., 33 n.l.

114. Bedford's trumpeters, Guillaume More, Henri Court, Jehan de Gand, Guillaume Normant, Jehan Haston played with others to entertain Henry V on campaigns in July 1420 at Melun, according to Monstrelet: '. . . devant la tente du roy, de nuit, sonnoient moult melodieusement par l'espace d'une heure ou environ, a jour faillant et au point du jour, huit a dix clarons d'Angleterre et autres divers instruments': J. Marix, op. cit., 77–8.

115. A. Pirro, op. cit., 34–35.

116. Ibid., 32.

117. A. Longnon, *Paris pendant la domination anglaise (1420–1436)* (Paris, 1878), 256.

118. J. Marix, op. cit., 148.

Many are the descriptions of lavish ceremonial, including music, which surrounded Bedford. Some of the best of these are to be found in the *Journal d'un bourgeois de Paris*.[119] Already in 1420, the two kings, Charles VI and Henry V, with their queens, princes and dukes, had made an entry into Paris, where the streets were crowded with priests carrying relics and chanting *Te Deum laudamus* and *Benedictus qui venit*. Spectacular celebrations followed in April 1423, when Bedford married Anne of Burgundy. When Bedford came triumphant into Paris in September 1424, similar scenes were enacted and much honour was done him in Notre Dame, with singing of hymns and songs of praise, and playing of organs, trumpets and bells; no Roman general had such a welcome, says the Bourgeois, drily. September 1429 saw this once again, when the duke of Burgundy accompanied his sister Anne and Bedford. A solemn *Te Deum* was performed by order of the duke in 1430, to celebrate the capture of Joan of Arc. When the Regent's wife died in 1432, it was noted that in the funeral ceremony the English chanted 'most piteously, after the manner of their country'.

Apart from the complicated question of cross-channel *contrafactum*[120] there exist a fair number of English manuscripts containing a mixed repertory of English and French songs, not to mention indications of earlier such mixed repertories as, for instance, in the *Red Book of Ossory*,[121] or the inclusion in the Old Hall MS of a famous 'musician motet' by John Aleyn, a member of the late fourteenth-century Chapel Royal but also composer of secular works in French and active in France.[122] Sir John Stainer printed most of the fourteenth and fifteenth-century mixed repertories in his *Early Bodleian Music*,[123] as do Dobson and Harrison in *Medieval English Songs*;[124] they include the important collection from the turn of the fourteenth century, MS Cambridge University Library Add. 5943, which has also recently been re-edited by R. Rastall.[125] Certain of the fifteenth-century English carols also include French lines and verses,[126] and a number of French songs, including some apparently composed or embellished by

119. Ed. A. Tuetey (Paris, 1881).
120. See also N. Wilkins, *Chaucer Songs* (Cambridge, 1980).
121. See N. Wilkins, *Music in the Age of Chaucer* (Cambridge, 1979), 95–6.
122. Ibid., 87–8.
123. Bodleian MSS Ashmole 1285, Rawlinson G.22, Rawlinson G.18, Douce 139, Bodley 381.
124. *Medieval English Songs* (London, 1979).
125. Ed. R. Rastall, (Antico Edition, 1976–79), nos. 11, 16, 17, 18; see also N. Wilkins, op. cit., 107–110.
126. J. Stevens, ed. cit., 36, 67, 113; 6 n.b. the 'Agincourt Carol'.

the king himself, also appear in the Henry VIII collection.[127] Apart
from these well-known examples, where we find the two languages in
juxtaposition, evidence of French influence in England may also be
detected in notational practice, as in the Old Hall MS, or in such
instances as the Robertsbridge Fragments, which give keyboard
arrangements of De Vitry motets from the *Roman de Fauvel* and
estampies, in an apparently English source copied *c.* 1330.[128]

Further examples of these various categories may yet be discovered,
as can be demonstrated by two examples from manuscripts in the
Parker Library of Corpus Christi College, Cambridge. Plate 18 shows
two fragments of an unidentified *Gloria* in late fourteenth-century
French Ars Nova notation (including red notes in the original). These
are binding strips from MS 329, a fifteenth-century MS probably from
the Cluniac Priory of Thetford; five end flyleaves are from a roughly
written account roll of 35–36 Edward III. Plate 16 and its transcription
are of an easy-going French secular piece in late thirteenth-century
conductus style, rather reminiscent of Adam de la Hale. It is, however,
on the reverse of a celebrated flyleaf from MS 8, the *recto* of which
contains two voices of the only known Motet with English text,
'Worldes blisce have god day!'[129]

We have done little but scrape the surface of Anglo-French cross-
influence in the late Middle Ages, but the connections are evident. No
wonder that the fifteenth-century carol writer placed these two countries side by side at the opening of his verse:

> England and France,
> Empires all,
> In every clime:
> Praise Ye the Lord.

127. J. Stevens, ed. cit., 2, 3, 12, 13, 14–15, 30, 31, 32, 34–5, 36, 37, 64–5.
128. See N. Wilkins, op. cit., 89–92.
129. Ibid, 99–100; M. Bukofzer, 'The first motet with English words', *Music and Letters*, xvii (1936), 232–3.

Index

MANUSCRIPTS

NAMES

SUBJECTS